SEX AND
THE OFFICE

SEX AND THE OFFICE

WOMEN, MEN, AND THE SEX PARTITION THAT'S DIVIDING THE WORKPLACE

Kim Elsesser

TAYLOR TRADE PUBLISHING
Lanham • Boulder • New York • London

Published by Taylor Trade Publishing
An imprint of The Rowman & Littlefield Publishing Group, Inc.
4501 Forbes Boulevard, Suite 200, Lanham, Maryland 20706
www.rowman.com

Unit A, Whitacre Mews, 26-34 Stannary Street, London SE11 4AB, United Kingdom

Distributed by NATIONAL BOOK NETWORK

British Library Cataloguing in Publication Information Available

Library of Congress Cataloging-in-Publication Data
Elsesser, Kim.
  Sex and the office : women, men, and the sex partition that's dividing the workplace /
Kim Elsesser.
    pages cm
  Summary: "In Sex and the Office, Kim Elsesser delves into how issues as varied as
sexual harassment, workplace romance, spousal jealousy, and communication styles
create barriers between men and women at work. These invisible barriers, which
Elsesser labels the "sex partition," tend to have the greatest impact on the careers of
women, because men typically still dominate senior management, and connections with
senior managers are essential for career advancement. Elsesser describes how senior male
employees prefer to stick with other men, especially when it comes to dinners, drinks,
late-night meetings, or business trips. When it's time for promotions or pay raises, these
same executives are more likely to show preference to the employees with whom they feel
most comfortable—other men. Elsesser doesn't blame men for the sex partition; instead,
she describes how some common organizational practices create barriers between the
sexes. She offers practical advice on how to break down the sex partition and reveals the
best strategies for networking with the opposite sex. Sex and the Office is sure to spark
new dialogue on the sources of the gender gap at work. "—Provided by publisher.
  Includes bibliographical references and index.
  ISBN 978-1-4930-0794-3 (hardback) — ISBN 978-1-63076-121-9 (electronic) 1.
Women—Employment. 2. Sex role in the work environment. 3. Sexual harassment.
4. Interpersonal relations. 5. Business networks. 6. Career development. I. Title.
  HD6060.E44 2015
  302.3'5—dc23

                                                                    2015006762

Printed in the United States of America

For Bradley

CONTENTS

PREFACE

While attending college at Vassar, I was inspired by the tradition of empowering women and education in a female-dominated environment. After Vassar, I headed to graduate school at MIT to study business and operations research (a field that applies advanced math to study decisions made by organizations). When I started at MIT, I recall being told that only 19 percent of the graduate students were women.

Coming from Vassar, MIT offered quite a culture shock. Rumor had it that a few MIT professors still thought that admitting women to MIT was a mistake, and that female students were too much of a distraction for the male students. I didn't think there could be a less female-friendly environment than MIT, until I landed a job on the trading floor at Morgan Stanley. There, a senior trader and I launched a quantitative proprietary trading group, which became one of the most successful in the company's history.

Female traders were almost nonexistent at the time. There were plenty of women on the trading floor, but they were mostly employed as assistants to the traders and salespeople. Occasionally mistaken for an assistant, I was asked to get coffee and order lunch by those who didn't know my role, and my male subordinates were occasionally forced to explain that I was their boss and not their assistant.

During my tenure in trading, I strived to understand why there were so few women at senior levels of management. After all, it wasn't so bad on the trading floor. That's not to say I completely fit in either. For example, my male anatomy, or lack thereof, came up in conversation with surprising frequency. Did I have the balls to do that trade? Was my dick big enough? Or, more frequently,

I needed to get some balls. It didn't take long to come up with snappy answers to these comments, and soon I was one of the boys. Or was I?

Certainly, within my small proprietary trading group, everyone established close friendships with one another. We worked long hours together and often socialized after work and on weekends. My manager and I spent an inordinate amount of time together. Building a trading group from scratch had innumerable challenges, and we spent a lot of time discussing each one. There were insinuations that we were more than friends—we weren't.

Although everyone within our trading group became friends, when it came to those coworkers outside our small group, friendship was much tougher. Sometimes it seemed like senior management avoided contact with me and that I made them uncomfortable. But that was no problem; Morgan Stanley sponsored many outings where I could get to know senior management and show them how fabulous I was.

For example, the equity division at Morgan Stanley had its annual officers' meetings at beautiful resorts, and these meetings provided long afternoon breaks. It would be easy to befriend senior management by the pool in the afternoon. It turns out the afternoon break was primarily for golfing. Although I had taken a golf class at Vassar, I certainly wasn't ready to go tee-to-tee with male managers who practiced every weekend. I went jogging alone while my male colleagues enjoyed an afternoon of golf together. I promised myself I would work on my swing.

Even if my golf swing wasn't up to par, there would be other opportunities to socialize with management. At one outing, as evening fell, I headed out to see what others were up to. "Where are you going?" I asked my colleague who was heading out of the hotel bar. It was time for the poker game, I was told.

"You're welcome to join us," he added as he left the bar. Join them? I didn't know how to play poker, and with the stakes they played for, I certainly wasn't going to ask for lessons. Instead, I headed to bed early.

It's not that I was explicitly excluded from these events. I certainly could have played poker or shot a round of golf, but I couldn't get much further from my comfort zone. Meanwhile, my male colleagues were chalking up lots of face time with the big shots in the department. I was determined not to let any more opportunities pass by. Not long thereafter, another opportunity knocked.

The head of my division was taking some managers out for drinks. "Do you want to join us?" they asked. Drinking? Yes, I could do that. There was one catch, I was told. The section of the club where we were headed was for men only. If I could get in, then we'd have our own private room to shoot pool.

I had long blonde hair, and like to think I didn't look much like a man, but I wasn't going to let this opportunity get away. No problem, I could do this. A coworker lent me a long trench coat, and another lent me a hat. I tucked my blonde locks into the hat, and felt pretty ridiculous. Is this how I was going to impress management?

At the club, words and a tip were exchanged with the doorman, and soon we were in a private room with a pool table. Now that I was inside, I merely had to demonstrate my brilliance while playing pool. I hadn't shot pool since high school, but I reasoned I could just apply my knowledge of physics. Angle of incidence equals angle of reflection—how hard could it be? I held my own.

In the years that followed, I continued to pursue outings with my male coworkers. The most memorable was an outing to a hostess bar in Tokyo. At Japanese hostess bars, a female hostess who works at the bar is assigned to each guest (all men, except for me), and your hostess pours your drinks and chats with you. At this particular hostess bar, frequented by expats in Tokyo, topless women performed pole dancing on a nearby stage.

And then there was the paintball outing. But that was too painful (literally) to describe. Let's just say it wasn't easy establishing friendships with senior managers, and it was difficult to watch the ease with which my male colleagues socialized with them. It occurred to me that this challenge of establishing valuable cross-sex friendships at work might extend to other women in the workplace. Thus began my research into obstacles to cross-sex friendships at work and its impact on women's careers. I left Morgan Stanley to pursue a PhD in psychology from UCLA. (Once again, culture shock. The graduate students were mostly women, as were half the faculty, and male anatomy never made its way into conversations.)

In 2006 I published an academic paper with Anne Peplau on obstacles to cross-sex friendship at work. After publication of that paper, many people came forward to tell me their own stories of how obstacles to cross-sex friendship impacted their careers. Their stories are featured in this book (names have been changed to protect anonymity), along with new research of my own and the latest research of other scholars. I examine why these friendships at work are so important to career success, discuss the barriers keeping men and women from crossing the gender line to initiate friendships at work, and offer suggestions for overcoming these barriers.

I

WHAT IS THE SEX PARTITION?

1

THE SEX PARTITION
AND HOW IT
IMPACTS YOU

*Friendship is unnecessary, like philosophy, like art. . . . It has
no survival value; rather it is one of those things which give
value to survival.*

—C. S. Lewis, author[1]

Allen is an ambitious entry-level employee at a prestigious consulting firm
and an experienced long-distance runner. A senior manager in Allen's
firm, Joe, is training for his first marathon. Sharing an elevator one morning,
Allen and Joe discover their common interest in running. Since Allen has been
running competitively for many years, Joe is eager to hear more about his training strategies. Later that same day, Joe stops by Allen's desk and invites Allen
to join him for a beer after work to discuss running. Allen agrees and, while at
the pub, Joe offers Allen a tip on how to deal with a difficult client which helps
Allen gain a higher profile within the firm. A mentor relationship develops, and
Joe continues to provide Allen with valuable advice and information. When a
new job opportunity emerges, Joe is eager to recommend Allen.

Now imagine Anita is in the elevator that morning instead of Allen. Just like
Allen, Anita is an ambitious entry-level employee and an experienced long-
distance runner. Are Joe and Anita as likely to uncover their common interest
in running during their morning elevator ride? Probably not, but let's say they
did. Is Joe as likely to ask Anita to join him for a beer after work? Again, probably not—he'd most likely feel awkward. What if Anita thinks he wants a date,
or worse, what if she thinks it's sexual harassment?

Let's say Joe overcomes these concerns and invites Anita to join him for a beer after work to discuss training for the marathon. Unlike Allen, Anita is caught off guard, and her mind fills with questions. A beer? Is this a date? If I go, will I give him the wrong idea? Even if he does just want to discuss running, what will my coworkers think? That I'm sleeping my way to the top? And what will my boyfriend think? Anita nervously declines his invitation, providing some excuse as to why she's busy. Anita never befriends Joe and never receives the career-boosting client tip. No mentor relationship blossoms for Anita.

When Allen met Joe for a beer after work, no eyebrows were raised and no questions were asked. But for Joe and Anita, the situation was much more complicated—almost not worth the effort. Situations comparable to this fictional anecdote play out in workplaces every day, and I believe they are a primary culprit in women's lack of advancement at work.

In order to avoid any suggestion of workplace romance or sexual harassment, opposite-sex coworkers are shying away from nonessential interactions, creating a barrier between men and women at work. Friendships with the opposite sex can be tricky enough to manage outside of work, but within the workplace, additional constraints encourage workers to stick to same-sex colleagues. These barriers between the sexes that get in the way of developing cross-sex friendships make up what I call the *sex partition*.[2]

The sex partition limits your pool of potential friends, and limiting your friends also limits your career. The benefits of friendships at work extend far beyond having buddies at the water cooler. Friends at work provide one another with valuable information, and friends with more senior employees can evolve into mentor relationships. The research evidence is irrefutable: Those with more work friends earn more money, get promoted faster, have better job performance, are happier in their jobs, and have better health than those with fewer friends.[3]

Any way you look at it, those with less access to work friends are at a real disadvantage. While the sex partition limits the friendships of both men and women, it packs a much greater punch for female employees. Since senior management is still predominantly male,[4] when it comes to befriending senior execs, women often have to seek out male friendships. Yet, one study reports that a shocking 64 percent of senior men were reluctant to have a one-on-one meeting with a junior woman at work.[5] If junior women can't get a meeting, they are not going to develop the working relationships with the senior executive men that are critical for career success.

What about men in female-dominated organizations? Wouldn't they also face sex partition issues when they try to climb the ranks? Surprisingly, they don't.

Men in female-dominated workplaces are often said to be on a "glass escalator" to the top management levels.[6] In other words, men's advancement is actually accelerated in these organizations. Why would men have it easier when they're surrounded by women? Despite the fact that there are more women than men in these workplaces, the senior-level management in these organizations is still often dominated by men. Junior-level men in these environments can buddy up to the boss, and it pays off. Take, for example, secretaries—96 percent of whom are women. Despite their dominance of the profession, female secretaries earn only 86 percent as much as male secretaries.[7] Male secretaries have an easier time than female secretaries bonding with predominantly male management, and it shows in their paycheck.

So essential are workplace friendships to career success, I contend the sex partition is the primary impediment preventing gender equity in the workplace. Statistics reveal that women's careers are still lagging well behind those of their male counterparts. Despite the fact that women are obtaining more bachelor's degrees and graduate degrees than men, women in the United States still earn only seventy-seven cents on the dollar compared to men and have meager representation in the top levels of corporations. In the Fortune 500, women hold only 14.6 percent of executive-officer positions,[8] 8.1 percent of the top earner positions,[9] and only 4.6 percent of the Fortune 500 companies are run by female CEOs.[10] Within the law profession, women are overrepresented at the lowest positions such as staff attorney (64 percent women), but only 17 percent of the highly paid equity partners are women.[11] Women in the United States government don't fare so well either. There are only seven women presently holding state governor positions, women make up a mere 18 percent of the 113th Congress,[12] and we have yet to elect a female president.

WHY ARE WORK FRIENDSHIPS SO VALUABLE?

I'm certainly not the first to suggest that women are held back by difficulties networking. The novelty of the sex partition lies in *why* women have so much difficulty establishing networks with men. But, before we get into the *why*, I want to make sure you understand just how critical friendships at work can be to your career.

Whether helping you fix a printer jam, writing a portion of your overdue brief, or just bringing you coffee on a late night, in my study of friendships at work, I was told friends at work "look out for you." Professionals reported learning from their friends at work and feeling more comfortable asking them questions. Mike, an urban planner, expressed how his friends at work help him "gather information, not just about how the company works, but who is doing what to whom and when, and what the real story was."[13]

Information we get from our friend network is not only valuable in itself, but it also provides power to the recipient. One of my coworkers, John, knew everything that was happening at work. If you wanted information you went to John. This gave John power, because he could decide what information he wanted to share, and how he wanted to spin that information. The information that we receive from our friends instills us with power, because it provides us with the ability to make good decisions and influence others. In fact, friendships can translate into power merely because those with friends are perceived to be well connected. In other words, having more friends at work gives an employee higher status that results in what is often termed referent power, or power gained from having the respect of others.[14]

This information, help with our jobs, and the listening ears we get from our friends at work also give us a feeling of social support, and the benefits associated with social support at work are overwhelming. Studies reveal traffic enforcement agents who received more social support issued more summonses, booksellers with social support sold more books, and auto parts manufacturers with support from coworkers worked more creatively.[15] As if that's not enough, those with more social support from coworkers have better health and are happier in their jobs.[16] Just one day with less support at work can result in a decline in your job performance.[17]

Information and social support are valuable, but perhaps the greatest career boost our friends can give us is assistance landing a new job offer. With the exception of my Howard Johnson's waitressing job, I have not obtained a job without the help of my contacts. From my much-coveted Vassar College campus job score-keeping for intramural sports to my Wall Street trading job, it was all about who I knew. I worked hard, so the people I knew felt comfortable recommending me, but I doubt I could have landed my jobs by blindly sending résumés or answering ads.

Recently, studies have confirmed what many have long known, that getting the good job depends on who you know.[18] Studies of workplace promotions consistently indicate that advancement most often results from tapping the right contacts.[19] Not surprisingly, those who are personally referred for a particular job are more likely to land the job than those who apply without a referral.[20]

Obtaining job offers isn't only useful for those interested in moving on. You want to negotiate a raise? Acquiring outside offers can be one of the most effective methods of negotiating a pay increase with your current employer. Having an outside job offer under your belt gives you leverage. You're not just asking for a raise, but you're providing evidence of your worth. Researchers speculate that one reason women find themselves at the bottom of the pay scale is that they're less likely to network for outside job offers.[21] Acquiring information about outside job openings requires a substantial friendship network, and, if women have more difficulty developing these relationships, they just won't receive the offers.

ACQUAINTANCES ARE VALUABLE, TOO

Although one of my best friends in college got me the score-keeping gig, most of my other jobs came from connections who weren't in my circle of closest friends. When it comes to work, acquaintances (sometimes referred to as "weak ties") can often be more valuable than close friends or relatives (or "strong ties").[22] Why are weak ties so valuable? Close friends tend to link you to other people who are similar to yourself, therefore, your strong ties typically have the same knowledge and contacts that you already have. Weak ties are more likely to offer connections to people you don't already know. Often weak ties are of higher prestige than strong ties, and therefore weak ties can lead to other higher-status contacts or better job offers.[23] Ultimately, job seekers who are referred by weak ties are more likely to attain higher-prestige positions than those who are referred by strong ties.

Don't write off your close friends just yet. Although the information obtained from weak ties is important, the information from more established friends is valuable, too. Closer friends tend to share more sensitive information and are more honest with one another.[24] In fact, the information received from closer friends tends to be more timely, more accurate, and of higher quality than information obtained from those who shared a less intimate friendship. Workers benefit, therefore, from both their close friends and their acquaintances.

MORE MEN IN YOUR NETWORK=MORE MONEY
IN YOUR PAYCHECK

Clearly, friends in your network are important, but it turns out some friends are more beneficial than others. Several studies reveal that the number of men in your network may have more of an influence on your paycheck than the number of women in your network.[25]

One revealing study illustrates how leveraging contacts with men in your network can impact your paycheck. The researchers began by counting the number of influential people that executives had encountered in their careers.[26] These were not necessarily friends or even acquaintances, just influential people that the individuals worked alongside sometime in their past. For male executives, overlapping with more influential contacts throughout their careers resulted in higher salaries. For female executives, no such relationship was found. The female executives' salaries were not related to the number of influential contacts they had encountered in their career. In other words, the male executives were able to leverage their contacts into higher pay, while the women were not. It's important to note, it was not the availability of influential contacts that differed—the women had typically worked alongside more influential people than men did. Instead, it was the ability to initiate relationships with these people, and then utilize these relationships, which ultimately resulted in greater remuneration. Ultimately, men were able to utilize their contacts better than women in the study.

What might explain this gender discrepancy in utilizing contacts? It may help to know that the influential contacts in this study were predominantly male. Therefore, the women had to forge primarily cross-sex friendships in order to leverage these contacts, while men simply needed to befriend other men. I believe difficulties establishing cross-sex friendships, the sex partition, was responsible for holding these women back.

It turns out the executive women in this study earned 17 percent less than their male counterparts. How much of this gender difference in pay was attributable to the gender difference in the ability to leverage contacts? All of it. The authors in the study assert that the ability to leverage contacts statistically *accounted for the entire gender gap in pay* for these executives.

It shouldn't shock you that male friends can offer more benefits than female friends. Look at the stats; men are still running most organizations. If you want friends in high places, a good portion of them will probably need to be men. Men also have connections to other men in high places. Connecting to men in middle management can link you to their connections to senior management.

Don't get me wrong—I'm not suggesting that female friends aren't valuable at work. I've had many that were incredibly valuable to my career. I'm saying that women generally have more difficulty befriending men, and since men still run most of our organizations, this is a real problem.

Now that we understand the value of friendship and networking, the goal of the remainder of this book is to examine *why* women have so much trouble establishing friendships with male colleagues. The reasons aren't the typical excuses—that women are too busy with childcare or not adequately assertive—though these issues may play a role. From sexual harassment training and fear of sexual harassment charges to awkward situations on business trips and un-requited romantic interest, a whole slew of issues are creating barriers between men and women at work.

These issues don't only impact women who want to be at the helm of large corporations. Stories in this book reveal how the sex partition impacts the careers of supermarket employees, dental hygienists, and university students as well as lawyers and corporate employees. If you're a woman and you work with men, most likely the sex partition is impacting you as well. There are no easy fixes, but I'll help you navigate around the sex partition at your workplace.

Until now, few have addressed these issues head on. Perhaps no one thought we could remedy them. Or perhaps fear of risking the progress we've made in reducing sexual harassment in the workplace has left organizations afraid to encourage interactions between men and women. However, given the barrier these issues are creating for women's careers, we have no alternative but to start discussing these problems. Silence certainly isn't going to make them disappear.

It's also important to note that the sex partition isn't anyone's fault. Men are not to blame and women are not to blame. Some organizational practices exacerbate the problem, but organizations aren't all to blame either. However, there are steps we can all take to break down the sex partition, and the final six chapters of this book focus squarely on workable solutions to this problem. Although accompanied by anecdotes, the description of the sex partition and the proposed remedies are solidly based on my own studies in combination with the latest research from psychology, sociology, organizational behavior, and management.

II

DOES HEIGHTENED AWARENESS OF SEXUAL HARASSMENT CREATE A SEX PARTITION?

2

FRIENDLINESS VS. SEXUAL HARASSMENT: WHERE'S THE LINE?

Every time a man and a woman are at the water cooler, Anita Hill's right there between them.

—Andrea Sankar, anthropologist[1]

I can recall several occasions when, as an equity trader at Morgan Stanley, I walked in on a conversation among male colleagues, and the conversation stopped dead. Silence ensued as my colleagues nervously tried to determine how much I had already heard. They weren't talking about me; invariably they were sharing gossip or jokes they deemed inappropriate for female company. Often I would try to pry these lewd jokes and stories from my colleagues. The male colleagues typically declined, asserting that if they shared their stories, they would be engaging in sexual harassment. After swearing over and over that I would not be offended, sometimes my colleagues would concede and share a watered-down version of their conversation. More often than not, they would assure me that I didn't want to hear it, or that they would share it later, and then they would disperse. One thing was clear—when I entered the room, the party was over.

My colleagues were correct that I was offended, but not by the content of their jokes. I was offended that I wasn't included as one of the boys. I was offended that they didn't feel comfortable enough to share their jokes with me. I was offended they thought I was going to bring sexual harassment charges against them. Heightened awareness of sexual harassment issues in the workplace hasn't eliminated the offensive jokes and stories in the office; instead, it has merely segregated by gender the sharing of such stories. The resulting problem for women and their careers isn't that these jokes have some inherent career value, but the sharing of these jokes and stories helps forge bonds that last well beyond the joking sessions. Those excluded from the jokes are excluded from the bonding as well.

Joan, a business consultant I interviewed, described her own isolation from the men at the office. She was often excluded from conversations and struggled to put male colleagues at ease:

> I feel like sometimes, [men] don't feel like they can relax when women are around as much. They feel like they have to be careful what they say, and they have to be careful what jokes they tell in front of the women in the office. Whereas when they're just all men they can joke around and talk about things they wouldn't want to talk about when women were around so it's harder to break that barrier. . . . I try to make the men feel like I understand them, that I'm not offended by all their stupid jokes and things like that. I guess after they understand that I'm not like every woman that's going to sue them for sexual harassment, then it's fine.[2]

Heightened awareness of sexual harassment issues in the workplace has left employees wary of interactions with the opposite sex, because employees fear that their friendliness might be misinterpreted by their coworkers. Men tend to be overly cautious in interactions with women at work, and female employees must put their male coworkers at ease and assure them that they're not in danger of a sexual harassment suit.

Cross-sex interactions are so fraught with complications that one recent study found a shocking 64 percent of senior men are reluctant to have a one-on-one meeting with a junior woman.[3] Two decades ago, a similar study found that over half of senior male executives were sensitive about making contact and reaching out to women in their organization.[4] Little has changed. Unfortunately, these are the same senior men that would make valuable mentors to the junior women. If these women have difficulty booking a one-on-one meeting with a senior exec, it's unlikely that valuable mentor relationships will blossom.

I'm certainly not suggesting heightened awareness of sexual harassment is all bad. Organizational sexual harassment policies not only warn potential offenders but also provide procedures for the harassed to come forward with their complaints without fear of retribution. Large numbers of employees are impacted by sexual harassment at work, and in 2013, 7,256 cases of sexual harassment were filed with the Equal Employment Opportunity Commission (EEOC), and many more cases are handled internally by human resource departments. A large majority of these cases are brought by women, but a growing number (17.6 percent in 2013) are filed by men.[5] Clearly, awareness of sexual harassment policies is critical so that all employees can feel safe and comfortable at work, and those who are sexually harassed should be encouraged to speak out.

However, it's equally critical that organizations become aware of an unintended consequence of this heightened awareness of sexual harassment. The increased attention focused on issues of sexual harassment has created a work environment where employees fear accusations from the opposite sex. As a result, workers behave in an overly cautious manner so their behavior will not be misinterpreted as sexual harassment. While cautiousness is admirable, overcautiousness inadvertently contributes to the sex partition.

WHAT IS SEXUAL HARASSMENT?

The male traders who refused to share their jokes with me may have been surprised to learn that occasional joking does not constitute sexual harassment. The senior execs who were reluctant to meet with a junior woman would be heartened to discover it's actually quite difficult to inadvertently sexually harass a colleague. Indeed, much of the fear that surrounds sexual harassment allegations results from a lack of understanding regarding what legally constitutes sexual harassment. For employees who are unclear about the definition of harassment, reducing contact with opposite-sex employees is a surefire way to decrease the likelihood of sexual harassment charges. Certainly, the less interaction you have with opposite-sex employees, the less likely you are to inadvertently sexually harass.

So, what exactly is sexual harassment? Sexual harassment is a form of sex discrimination that violates Title VII of the *Civil Rights Act* of 1964 (Title VII prohibits discrimination by employers on the basis of race, color, religion, sex, or national origin). Therefore, sexual harassment has a relatively short history in the United States (the first sexual harassment cases were not brought until the 1970s). The EEOC defines sexual harassment in its 1984 Policy Statement on Sexual Harassment as:

Unwelcome sexual advances, requests for sexual favors, or other verbal or physical conduct of a sexual nature when:

1. Submission to such conduct was made either explicitly or implicitly a term or condition of an individual's employment.
2. Submission to or rejection of such conduct by an individual was used as the basis for employment decisions affecting such individual.

3. Such conduct has the purpose or effect of unreasonably interfering with an individual's work performance or creating an intimidating, hostile, or offensive working environment.

Thus, instances of sexual harassment can be broken down into two categories, often labeled quid pro quo and hostile environment. Quid pro quo (literally "this for that") harassment occurs when the unwelcome conduct is a condition of an individual's employment or becomes the basis of an employment decision. Although sometimes difficult to prove with no witnesses, there is little disagreement or ambiguity over whether these behaviors are harassing in nature. A supervisor who bargains, "Have sex with me and you've got the job, or the promotion, or the raise," clearly engaged in quid pro quo harassment. Similarly, if the supervisor threatens, "If you don't have sex with me, I'll fire you," there is little ambiguity as to whether this behavior constitutes sexual harassment.

The second type of harassment, hostile environment harassment, is more ambiguous. The definition—conduct that has the purpose or effect of unreasonably interfering with an individual's work performance or creating an intimidating, hostile, or offensive working environment—is far less clear-cut. The problem is that behavior that seems hostile or intimidating to one person may go unnoticed by another. It's sometimes easier to avoid opposite-sex interactions rather than trying to discover what types of behaviors are offensive to each employee.

SOMETIMES SEXUAL HARASSMENT IS CLEAR-CUT— MOST TIMES IT ISN'T

Not all cases of hostile environment sexual harassment involve ambiguity. Take the case of Ashley Alford. In 2011 a jury awarded Ashley Alford $95 million for sexual harassment she endured while employed at a national furniture chain. No one would question that the behavior Alford was subjected to constituted sexual harassment. According to Alford's allegations, it started when her supervisor, Richard Moore, began pinching her.[6] The pinching quickly escalated to groping of her chest and buttocks. Moore purchased clothes and chocolates for Alford, and he then demanded that she provide him "sucky-sucky" in exchange for the gifts. Alford called the organization's sexual harassment hotline to report the harassing behavior, but no investigation took place, and Alford was never privately interviewed about her experiences. Moore's boss called both Moore and Alford together to discuss the matter, then allegedly told Moore that he had to "watch his back" because sexual harassment allegations had surfaced. Moore was allowed to continue supervising Alford.

From there it only got worse for Alford. One day while Alford was sitting on the stock room floor, Moore approached her from behind, unzipped his pants, and hit Moore on the top of her head with his penis. On another occasion, Moore restrained Alford against her will, lifted her shirt, pulled out his penis, and while still holding Alford, masturbated and ejaculated on her. In this case the sexual harassment escalated to sexual battery. Thankfully, most cases of harassment are not quite so severe. Allegations relating to a hostile environment are often far less clear-cut.

On Wall Street I was told that several of my own male coworkers would gather at the start of each workday to rate their female coworkers' attractiveness on a one-to-ten scale. This represented one more male bonding routine from which all female employees were naturally excluded. Each day they would try to reach consensus on which female employee was the most attractive that day. One would argue that Marianne's cleavage gave her an advantage, while another would suggest that a particularly tight outfit on Susan should put her over the top. Although it was clearly unprofessional behavior, it certainly didn't interfere with my work performance. Compared to what Ashley Alford endured, the behavior seems almost innocuous. Would this behavior constitute a hostile working environment according to the definition? Some would probably say it would while others would say not. So how do the courts decide what constitutes a hostile environment?

In 1993 the Supreme Court suggested an approach to more ambiguous sexual harassment cases based on the case, Harris v. Forklift Systems, Inc. Teresa Harris, the plaintiff in this case, worked as a rental manager for Forklift Systems and complained of comments and behaviors directed at her by the president of Forklift, Charles Hardy.[7] According to Harris's allegations, in front of others, Hardy suggested that the two of them "go to the Holiday Inn to negotiate [Harris's] raise." Again, in front of others, on several occasions Hardy told Harris, "You're a woman, what do you know" and, at least once, called Harris a "dumb ass woman." He made sexual innuendos about Harris's and other women's clothing, and he occasionally asked Harris and other female employees to get coins from his front pants pocket. He threw objects on the ground in front of Harris and other women and asked them to pick up the objects. Harris complained to Hardy about his conduct, and he apologized, told her he was just joking, and that he would stop. However, a month later the harassment began again. While Harris was arranging a deal with a customer, Hardy asked her, in front of other employees, "What did you do, promise the guy . . . some [sex]

Saturday night?" Harris quit her job and sued Forklift, claiming that Hardy had created an abusive work environment based on her gender.

Perhaps shockingly, the lower courts ruled against Harris, stating that the abuse was not so severe as to affect Harris's psychological well-being. The case went to the United States Supreme Court which ruled in Harris's favor, with Justice Sandra Day O'Connor stating that as long as the environment could "reasonably be perceived, and is perceived, as hostile or abusive there is no need for it also to be psychologically injurious."[8] O'Connor stipulated that the harassing conduct didn't need to go as far as to cause a "nervous breakdown" but needed to be serious enough to detract from the job performance of the victim. The court suggested that in determining whether a particular behavior constitutes a hostile environment, one should consider the frequency, severity, threatening, and humiliating qualities of the behavior. Was it a "mere offensive utterance," or does it impact the victim's job performance? Furthermore, instead of assessing how the behavior impacted the victim, the emphasis should be on whether a reasonable person would find the conduct hostile. If a reasonable person would not find the behavior offensive, then it's not harassment.

This "reasonable person" standard continues to be applied in courts to assess the severity of hostile environment harassment. But is a reasonable person more like a reasonable man or a reasonable woman? Do reasonable men and reasonable women view harassing behavior in the same way? In the case of Harris v. Forklift, Hardy thought his behavior was "just joking," yet most women would probably side with Harris that the behavior was abusive.[9] Many scholars have argued that the standard should consist of whether a reasonable person who is the same sex as the victim would perceive the behavior as harassment. Instead of a "reasonable person," if the victim is female, then the standard would be that of a "reasonable woman," and if the victim is male, then the standard would be that of a "reasonable man."

The Supreme Court stopped short of adopting a gender-specific standard, and the "reasonable person" guidelines remain. Yet there is research evidence that women are more likely than men to label certain behaviors as harassing.[10] Men and women don't disagree about quid pro quo harassment. These situations are easily identified by both genders as harassment. However, when it comes to labeling certain behaviors hostile environment, gender differences start to emerge.

Does putting pressure on a colleague to go out on a date constitute harassment? Men and women tend to disagree. Women are more likely to label this as harassing, and men are less likely to see it that way. What about hugging or kissing a coworker? Once again, women are more likely than men to label this as harassing. Harassment researchers suggest that these differences may result from different perceptions of the same behavior. Men may view touching or date requests as complimentary toward the women, but women don't necessarily see it that way.[11]

It's not surprising that women are more likely than men to perceive particular behaviors as harassing. Since women are more likely than men to be on the receiving end of harassment, it makes sense that they're more sensitive to harassing behaviors. However, it's men's uncertainty regarding what behaviors women may label as harassing that encourages men to hold back in their exchanges with women. Since men may see things differently than women, to be on the safe side, some men avoid any interaction that could even remotely be perceived as harassing. They may avoid unnecessary interactions with women altogether.

However, these concerned men should be relieved to learn that the EEOC makes it clear that "the law doesn't prohibit simple teasing, offhand comments, or isolated incidents that are not very serious. Harassment is illegal when it is so frequent or severe that it creates a hostile or offensive work environment or when it results in an adverse employment decision (such as the victim being fired or demoted)."[12] In other words, most sensible individuals need not worry about inadvertently sexual harassing a colleague. Unfortunately, many organizations don't see things this way and often chastise their employees for friendliness toward an opposite-sex employee.

3

FEAR OF SEXUAL HARASSMENT CHARGES=FEAR OF WOMEN

We fear things in proportion to our ignorance of them.

—Christian Nestell Bovee, writer[1]

Suzanne, a hospital manager, shared with me how one of her closest friendships began. The friendship began when a female colleague complimented her on her outfit. You can imagine how this might have transpired. "I love your suit, where did you get it?" And a conversation ensued about Suzanne's favorite shopping destinations.

Now imagine what may have occurred if a man offered that compliment. Josh, a manager I spoke to, told me about when he offered a compliment to a female colleague. Josh admired his female colleague's business suit. This time, no extended conversation ensued. No friendship developed. Instead, Josh was called in by his human resources department for questions surrounding sexual harassment allegations. Josh describes what happened this way:

> It was just this week when HR said to me that they had to ask me some questions. And there were two specific things they asked me. One is, had a particular employee struggled with a box as she was coming into the lobby, and had I opened the door for her. I didn't remember the incident all that clearly, but I said that was possible. Then they asked, "Did you say, 'It's good to see you sweat'"? I said I don't remember specifically, but it seems possible. When she [the human resources employee] first asked that question, because it had no previous context, I had no idea where she was going with it.

Then the next question [from the human resources department] was, "Have you ever complimented this person on her clothes?" And then all of a sudden I said, "Oh, where are you going with this?" First of all, this is a person who did wear very nice clothes, but otherwise, believe me I had no interest in her whatsoever. If I said that's a nice suit or something, nothing was meant by that. I know sometimes that comment can be a euphemism for "nice tight sweater," but this is not a case of a woman who had a shapely figure or wore revealing clothes. She wore tailored stuff and there was no turn-on there, so anything that was interpreted, it had to be entirely on her part.

And as for the comment "nice to see you sweat," my God the last thing I would have ever hinted was a sexual reference. It was good to see her working hard, carrying a box, basically because she's lazy.[2]

For these two employees, compliments had dramatically different outcomes. Josh's compliment resulted in questioning by his human resources department, while Suzanne's compliment resulted in a new friendship. Human resources departments are sending a message to their employees that interactions that are perfectly safe and natural with same-sex employees can land you in trouble with opposite-sex employees. Take Josh's comment, "It's good to see you sweat." Had Josh, instead, opened the door for a male colleague carrying a box and commented, "It's good to see you sweat," it is extremely unlikely it would have been perceived as inappropriate. If it had been a man, human resources would not have become involved.

After his run-in with the human resources department, Josh changed his behavior toward all women at work. As many in his position would, he feared sexual harassment charges would result from casual conversations with female colleagues, and he severely limited his future interactions with female employees.

BACKLASH STRESS CREATES A GENDER DIVIDE

Stories like Josh's spread around workplaces, instilling a fear that innocent remarks will be misinterpreted. These stories intensify concerns that remarks, particularly those taken out of context, could be perceived as sexual harassment. Indeed, the fear regarding sexual harassment charges is so common among men, one researcher created a psychological term to describe it. The term "backlash stress" was created to label the stress that results from insecurity surrounding what constitutes sexual harassment. Technically, the official definition of backlash stress is "fear of being accused of sexual harassment or from uncertainty about the norms for interacting with women in the workplace."[3] In one study, several male employees at a midwestern university described their experience with backlash stress:

> I would call the specter of sexual harassment an extreme burden on my daily work practices. I do not manage or direct women, but I feel compelled to address all women differently than I would men.[4]

> I feel the need to be "on guard" to prevent any behavior which may be misinterpreted by women, particularly younger women with very sensitive natures.[5]

> The problem with sexual harassment is constant worry and self-checking to make sure something I do innocently is not misconstrued.[6]

Workers who experience sexual harassment backlash stress are more likely to be tardy or absent from work and tend to be less satisfied with their coworkers and supervisor. However, a greater consequence for the organization may result from the deterioration of communication between male and female employees. Those overly concerned that their actions will be misconstrued will most likely avoid interacting with opposite-sex coworkers.

WHY IS SEXUAL HARASSMENT ON EVERYONE'S MIND?

Clearly backlash stress is the result of a heightened awareness of sexual harassment, but why is sexual harassment engrained so prominently in the minds of employees? Primarily, the organization has incentive to keep it on the minds of employees. In addition to legal requirements in some states requiring sexual harassment training, organizations have their own financial incentives to heighten their employees' awareness about sexual harassment and to offer training and reporting procedures. While a few organizations may have a genuine motivation to protect their employees from sexual harassment, the primary motivation stems from a desire to control the organization's liability in harassment lawsuits.

This fear of liability stems from a 1998 case where the Supreme Court ruled that an employer can be liable for sexual harassment in their organization even if the employer is not aware of the harassing behavior. In the Supreme Court case Faragher v. City of Boca Raton, the plaintiff, Beth Ann Faragher was a lifeguard with the City of Boca Raton. Faragher claimed that two of her supervisors had created a sexually hostile atmosphere at work by repeatedly subjecting her and other lifeguards to uninvited and offensive touching, making lewd remarks (e.g. "I want to eat your clit"), and speaking of women in offensive terms (e.g., referring to the female lifeguards as "tits").[7] This case is not notorious because of the size of its financial reward; Faragher was suing for only a dollar. The uniqueness of this case, and the reason it was appealed to the Supreme Court, was to determine whether the City of Boca Raton, unaware of the lifeguards' behavior, was liable for the harassing actions of these two lifeguards. The question of whether employers can be liable in cases of sexual harassment, particularly if they were not aware of the harassment, had not been clarified prior to this case.

The 7–2 decision from the Supreme Court stated that employers are responsible for their own ignorance regarding sexual harassing conduct in the workplace. In this particular case, they ruled that the harassment was so pervasive that the city should have known about it. More specifically the court ruled that the employer must prove it "exercised reasonable care to prevent and correct promptly any sexually harassing behavior."[8] In this case, the City of Boca Raton failed to disseminate its sexual harassment policy to the lifeguards, failed to oversee their conduct, and failed to provide a mechanism for bypassing harassing supervisors in the complaint process in its sexual harassment policy.

Feminists lauded the decision, and it was viewed as a milestone in ceasing harassing behavior in the workplace. However, a rarely discussed drawback of this finding is that it encourages organizations to err on the conservative side and to disallow any behavior that might even be close to harassment. This hypervigilance rubs off on employees, who, in turn, become more conservative in interactions with cross-sex employees.

Organizations naturally want to limit their liability and ultimately want to avoid sexual harassment litigation in order to protect their bottom line. While press coverage that often accompanies sexual harassment cases is not flattering and can impact a business's reputation, deter customers, and reduce revenues, these costs pale in comparison to the costs associated with jury awards and class-action settlements. Dollar figures in headline-making cases are large enough to instill fear into any employer. Recent headlines touted the $95 million Ashley Alford was awarded for her bout with sexual harassment.[9] Unfortunately for Alford federal caps on sexual harassment awards will reduce her payout to closer to $40 million. Other headlines hype the $168 million awarded to Ani Chopourian, a physician's assistant who suffered repeated instances of hostile environment sexual harassment while employed at Mercy General Hospital in Sacramento, California.[10] These headline-grabbing large settlements are the exception rather than the rule, and the average settlement in a sexual harassment case tends to be closer to $6000.[11] When cases settle for small monetary amounts or when the payout is under $10,000, they don't typically make headlines. The public and organizations are left with the notion that sexual harassment payouts are huge and should be avoided at all costs.

Discouraging sexual harassment is a worthy goal. And if large payouts incentivize organizations to eliminate harassment in the workplace, then all is good. Organizations should be lauded for their efforts to create a hospitable work environment. Unfortunately, that's not the end of the story. Organizations are not only incentivized to eliminate harassment but also they're motivated to go overboard to discourage any behavior that could be perceived as slightly annoying, even by the most sensitive employees. This is where problems arise. Well-meaning organizations are inadvertently strengthening the sex partition. The hypersensitivity toward sexual harassment is creating a barrier between men and women at work.

POPULAR MEDIA CONTRIBUTES ITS SHARE ON SEXUAL HARASSMENT

Organizations are not the only source of information (or misinformation) regarding sexual harassment. Media coverage of celebrity harassment cases provides another source of the heightened awareness. Most claims of sexual harassment go unnoticed by the public, but when a celebrity faces sexual harassment allegations, a media circus often ensues. You may recall reading about:

- Bill Clinton vs. Paula Jones
- Brittany Spears vs. her bodyguard, Fernando Flores
- Hewlett Packard CEO Mark Hurd vs. unidentified female contractor
- Bill O'Reilly vs. former *O'Reilly Factor* producer Andrea Mackris
- Presidential candidate Herman Cain vs. several accusers
- San Diego mayor Bob Filner vs. twenty accusers

In addition to increasing sensitivity to issues surrounding sexual harassment, the media doesn't always help clarify what behaviors constitute sexual harassment, and instead may fuel the uncertainty surrounding this issue. Furthermore, the highly publicized repercussions for those accused (and not necessarily even found guilty) of sexual harassment may induce more fear of sexual harassment charges in the rank and file.

Take the media frenzy that occurred when sexual harassment allegations emerged against 2012 Republican presidential candidate Herman Cain. During his bid for the presidency, news surfaced of four women who alleged that the presidential candidate sexually harassed them between 1996 and 1999, while he was at the helm of the National Restaurant Association.[12] As a result of the accusations, which Cain labeled false, he withdrew from the 2012 presidential election. The media attention on Cain was unrelenting and for good reason. Not only were the accusations titillating, but a harassing past would certainly be relevant to Cain's potential to lead the country.

One interview with Herman Cain illustrates how the media can augment the confusion and ambiguity surrounding harassment, while reinforcing the sex partition by suggesting men and women need to be cautious in their interactions with one another. In the following excerpt, conservative radio talk show host Sean Hannity was trying to uncover what, if any, harassing behaviors Cain performed while at the National Restaurant Association.[13]

Hannity: What did she [the accuser] allege?[14]

Cain: I don't know, Sean, other than the one thing that I talked about in terms of making a gesture to basically say that my wife was short, and she was as short as my wife. Now he [the accuser's lawyer] may be coming from the fact that he was her attorney when the charges [were] made. He still thinks that there's something. In other words, I don't know where his head is. He is not accepting the fact that the charges were found baseless is all I can conclude. Ok? So, I have no idea what they were, and when Greta [referring to an interview with Fox News reporter Greta Van Susteren] pushed me on it, I still couldn't come up with but one thing that might have been included in it.

Hannity: Is there anything that you can think of that might have been misconstrued? You talked about somebody's height—did you tell a woman that she looked good? That dress looks hot?

Cain: Nope.

Hannity: Anything, any flirtation that you can think of?

Cain: Nope, nope, I didn't, Sean. Let me tell you why, because being in business I learned a long time ago, that unless I am really, really comfortable with a fellow employee I don't pay women compliments, unless I know them well enough that they're not going to take it the wrong way. I know in this particular case, I didn't make those kind of compliments. I didn't say that she looks hot or whatever this sort of thing. Why? Because when you are in a leadership position you run the risk of it being misunderstood. So, I know I didn't do that kind of stuff.

Basically, Mr. Cain was describing the sex partition. He describes how his awareness of sexual harassment issues discourages him from interacting with his female coworkers. Specifically, he doesn't pay women compliments unless he knows them well enough to be sure they're not going to take it the wrong way.

Those in leadership positions, he warns, are particularly prone to misunderstanding by women. With a presidential candidate suggesting that male leaders should restrict their interactions with women in order to reduce any chance of misunderstanding, the sex partition no doubt gains strength.

It's important to note that paying a woman a compliment is *not* sexual harassment. Hannity asks Cain if he told a woman that she looked good or flirted. Telling a woman that she looks good is not sexual harassment either, nor is an isolated flirtation. However, this line of questioning certainly implied that telling a woman she looks good or an isolated flirtation constitutes sexual harassment. Male employees listening to the radio program could head to work with the message that similar comments toward their own female colleagues could result in sexual harassment allegations.

Recall, however, that sexual harassment law "doesn't prohibit simple teasing, offhand comments, or isolated incidents that are not very serious."[15] Legally, it would be okay for Cain to compliment women in the office. Even if his compliments inadvertently crossed the line from polite to creepy, if he stopped when told his behavior was unacceptable, his behavior would most likely not constitute harassment.

Furthermore, Cain's denial that he engaged in any sexual harassment reinforces the idea that men's innocent behavior may be misinterpreted by women at work. His message, that he withdrew from a presidential bid because of false sexual harassment allegations, perpetuates the perception that drastic repercussions ensue when women misinterpret male friendliness.

It's also important to note that there was no subtle misinterpretation in the allegations against Cain. No, Sharon Bialek, one of the women who alleged that Cain harassed her, wasn't concerned about compliments. She wasn't offended that he told her that she was the same height as his wife, or that she looked good. Regardless of whether her version of events is true, there could be no misunderstanding them. Bialek claimed that she dined with Cain, who offered to help her find a new job. Driving from the restaurant, she claims that Cain parked the car and then "suddenly reached over and put his hand on my leg, under my skirt and reached for my genitals. He also grabbed my head and brought it towards his crotch."[16] When she expressed her shock at his actions, she claims Cain told her, "You want a job, right?"[17] Although only Bialek and Cain know exactly what happened that night, Cain's message that he was misunderstood merely perpetuates the attitude that caution needs to be taken in interactions with women at work.

Cain is not alone—other famous cases of sexual harassment have brought down men in high positions. Mark Hurd, for example, was at the height of his career when charged with sexual harassment. Hurd took over a struggling Hewlett Packard (HP) in 2005. By 2010 Hurd turned the company around, and the *New York Times* reported that Hurd had "pulled off one of the great rescue missions in American corporate history, refocusing the strife-ridden company and leading it to five years of revenue gains and a stock that soared 130 percent."[18] Hurd was negotiating a three-year contract with HP that would pay him $100 million when sexual harassment charges surfaced. HP investigated the charges and found that they were unsubstantiated.[19] The investigation, however, uncovered expense reports that Hurd had filed indicating a misuse of company funds, and Hurd was asked to resign, ostensibly because of the expense reports. Hurd believed the true reason the board decided to oust him stemmed from potential public relations problems that would follow sexual harassment allegations.[20] Even though the investigation could not substantiate that harassment took place, Hurd suggested that the allegations alone brought him down, and not the expense reports.

Both positive and negative messages are sent through the extensive media coverage of these two cases. The positive message is that sexual harassment will not be tolerated no matter how powerful the perpetrator. The second, more subtle, message suggests that mere allegations of sexual harassment can bring down powerful men, even if the evidence of harassing behavior is sketchy or nonexistent. It is this second message that strengthens the sex partition by escalating fears of sexual harassment allegations.

FALSE ALLEGATIONS ADD TO THE FEAR SURROUNDING SEXUAL HARASSMENT

Cain and Hurd both asserted that the sexual harassment claims against them were false. In general, employees believe that false sexual harassment allegations are relatively common. According to a 2011 *Newsweek* poll, 85 percent of those surveyed felt that employees are unfairly accused of sexual harassment at least some of the time.[21] Yet another poll revealed that 25 percent of men worry that they will be falsely charged with sexual harassment at work.[22] If one avoids harassing behavior, fear of legitimate claims of harassment is minimized. However, how can anyone avoid false allegations without avoiding cross-sex interactions altogether?

Indulge an analogy to shoplifting. Typically, if you don't shoplift, chances are pretty slim that you'd be falsely accused of shoplifting. And, if by some chance, you were falsely accused of shoplifting, due process would most likely exonerate you. Therefore, most of us have no trepidation when entering a store. Now, imagine instead that false shoplifting allegations were prevalent, and that those suspected of shoplifting were typically prosecuted by store security without due process. Chances are you'd develop an aversion to shopping, and you would think twice before stepping into a store. Similarly, the general perception that false harassment charges are common, and that those accused of sexual harassment are not afforded due process, results in an aversion to interactions with opposite-sex employees.

False allegations of harassment are of course feared, because they can have a devastating impact on the accused. Even if the accused is found not guilty, coworkers can still assume guilt despite evidence to the contrary, families are affected, and all male employees (not just the accused) are likely to shut down their interactions with female coworkers. One professor I spoke with, we'll call him Rohit (not his real name), shared with me the impact that false allegations had on him. Although the case was formally closed over a decade ago, the repercussions persisted long after.

Rohit's ordeal began in a class he taught that tackled controversial issues. In the class, some female students disagreed with a classmate's viewpoint on the likelihood of false allegations of rape. The students complained to the school's sexual harassment officer, and Rohit was initially charged with creating a hostile environment for women in his class. However, after the first few months of the investigation into the hostile environment allegations, the charges escalated to rape. That's right, one of the students who claimed he created a hostile environment in class was now accusing him of raping her as well. Why didn't these charges surface at the beginning? The alleged victim thought the hostile environment charges would be "enough."

Even though Rohit had alibis when these alleged rapes supposedly occurred, a university panel found him guilty. Fortunately, the university chancellor reversed the panel and dismissed the case, and Rohit won a defamation case against his accuser. It may sound like everything turned out fine. After all, Rohit was not found guilty and even won a defamation case against his accuser. But things weren't okay for Rohit, his family, his coworkers, or his female students—and more than ten years later, they're still not back to normal.

Despite the verdict in his favor, people still assumed Rohit was guilty. The day of the verdict, Rohit says the local newspaper ran a piece on how the outcome (in Rohit's favor) was a travesty of justice. At the university, some of Rohit's colleagues, other professors who had invited him to speak to their classes each semester, pretended not to know him any longer. "I'd walk on campus, I'd say 'hi' and they'd turn their head."

And the toll the ordeal took on his family? Rohit told me that if it wasn't for his wife and two children, he would have contemplated suicide. That's how much of a nightmare the whole situation was for him. Even his eight-year-old daughter suffered consequences. A previously independent little girl began wetting her bed, wouldn't sleep alone, and was afraid to go to school. One reporter who called their home told the scared little girl who answered the phone that her father was in "big trouble."

And, of course, the allegations affected his female students. Not only was Rohit less likely to interact with his female students, but do you think his fellow professors wanted to endure what Rohit had experienced? They also shut down interactions with female students. Rohit told me how his open-door policy quickly became a closed-door policy.

> When I first started teaching, I had an open-door policy. Students could come in any time my door was open, and they could talk to me about anything. I had a real easy relationship with my students. Obviously, that all changed. After the whole thing began, I had a closed-door policy. You didn't come to my office unless you had an arrangement with me, and I would avoid making appointments with female students. If a female student wanted to talk to me, I told them to see me in class. I'd tell them, right before the beginning of class, come up in front and ask me your questions—in other words, with everybody else sitting there. I did everything I could to avoid meeting female students outside of class. And I'd say that continued for close to ten years. None of my colleagues had exactly the same open-door policy I did, but some of them were close, and that all stopped. None of us wanted to deal with female students anymore.

None of the professors *wanted to deal with female students anymore.* And that's just the people that Rohit knew. What about the others that read about his ordeal in the local papers or heard about it on the local news? It would be a safe bet that many that heard about his story were also more reluctant to interact with their female colleagues. For Rohit, things never returned to normal. Although he'll now allow female students in his office, his blind trust of female students is gone forever. Wariness around women is his new normal.

I asked Rohit how such an event could transpire at his university. Rohit explained that the sexual harassment officer on campus overzealously sought to find sexual harassment, even when it wasn't there. She spoke to students and warned them that sexual harassment was pervasive, and that they must be constantly on guard. He told me:

> The sexual harassment booklet that was sent around to the students and the faculty was so insane, and the sexual harassment officer who promoted it found sexual harassment everywhere she looked. In it, she said if we upset a student or say something in class that upsets a student, that can be sexual harassment.

When she came to our department, she explained there are two basic types of sexual harassers. There are those that are stodgy, they dress up and like to wear nice clothes, they want you to call them Professor this or Doctor that, and they seem to be beyond reproach. And you have to watch them, because once they establish their sense of superiority, then they take advantage of you. The other type are the ones that are loose and laid back, they're relaxed, they wear casual clothing, they don't mind if you call them by their first name, and they get to be friends with you. Those are really the sinister ones, and you have to watch out for them, too. Basically, she just described all males on campus.

She would go around the campus talking to the students and faculty, and she created such fear in the faculty. People were afraid to say anything against her. You had to join with her, because if you weren't a part of that group, you could become part of the outgroup. And that's how she got people to support her insanity.

In other words, the members of the faculty were too afraid to stand up to the sexual harassment officer and clarify that upsetting a student in class does not constitute harassment. Obviously, neither a professor's style of dress nor how he or she prefers to be addressed are related to his or her likelihood to sexually harass. Students who are lucky enough to have the ear of a professor should take that opportunity, not be discouraged from it. The harassment policy at this university seemed to suggest it was best to avoid all professors. It's tough to learn that way. Fortunately, in light of Rohit's ordeal, they modified the policy. It's now toned down a bit.

Rohit's story isn't an isolated case. Stories of false harassment charges and overzealous pursuit of harassers are all too frequent. Professor of psychology Russell Eisenman, who studies sexual harassment, reported several instances of false harassment charges and situations where students were coerced into filing charges.[23] In one instance, a student was coerced into filing charges after a male professor asked her for a date. The student told a female professor about the date request, and this professor recommended that the student file sexual harassment charges. When the student wavered, the female professor gave the student an incomplete in her course, threatening to alter her grade if she did not file the charges. The student filed the charges, the male professor was convicted and penalized, and the student received an A in the female professor's course.

In another instance a female professor helped a student file a complaint against a male professor who had allegedly hugged the student in his office and spoke to her about sex.[24] He was convicted by a university panel and punished. However, the female professor then urged the student to file assault and battery charges with the police. She did file charges but then told a fellow student that the charges were not true. She had merely filed the charges to appease her female professor. After a long court battle, the professor was acquitted of the assault and battery charges.

Hearing stories of false allegations, it's not surprising that male executives fear sexual harassment charges. Some feel the "he said, she said" nature of sexual harassment allegations allows them to be used as a tool to get back at a disliked colleague, while others allege that overzealous feminists use sexual harassment charges to get back at men in general.[25] Male participants in one study described their fears of sexual harassment charges, and voiced concerns that sexual harassment can be used to target men:

- It [sexual harassment] is way too powerful a tool for a woman to use against men.
- It can be very uncomfortable, because some people can abuse the sexual harassment issue. Some women can use it as a tool.
- Harassment is way overused as a way to get back at people you don't care for.
- The accused harasser becomes the victim too easily. Anyone could accuse anyone on any given day and win.
- Something once said casually and innocently is now blown way out of proportion.[26]

What could polarize men and women in the workplace more than the suggestion that sexual harassment allegations can be falsely applied to get revenge upon a disliked coworker? The sentiments from these men clearly indicate anger and frustration at being potential targets of sexual harassment scams. The natural response to these feelings would be to withdraw and restrict interactions with female coworkers.

Accusations of sexual harassment can have consequences that run the gamut from losing one's job to losing the respect of family, friends, and coworkers. Clearly the repercussions of harassment charges were severe for Rohit. What about innocent until proven guilty? Within an organization, harassment cases are typically decided by a human resources representative without formal legal training. Often there is no fair hearing of both sides and no "reasonable doubt" standard prevails in determining guilt.

In fact, employers have incentive to favor the victim of sexual harassment. Ethics professor Mane Hajdin claims that "an employer that ends up erring in favor of the alleged harasser, even if only slightly, may easily find itself in court, while an employer that errs in favor of the alleged victim is unlikely to find itself in similar trouble, unless the error is extreme."[27] As a result employers have incentive to give the benefit of the doubt to the victim over the alleged harasser. While beneficial to victims of harassment, this strategy of presumed guilt of the accused further fuels the fears associated with sexual harassment charges.

Awareness of false allegations can lead men to limit their interactions with women and favor spending their free time with other men. One university professor told me how he became more cautious in his interactions with female students after hearing rumors of a colleague who was allegedly set up with false sexual harassment allegations. As a result, he described to me how he's more cautious in his interactions with female students.

> If I was teaching a night class that gets out at ten at night, and wanted to meet right after class with a student, I'd be much more comfortable meeting with a male student than meeting with a female student. I think about how this is going to be construed by the female student, "Hey, why don't you stop in at 10:15 at night." And that could be interpreted in a different way by a female student. It would seem creepy. Maybe I just have an avoidance of seeming creepy. With male students that doesn't enter my mind at all, I just tell them to stop by, and it's not a big deal. And I don't think it's going to be misconstrued as creepy.

As a result, there is an opportunity to get to know his male students better, and this translates into advantages for them. He continues:

> There would be a higher probability with male graduate students, if we had to kill time, for me to say, "Hey do you want to go grab a beer," or "I have to go eat, why don't you come with me" than with a female grad student. I can get to know a student better, and that might help them get a better letter of recommendation or personal recommendation from me down the road.

For this professor, the effects of the sex partition may seem small. Ostensibly, for female students, missing out on late-night meetings or dinner discussions may not be career altering. However, an opportunity exists for male students that clearly does not for female students. Male students have greater opportunities to befriend this professor and may walk away with a superior letter of recommendation as a result.

ACQUAINTANCES VS. CLOSE FRIENDS—WHO BEARS THE BRUNT OF THE SEX PARTITION?

In his interview with Sean Hannity, Herman Cain mentioned that he only offers compliments to women he knows well, suggesting that the fear of sexual harassment charges may have a larger impact on acquaintances than on close friends. The sex partition obstacles are not impenetrable, and there are certainly cross-sex dyads that are able to overcome these barriers and establish a close friendship at work. It seems that fear of sexual harassment charges may not constitute an issue for these closer cross-sex friendships.

Many of those I interviewed reiterated Cain's sentiment that caution is primarily required in interactions with those you don't know well. Andrew, a male management consultant, described how he needs to be comfortable with colleagues before he shares an inappropriate joke:

> If I make an off-color joke or something like that, I'm more likely to do that with a male than a female. Not that I go around telling dirty jokes all the time, but if I get a funny e-mail that I find humorous, I would certainly segregate by gender who I'd send that to. So it is harder to develop a real friendship. I have to have comfort, even though I am not necessarily operating strictly within the professional decorum boundaries, that it's not going to reflect back on me professionally through that person's eyes. And it's easier to get a feel for that with a same-sex person.[28]

You're probably thinking Andrew should keep his inappropriate jokes to himself at work. And you're right. However, rules that attempt to shut down this behavior don't seem to be effective. Instead, they merely restrict the sharing of such jokes to same-sex colleagues and a few cross-sex colleagues that can take the joke. As a result, it's women who are left out of the bonding that results from the joking sessions.

In her book *Gender on Trial*, Holly English recounts an interview with a male partner in a law firm who concurred that fear of sexual harassment led him to ask different questions of female coworkers he knows well and those he does not.

> I think that it takes longer for a male partner, me specifically, to let my hair down when supervising a woman associate than with a man. You kid around in a different way, talk about different things. The fear of lawsuits is in there at all times at some deep level. We don't want to create a hostile workplace so we create a stultified workplace. A guy is more easily prone to ask a guy who he was seeing, but I wouldn't ask a woman that unless I knew her well enough. I would be less reluctant to ask what a guy did over the weekend. I'd be more careful in my language, I'd swear a bit with a guy. I wouldn't do that with a woman. I sort of regret that I have to be that way.[29]

While it's good news that concerns surrounding sexual harassment have less impact on close cross-sex friendships, trouble developing acquaintance relationships can be problematic. Recall the importance of acquaintances or weak ties for career advancement. These are the folks more likely to get you a new job and connect you to new circles. And close friendships typically evolve from these acquaintance relationships too. Obstacles that impact acquaintances may ultimately hinder the development of close friendships.

ATTRACTIVE WOMEN MAY HAVE EVEN MORE DIFFICULTY ESTABLISHING FRIENDSHIPS

Just as acquaintances may be harder hit by the sex partition, attractive women may also suffer greater obstacles to cross-sex friendship development at work. Imagine that a senior male executive decides to mentor a junior woman. They frequently engage in closed-door meetings in his office and occasionally meet up outside of work. How does the interpretation of this scenario change if the woman is extremely attractive or extremely unattractive? Sadly, the executive's motivations are more likely to be questioned when the woman is attractive. As a result, men may be even less likely to engage in one-on-one meetings with very attractive women. As a result, attractive women may have more difficulty establishing cross-sex friendships and mentor relationships than their more homely female colleagues.

Most of us have a schema or a mental picture of how sexual harassment transpires in the workplace.[30] In this mental picture of sexual harassment, the perpetrator is typically male and the target is typically female—an attractive female, that is. Most people believe unattractive people are less likely to be sexually harassed, and thus are less likely to believe sexual harassment charges when they come from a less attractive employee.[31] Therefore, employees may be more cautious when interacting with an attractive woman.

In general, attractive people receive a lot of breaks at work and are generally perceived as more intelligent, more likely to be hired, and they typically earn more money than those who are less attractive.[32] Interestingly, attractive women don't seem to fare quite as well as their good-looking male counterparts. One study followed MBA graduates who had each been rated on their physical attractiveness.[33] Ten years after their graduation, attractive men earned an additional $2600 for each additional unit of attractiveness, but attractive women only outearned unattractive women at a rate of $2150 for each additional unit of attractiveness. Attractive women still have an advantage, but their advantage is not as great as that experienced by attractive men. I would argue this discrepancy results from the greater burden the sex partition imposes on attractive women.

Ironically, men at work need not worry so much about attractive women bringing harassment charges, because research indicates that attractive women are less likely to label certain behaviors (including sexual joking, requests for romantic or sexual relations, touching and grabbing) as sexually harassing.[34] Most likely because attractive women are more accustomed to flattery and other flirtations from men, they are less likely than unattractive women to label these behaviors sexual harassment.

WORK IS A NO-FLIRTING ZONE

Flirting is another avenue to friendship that is curtailed in the workplace due to sexual harassment awareness. In their book *Flirting 101: How to Charm Your Way to Love, Friendship, and Success*, Andrew Bryant and Michelle Lewis suggest that those who have the ability to flirt generally establish more cross-sex friendships. The best flirters are typically skilled conversationalists and good listeners who can initiate new conversations and forge new relationships.

Although many typically think of flirting as signaling sexual interest, flirting need not have a seduction component. People often flirt merely to make others feel good about themselves.[35] Evolutionary psychologists believe humans' ability to flirt is hardwired.[36] From an evolutionary perspective, good flirters are able to attract more potential mates, which is advantageous for passing along genes to future generations. Humans are not the only flirters—all mammals flirt, as do birds, fish, and even fruit flies.[37]

In the workplace, however, there is a fine line between flirting and inappropriate behavior. As Bryant and Lewis describe, "Knowing where that line is will protect you from ending up in bed with someone you really only wanted to talk to, or from making a terrible mistake in work situations."[38] Fear of making a terrible mistake or crossing the line at work keeps many coworkers from using flirting as a tool for developing cross-sex friendships at work.

While completing a research study on sexuality in the workplace, Christine Williams, Patti Giuffre, and Kirsten Dellinger spoke to a female urologist who described the effect of sexual harassment regulations on flirting in the operating room:

> Sexual banter happens partly because of the high stress situations. In the operating room, it's even more stressful. You all go in and put on these scrubs. It removes social and sexual boundaries. . . . [There's] teasing and joking and pinching and elbowing. It's fun. That's one reason people like being in that arena.

That's part of the camaraderie. . . . I think it's been limited somewhat by all of the sexual harassment cases. It's sad that if someone who I'm working with nudges up to me and elbows me, and I say, "I'm glad I wore my metal bra today to protect myself from your elbow," I can't say that in peace anymore. It's a way that men and women interact. It's a form of flirtation.[39]

Clearly, flirting behavior that "crosses the line" should not be tolerated in the workplace, especially if it makes some employees uncomfortable. Yet cross-sex friends often flirt to develop and maintain their friendships. Efforts aimed at eliminating this behavior in the workplace exacerbate the sex partition.

IS THE SEX PARTITION ALL ABOUT THE MEN?

Thus far, the evidence suggests that men are more reserved in their interactions with women because of their fears regarding sexual harassment charges. Where are the women in this? In general, women don't fear sexual harassment charges, but instead sense their male colleagues' discomfort with women. Women feel that in order to fit in, they need to put the male colleagues at ease.

Recall Joan at the beginning of this chapter who described how her male coworkers typically feel uncomfortable around women, and friendship can only develop after they perceive no risk of sexual harassment charges. Elizabeth, a female attorney, noted a similar discomfort from the male law partners in her firm:

My own experience when I worked with certain male partners, I think when they worked with male associates they would be more free to, as some attorneys do, probably a lot of senior management do, swear or act in a certain way. You felt as though they didn't feel comfortable doing that in front of you, which was fine, but then you felt that also they just didn't feel comfortable. They felt uncomfortable with you entirely. You could tell they were trying to think about how they should act, which made it an uncomfortable relationship. You wanted to say, "Hey, act how you want, I don't really care, I'm very easy going, just do whatever." You could just sense that they felt they had to act differently, and that it made them just prefer to not be alone with you in an office and not have to, you know, they would rather work with a male associate.[40]

These women clearly sensed that the men in their organizations hold back in their interactions with women, making it harder to "break the barrier" and establish a friendship with these men. As a result of the gender differences that emerged in these interviews (that men are more likely to withdraw or hold back due to concerns regarding sexual harassment, and the women report having to relax these fears in the men in order to establish a friendship), women may face a double-edged sword. To be included as "one of the guys," they may have to endure behavior they find objectionable. If they complain about the objectionable behavior, the women will most likely be excluded from the male networks.

I'm not suggesting the sex partition is men's fault. It's really not anyone's fault. It's true that men may be more reserved in their actions around women, but that's because we're inadvertently encouraging men to do just that. We're instilling a fear of sexual harassment charges that's polarizing women and men at work. Fortunately, we can improve the situation. I devote later chapters to detailed solutions and work-arounds, but the single most important catalyst for change is starting a dialogue. Talking frankly about the sex partition at work with peers, managers, and subordinates will facilitate communication between the sexes. Through open communication, employees can get a sense of exactly where the boundaries lie in their workplace. Would the female urologist's coworkers really be offended if she made a joke about her metal bra? I suspect not. She feels the camaraderie is missing because she can't be free to make these comments, but if she talked to her coworkers about her concerns, perhaps the camaraderie and her free speech could be restored.

DOES SEXUAL HARASSMENT TRAINING IMPLY WOMEN ARE WEAK?

There's no denying that some women could use the protection of a stronger person—but so could some men.

—Katherine Dunn, author[1]

The Endangered Species Act protects helpless animals, child labor laws protect vulnerable youngsters, and sexual harassment laws and training are provided for whom? Although the training is purported to be for both men and women, most employees still think of sexual harassment as a women's issue. Therefore, most would argue that sexual harassment training is predominantly provided for the protection of female employees. However, just like the endangered animals and the vulnerable youth, the suggestion that women need protection carries with it images of weak women who can't fend for themselves. Could sexual harassment training inadvertently be reinforcing stereotypes of women as weak and in need of protection?

The EEOC recommends that all employers offer sexual harassment training to their employees, and in some states, state law mandates that training be provided. In particular, California legislation requires that all employers who employ fifty or more persons provide supervisors with two hours of training in the prevention of sexual harassment within six months of hire or promotion, and every two years thereafter. Maine has an even stricter law requiring those with fifteen or more employees to offer sexual harassment training. It is estimated that United States employers spend about $10 billion annually on employment-law training, and sexual harassment prevention is one of the main topics.[2]

The goal of workplace training in sexual harassment is clear: to reduce the likelihood that harassing behavior will occur in the workplace. However, if sexual harassment prevention efforts are reinforcing stereotypes of weak women, then perhaps more is not better.

WEAK WOMEN—STRONG MEN

The suggestion that sexual harassment training inadvertently implies female weakness is not new. Training videos used to teach employees about sexual harassment tend to be gender neutral, portraying men as victims of sexual harassment as often as women. Despite these efforts to appear gender neutral, we all know that the large majority of sexual harassment cases are still brought by women against men, and sexual harassment is still largely perceived as a women's issue. Unfortunately, women may be perceived as needing this extra protection because they are unable to handle such issues on their own. Perceived weakness does not bode well for women's career advancement or for their networking potential. If women are perceived as unable to handle an isolated comment about their appearance, how are they supposed to handle a role in the C-suite? And who wants to mentor or befriend a weak employee?

Although feminists have spoken out on this issue, their protests have been largely ignored. For example, author and social critic Camille Paglia summarized: "What troubles me about the 'hostile workplace' category of sexual harassment policy is that women are being returned to their old status of delicate flowers who must be protected from assault by male lechers. It is anti-feminist to ask for special treatment for women."[3]

Author and journalist Katie Roiphe wrote, "In fact, the majority of women in the workplace are not tender creatures and are largely adept at dealing with all varieties of uncomfortable or hostile situations. Show me a smart, competent young professional woman who is utterly derailed by a verbal unwanted sexual advance or an inappropriate comment about her appearance, and I will show you a rare spotted owl."[4]

Even the United States Ninth Circuit Court suggests that women live in constant fear of sexual assault from men. The court writes:

> We realize that there is a broad range of viewpoints among women as a group, but we believe that many women share common concerns which men do not necessarily share. For example, because women are disproportionately victims of rape and sexual assault, women have a stronger incentive to be concerned with

sexual behavior. Women who are victims of mild forms of sexual harassment may understandably worry whether a harasser's conduct is merely a prelude to violent sexual assault. Men, who are rarely victims of sexual assault, may view sexual conduct in a vacuum without a full appreciation of the social setting or the underlying threat of violence that a woman may perceive.[5]

The court is asserting that women are concerned about mild forms of sexual harassment, because they are fearful of sexual assault from men. Sexual assault is inexcusable, and obviously should never be tolerated. In the horrible circumstances when it occurs, it's a frightening and often life-changing event. However, I'm not sure that most women fear that mild forms of harassment will escalate to assault. And suggesting that women fear that everyone is a potential assaulter doesn't exactly inspire cross-sex networking. I appreciate their concern, but the court does not exactly inspire men to team up with a woman on their next business venture.

SURPRISING RESULTS FROM MY STUDY

Despite the suggestion that sexual harassment prevention efforts increase the perception that women are weak or fragile, no one to date has conducted research on this issue. In order to assess how sexual harassment protection may impact perceptions of women, I conducted an exploratory experimental study of 111 university students. The goal of the study was to determine if watching a sexual harassment training video altered perceptions of women. Since the sex partition focuses on friendship, the study examined how viewing a sexual harassment training video altered perceptions of one's closest female friend and closest male friend.

The study involved sixty-nine women and forty-two men enrolled at a state university who participated in the study for course credit. (Refer to Appendix A to review the details of the study methodology, the participant demographics, and statistical data analysis.) Due to the nature of the study, only students who had some work experience were included in the study.

In order to disguise the goal of the study, the participants were told they were completing a two-part study to both evaluate a training video and to assess their friendships. Unbeknownst to the participants, the computer program automatically divided them into one of two experimental conditions. Half of the participants watched a typical sexual harassment training video and half watched a fire-safety training video. If sexual harassment training did indeed impact perceptions of women, then those who watched the sexual harassment training video would be more likely to rate their female friends as weaker than their male friends. For those who watched the fire-safety video, we would expect no such effect.

The sample sexual harassment training video was chosen because it seemed liked a typical training tool and was produced by a popular sexual harassment training provider. Although the video was short (under ten minutes in length), it covered all the basics. The video defined the two types of sexual harassment (quid pro quo and hostile environment), described the punishments for harassers (from warnings to termination of employment), and provided suggestions for a harassment-free environment (e.g., treat everyone with respect). In the video, both men and women were depicted as harassers, and suggestions for those harassed included confronting the harasser and reporting the harasser to management. The video was accurate and informative, and it seemed like a reasonable training tool.

Once again, if sexual harassment training had a negative effect on perceptions of female strength, we'd expect that those who watched the sexual harassment training would be more likely to rate their closest female friends as weaker than their closest male friends. Indeed, that is exactly what the results indicated. Participants who watched the sexual harassment training video were more likely to rate their closest female friend as emotionally weaker than their closest male friend. It is interesting to note that this result did not differ between male and female participants. That is, both men and women were more likely to rate the closest female friend weaker after watching the sexual harassment video. It is also important to note that there was nothing unusual about this particular video that would encourage this result.

REPERCUSSIONS FOR WOMEN AT WORK

The repercussions of these results are substantial. First and foremost is the source of the problem: sexual harassment training. Recent legislation intended to help women in the workplace by requiring organizations to institute sexual harassment training may inadvertently be hindering women as well. The sexual harassment training that is being rolled out to employees in organizations throughout the country may be reinforcing stereotypes that women are weak.

Furthermore, the focus of the sex partition is on friendship and mentor relationships. The results of this study indicate that perceptions of close friends were impacted by the sexual harassment training video. Power is an important element of friendship, and in the workplace, powerful coworkers are more desirable friends.[6] If women are perceived as weaker, they will have more difficulty developing valuable friendships with their male coworkers.

The perception of female weakness also has consequences for the development of mentor relationships. A senior executive doesn't choose weak employees to mentor but instead prefers up-and-coming employees with potential in the organization. Those who are perceived as weak are less likely to establish valuable mentor relationships.

It is important to acknowledge this study was exploratory in nature. More research will be required to replicate these results and assess what aspects of the sexual harassment training resulted in the adjusted perceptions of women. Was it the mere mention of the sexual harassment issue or something specific related to the particular video I chose? Also this study was conducted with primarily young university undergraduates, but I believe the result would be magnified if older employees with more work experience were studied. Years of exposure to sexual harassment through training, the media, and personal experience may make more seasoned employees more likely to perceive sexual harassment as a women's issue and therefore to perceive women as weak for needing such protection. Clearly, further research is required to assess the generalizability of this study to older employees.

The participants in this study were questioned about their friends within a few minutes of completing the sexual harassment training video, so the duration of the effects is not known. It isn't clear whether questioning them about their friends an hour, a day, or a week after watching the video would produce the same results. Clearly, the longer the effects endure, the more detrimental for women in the workplace.

KERNEL OF TRUTH—*ARE* WOMEN WEAKER THAN MEN?

The results of this study raise an interesting question regarding the strength of men and women with regard to dealing with sexual harassment. On average, men are physically stronger than women, but what about emotionally? Is there a kernel of truth to the notion that women are weaker than men when it comes to experiencing sexual harassment? If women are indeed weaker than men, then the same sexual harassment experiences would exert a greater impact on women than on men. However, research indicates that women do not report more severe outcomes from sexual harassment than their male counterparts.[7]

Specifically, the gender differences in the effects of harassment were examined in over eighty-nine thousand male and female employees.[8] For both men and women, sexual harassment was associated with a plethora of negative outcomes, ranging from distress to poor health to negative job outcomes. However, men and women who were harassed did not differ in their experience of these negative outcomes. In other words, sexual harassment does not have more of an impact on women, but men who are harassed experience the same level of distress and negative job outcomes as women do. These findings should be included in sexual harassment training to dispel the myth that women need protection from sexual harassment because of some gender-related weakness.

The results of this study suggest that recent legislation intended to create a workplace more hospitable toward women may be contributing to gender inequity at work. Creating a less hostile work environment is clearly a noble goal, and I'm certainly not suggesting we abandon it. We just need to increase our awareness of the unintended consequences of sexual harassment training, so that they can be addressed. I have little doubt that sexual harassment training can evolve to provide the same information, but with fewer repercussions for women.

So far, we've covered how heightened awareness of sexual harassment in the workplace and fear of sexual harassment charges hinder cross-sex interactions at work. And the training we provide to prevent sexual harassment may change perceptions of women in the workplace. But are there still more aspects of this training that contribute to the segregation of the sexes at work? Lamentably, yes, there's more.

5

SEXUAL HARASSMENT TRAINING: MORE REPERCUSSIONS

Ignorance of all things is an evil neither terrible nor excessive, nor yet the greatest of all; but great cleverness and much learning, if they be accompanied by a bad training, are a much greater misfortune.

—Plato[1]

Traders are generally an impatient lot. They speak quickly, walk fast, and hate to waste time. In one high-rise building where I was employed, the equity trading floor was on the fifth floor. An express elevator would whisk traders up to their desks. Although many high-rise buildings offer express elevators to higher floors, few offer express rides to floor five. At Morgan Stanley, where time was money, traders could not waste their time waiting in an elevator while passengers disembarked at lower floors. In order to save more time, shoe shiners would visit the trading floor, so that traders wouldn't miss out on any important trades while scuff marks were removed from their shoes. A separate cafeteria was provided on the trading floors, so that rushed employees who did not have the time to make it to the corporate cafeteria (another elevator ride) could grab some lunch. My boss even requested a revolving door be placed between our adjacent offices. Walking out of his office door and into mine required too much time. That was the culture. Time was money.

Imagine the reaction of these time-sensitive traders when told they were required to attend sexual harassment training. The perception was that sexual harassment training was for the benefit of the few female employees, and so, it was the women's fault the men had to endure the training.

WHO LIKES GOING TO WORKPLACE SEXUAL HARASSMENT TRAINING?

It's probably safe to say that most professionals don't look forward to attending sexual harassment training in their organization—it's just one more meeting to fit into a busy schedule. However, if employees believe that the training is primarily intended to benefit women, resentment at having to attend this training may be directed toward female employees. The true reason that sexual harassment training is typically provided is not for women or men, but to reduce legal liability. Nonetheless, most people still think of sexual harassment as a woman's issue. By consequence, resentment at having to attend the training may be directed at women in the workplace.

Again, I'm certainly not suggesting that we eliminate sexual harassment training. We do, however, need to be aware of this frustration, because it's one more issue that can alienate men and women at work. If we're going to spend hours talking to our employees about creating a hospitable work environment for both sexes, then let's make sure that's the outcome. Sexual harassment training needs to be accurate, informative, and motivated by establishing a welcoming work environment for men and women. Busy people will still probably resent having to attend, but if they feel their concerns are addressed, their resentment may be minimized.

WHEN ALEXANDER MCPHERSON SAID "NO" TO SEXUAL HARASSMENT TRAINING

In order to limit legal liability, organizations take sexual harassment training very seriously, but often the concerns of individuals get lost in the process. So eager are they to cover their legal butt, trainers can forget that the point of the training should be to create a hospitable work environment for everyone. As a result, those who have reservations about the training can be ignored or even punished.

Alexander McPherson, a professor of molecular biology and biochemistry at the University of California-Irvine, refused to complete his university's sexual harassment training. Why? He felt it was an attack on his integrity. In other words, he felt that forcing him to take sexual harassment training implied that he needs it. If the university felt he needed to take sexual harassment training it must be because they thought he might sexually harass someone. Although sexual harassment training is about tolerance and ensuring employees are comfortable in the workplace, the university refused to acknowledge McPherson's reservations regarding the training. In fact, the great lengths his university was willing to go to in order to ensure his complicity with the training demonstrates the significance that sexual harassment training has achieved within organizations.

McPherson and other faculty and supervisors at UC-Irvine were asked to complete sexual harassment training so the university would be in compliance with California law AB1825 (the California state law requiring institutions with more than fifty employees to provide training to supervisors). McPherson was willing to complete the training if the university was willing to sign a statement indicating he was under no suspicion of sexual harassment.

Had the university stepped in and addressed McPherson's concerns, the problem would have ended there. However, because sexual harassment training is motivated by legal issues and not people issues, the university refused. After McPherson's story appeared in the *Orange County Register*, things started to get ugly. The university began by stripping McPherson of his supervisory duties. McPherson was not fazed and persevered. He told me:

> I had to teach a course, and they said you can't supervise your teaching assistants. So, they took away all the teaching assistants. Well, they thought that this was a terrible punishment. It meant I had to grade the papers, but big deal. In the old days, I used to do all of that anyway. They let me teach—funny how I could supervise my students but not my TAs.

When the university realized this punishment was not sufficiently severe to coerce McPherson into training, they came down even harder. McPherson had just been awarded a $1.5 million grant from the National Institutes of Health (NIH). This grant supported McPherson's laboratory and, in particular, the salaries of two senior researchers in his lab. As is the case with many grants (despite the fact that McPherson developed the grant proposal and was the principal investigator on the grant), the NIH grant was legally contracted to the university. Therefore the university had the right to refuse the grant.

The university threatened to strip McPherson of his grant due to his lack of participation in sexual harassment training. McPherson explained:

> Had they killed that grant [my senior researchers] would have been out on the street after twenty years, because I couldn't pay them. So this was the leverage they were using on me. Both of [the researchers] at that time were pretty near retirement age, and they'd been with me since 1989. These people are as close to me as family, and I had to protect these people.

In order to pay his researchers, McPherson needed the grant. Therefore, McPherson completed the training, but he never received any written statement from the university. At least his grant was not declined. What did McPherson think of the training?

> In the end I did take the sexual harassment training online. It was trivial. It required me to sit there for forty-five minutes, and at the end answer these questions that were absolutely idiot questions. You didn't even need to take the training—your grandmother taught you this.
>
> One of the things I learned from the sexual harassment training was that it had only marginally to do with sexual harassment. It was mostly training on how to avoid getting the university sued. That's what it was all about. This is nothing but a giant protection of the university racket. There was no sincerity behind it to prevent sexual harassment, but that's not their objective. Their objective is to keep us from getting sued. And as long as they at least make the pretense that they are doing everything they can to prevent this, then it protects them from lawsuits.

If the university had been sympathetic to McPherson's concerns, he would have complied and completed the training. Taking into account that some employees may be antagonistic toward the training should be an integral part of all sexual harassment training. Training programs that incorporate flexibility and understanding toward reluctant employees may curtail resentment.

One of the craziest aspects of McPherson's story is the university's reaction. Inspired by McPherson's reluctance to partake in sexual harassment training, the University of California took up the issue of how to enforce sexual harassment training compliance by faculty. It turns out, a proposed punishment for those not participating in the training was more severe than the punishment typically given to sexual harassers![2]

Perhaps it's a sign we've gone a little far when the punishment for lack of participation in sexual harassment training exceeds the punishment for sexually harassing. We need to take a step back and remember what the goals of the training are, and be sure to address concerns about the training.

Other anecdotal evidence corroborates how obsessed organizations have become with regard to compliance with sexual harassment training. *US News and World Report* described how a team of Indiana firefighters volunteered to help rescue victims of Hurricane Katrina. When they arrived in Atlanta, Federal Emergency Management Agency (FEMA) staffers told them that their job was to hand out flyers, but their first task was to attend a multi-hour course on sexual harassment and equal employment opportunity.[3] Evidently, this is standard operating procedure at FEMA. Another example comes from CIA agent Robert

Baer's memoir, *See No Evil*, where Baer describes asking headquarters to send someone who spoke Afghan languages.[4] CIA headquarters offered to send a four-member sexual harassment team instead.

THEY SAID *WHAT* IN SEXUAL HARASSMENT TRAINING?

I am certainly not suggesting we make sexual harassment training optional, but I do believe we should be more sensitive to the concerns of the participants. Most importantly, if organizations go to such great lengths to ensure that every employee attends sexual harassment training, they should at least ensure the information they provide during that training is accurate. Unfortunately, that's not always the case.

Although regulation addresses the frequency and length of sexual harassment training, the substance of the training is somehow overlooked. Basically employers are told the importance of sexual harassment training but not the most effective approach to implementation. As a result, organizations ranging from automobile manufacturers to supermarkets must discover how to best instruct their employees about sexual harassment—not exactly their area of expertise. These organizations may rely on their own legal and human resources departments or hire outsiders to provide training. But even those who choose to outsource are forced to select from a proliferation of sexual harassment training providers.

As a result, the quality of training varies greatly from employer to employer. Negative experiences with the training not only lead to anger and frustration with required participation but also may result in negative feelings toward women. If employees are annoyed regarding their forced participation in sexual harassment training and feel that the training is intended to benefit women, then their irritation may be extended to women in the workplace.

The causes of frustration with the training vary. One of the most common complaints is that it is a waste of time. Employees often think they already know what constitutes sexual harassment and that they learn little from the training itself. If the information is provided with a condescending tone, the backlash may be even greater. Bill Whittle of the *National Review* describes his recent experience with sexual harassment training as follows:

> To be subjected to two hours of second-grade style, "who can tell me what Johnny did wrong by telling Sarah she has a hot body" lecturing infuriates me on many levels. To begin with, I do not need to be told this is inappropriate behav-

ior. I already know that is inappropriate behavior. I learned that was inappropriate behavior not from the state of California or a battalion of corporate lawyers,
but from my parents who raised me to be polite, well-mannered, and who spent
much of their own youth trying to form me into a civilized gentleman.[5]

Another complaint about sexual harassment training is that the training itself
can be offensive. Several letters and e-mails written to Alexander McPherson
described personal experiences with sexual harassment training that left participants offended, frustrated, and confused. (McPherson's ordeal was widely
publicized, and he was kind enough to share the e-mails and letters he received
in response to his predicament.) Some of their experiences were appalling. One
professor wrote:

> While at [the university] all faculty were required to take "sensitivity training."
> We were commanded to pair with a professor of the opposite sex. Then we were
> commanded to feel each other. I refused on the grounds that as a married man
> I had no intention of feeling any woman except my wife. I was forced to feel the
> woman's arm or face disciplinary action. I felt her arm. Does it strike you as il-
> logical that we are commanded to feel women who are strangers, then laws are
> passed making it illegal?

Clearly, sexual harassment training should not force men and women to
touch one another, but without any oversight on the content, anything can
be included in the training. Another employee described his experience with
sexual harassment training that he found offensive:

> As an employee of a university, it was mandatory (in order to keep my job) to
> accept the same policies that Professor McPherson did not accept. While taking
> the [sexual harassment] training course I was appalled by the example situations
> that were presented. I honestly felt like I was harassed by exposure to the training
> situations. There were several uncomfortable scenarios that were very unlikely
> to involve me. The perverted scenarios were presented as if they were common.
> I agree that nobody should harass their coworkers, but the training scenarios
> presented were vulgar.

Yet another described how he felt the training was demeaning to men: "Participants were told that because they are men they are prone to sexually harass."
Consistent with the findings that the training leaves perceptions that women
are weak, one employee expressed his disdain for sexual harassment training
for just this reason. He wrote, "Europeans must be laughing at our weak and
defenseless women who don't have the guts to send some jerk to hell and must

depend on the state's legal system to protect them. In Europe women have no trouble telling someone to buzz off."

In addition to descriptions of condescending, boring, and offensive training sessions (as if that's not bad enough), sexual harassment training can also instill fear into employees. In his research on sexual harassment and training, Russell Eisenman describes a sexual harassment training session in which the seminar leader accidently admitted to using sexual harassment allegations to punish a disliked employee. Eisenman writes:

> The person directing the sexual harassment seminar made what may have been a Freudian slip, saying "We would not try to fire someone for a minor behavior, even if it was sexual harassment, unless it was someone we are trying to get." She then realized how awful it sounds to say that they might use their power arbitrarily to "get" someone. So, she "corrected" herself saying "I do not mean we would try to get someone. . . ." This is part of the problem. Sexual harassment, especially the "hostile environment" type, is so vague that even attorneys cannot agree what is and what is not sexual harassment. Thus, the concept can be used to get someone, if that person is politically disfavored. Or, the person may have done something relatively minor, such as tell one dirty joke, and they can be fired for sexual harassment.[6]

Such arguments only add fuel to the polarization of men and women in the workplace. The suggestion that someone could be fired for minor behavioral infractions could instill sufficient fear in employees so that they refrain from interactions with opposite-sex coworkers.

One professor that I know, let's call him Ryan, told me how just this year he thought some in his department used sexual harassment to try to "get him" because they disapproved of his area of research (shhh, it involved unusual sexual practices!). The research was really the work of one of his graduate students. When the title of her thesis was announced at graduation, he could sense the disapproval from his colleagues. Although some colleagues clearly deemed the research topic inappropriate, the university research board had already given their stamp of approval for this line of research. Ryan felt that since his colleagues couldn't complain directly about his research, they'd find another way to get him. They reported him to the human resources department.

Ryan was called in by his human resources department and initially probed about his teaching. "Do you discuss anal sex during class?" was one of the first questions shot at him. Not knowing where this investigation was going, he explained that his health course covered the AIDS epidemic. It would be hard to discuss the spread of AIDS without mentioning anal sex, he explained.

Clearly, questions about his teaching weren't going anywhere, but a guy that does sex research must have done something inappropriate. The questioning continued. The human resources representative asked Ryan if he ever asked female colleagues to lunch. When he replied yes, the follow-up question was, "Don't you know that asking a woman to lunch is different than asking a man?" When Ryan defended himself by stating the department was predominantly female, and if he didn't want to dine alone, he had to ask women to join him, an investigation ensued. Several of Ryan's female colleagues were questioned as to whether Ryan had ever asked them to lunch. Thankfully, his female colleagues supported the notion that he was their friend, and reported that, indeed, they did dine with their friends—even male friends like Ryan.

Ryan's human resources department is sending a message that having lunch with an opposite-sex colleague is harassment. It's not. Needless to say, Ryan felt attacked and is now very hesitant to interact with his female colleagues. The suggestion that dining with opposite-sex colleagues could land you in trouble would instill fear into anyone. Ryan has also significantly reduced the number of students he is willing to work with. Those few students with whom he discusses his research must sign a waiver first.

If a new female faculty member is hired, it's unlikely Ryan will go out of his way to get to know her. He certainly won't be asking her to join him for lunch. She won't be able to garner the advantages of his years of experience in the department. Although Ryan's department is predominantly female, he told me the department has been chaired by men since his arrival twelve years ago. Connections with both sexes are necessary to get ahead, and at least in Ryan's university, they seem to be shutting down cross-sex interaction.

HOW DOES BACKLASH IMPACT SEXUAL HARASSMENT TRAINING?

While Ryan felt attacked by human resources and his own department, other men feel attacked by the sexual harassment training provided by their organization. In fact, sometimes they feel so attacked in sexual harassment training that the training actually backfires. A primary goal of sexual harassment training is to make employees more sensitive to sexual harassment issues in their workplaces. But sometimes just the opposite happens. Researchers Shereen Bingham and Lisa Scherer examined the impact of sexual harassment training and obtained shocking results.

Surveying half of their participants before they attended sexual harassment training and the other half after they completed training, they examined sensitivity to sexual harassment. If sexual harassment training was accomplishing its goal, those who attended sexual harassment training would be more sensitive to issues surrounding sexual harassment than those who had not.

Perhaps shockingly, that's exactly the opposite of what they found. Men who participated in sexual harassment training were *more likely* than men who did not to blame the victim and to think it was okay to sexually coerce a subordinate. Men who participated in training were also less likely to report sexual harassment in their workplaces.[7]

For men, the sexual harassment training had the exact opposite effect from what was intended. This negative effect of sexual harassment training was unique to men. Women who had completed training did not differ from women who had not had training on any of these issues. How do the researchers involved in this study explain their results? They argue that the men felt attacked and were attempting to defend themselves. Although the sexual harassment presentation clearly stated that both sexes engage in harassment, everyone knows that offenders are typically men. So, as a result of feeling attacked, the male participants experienced backlash against the policies. They were more likely to blame the victim and less likely to recognize sexual harassment when they saw it.[8]

When sexual harassment training is having the opposite of the intended effect, clearly intervention is necessary. It's important to note, as far as we know, there was nothing unique about the presentation of the sexual harassment training that caused this result. It was the insinuation that accompanies the training that allegations of sexual harassment give women power over men. In reality, sexual harassment training should focus on the rights of both the victims and alleged harassers, making it clear that a thorough investigation will ensure that all parties are treated fairly.

When not scaring men, sometimes the suggestions for avoiding sexual harassment are just too time-consuming and impractical. As an example, one published list of suggestions to help managers handle the sexuality and intimacy in cross-sex mentor relationships suggested that mentor and mentee should abide by the following guidelines.[9] First, they suggest that the mentor and mentee should refrain from calling each other by nicknames. I guess this makes sense if your nickname is "Cutiepie," but "Bob" for Robert seems okay. There's more. They suggest that the mentor and mentee should keep a journal with all times and places met and what was discussed. In addition, the pair should let others know about their scheduled appointments. Finally, they advise, the pair should be trained by human resources on the dangers of sexualizing the mentor relationship. These, along with the other suggestions they provide for establishing cross-sex mentor relationships, would no doubt reduce the likelihood of impropriety or perceived impropriety of these relationships.

The problem lies in the emphasis on the sexual aspects of mentor relationships. By suggesting that these relationships are more complicated and time consuming, they are basically recommending that employees should avoid cross-sex mentoring. While the suggestions they provide would most likely decrease the chances that a sexual relationship would develop, most employees would probably find it easier to just stick to same-sex mentor relationships.

As extreme as these guidelines may seem, other organizations are even more zealous in their suggestions to employees. Some, in an effort to prevent sexual harassment, suggest curtailing interactions between coworkers to eliminate any possibility that sexual harassment could occur. In doing this, the organization is most likely decreasing its own productivity. Informal friendships within an organization tend to increase collaboration, spark creativity, and increase information flow.[10] Organizations that discourage these informal networks are at a clear disadvantage.

Nonetheless, a fast-food restaurant provides an example of just such a policy. In a sexual harassment seminar, restaurant employees were instructed not to talk to each other at work about anything personal.[11] Instead, the employees were told they could only talk about job-related matters while at work. The goal of the policy was to avoid the possibility that someone may inadvertently sexually harass another.

At a law firm, where employees are typically lawyers who have been educated in the finer points of sexual harassment, one would expect misinformation would be less of a problem. However, one male lawyer points out what he garnered about social interaction from a seminar he attended:

> I was at a seminar, and a defense lawyer, a partner in a huge law firm, said the advice he gives is, do not interact with women subordinates socially, period. Don't ever go to lunch with one, don't ever go for drinks after work, don't ever do stuff on weekends. I knew this guy. I knew he's a real social guy, a party guy. I raised my hand and said, "Isn't social interaction helpful to one's career; aren't you more apt to give [an associate] work if you go out for drinks with him?" He said, "Yes, that's true." So I said, "What you're saying is that to avoid sexual harassment you're going to have to engage in conduct that's discrimination."[12]

Ironically, as this lawyer highlights, avoiding women in order to steer clear of any legal sexual harassment issues is, in itself, illegal. It is discriminatory to exclude women from activities that may further their career. Excluding all female employees to avoid potentially offending a few doesn't seem like a great strategy anyway. In other words, the proposed solution potentially has a greater negative impact on female employees than the original problem it was trying to solve.

COMPLIMENTING A COWORKER—IS THAT SEXUAL HARASSMENT?

In order to eliminate any possibility of legal liability, organizations often adopt an overly cautious stance in their sexual harassment training. So heavy-handed are many training seminars that the current approach toward sexual harassment training has been compared to fixing a watch with a sledgehammer.[13] Unfortunately, this overzealous approach to sexual harassment training may increase rather than decrease the ambiguity about what constitutes sexual harassment—and recall that ambiguity regarding what constitutes harassment strengthens the sex partition.

A study by Mary Pilgram and Joann Keyton illustrates how participants emerge from sexual harassment training more confused than when they started.[14] Participants in this study were questioned both before and after participating in sexual harassment training which consisted of a widely used, commercially produced online sexual harassment training program. After participating in the training, participants were more confused about what behaviors were considered harassing.

An example from this study illustrates the point. Participants were given the following true or false question both before and after participation in the sexual harassment training: "True or False. It is considered sexual harassment to tell a classmate of the opposite sex that he/she looks nice." As you know from reading this book, the correct answer is false, and 87 percent of the participants answered this question correctly before participating in the sexual harassment training. However, only 54 percent answered it correctly *after* participating in the sexual harassment training. Participating in the training caused the participants' knowledge about sexual harassment to decrease!

Pilgram and Keyton suggest that "perhaps the training caused the participants to be overly sensitive and more cautious in identifying what constitutes sexual harassment after the training, supporting the complex nature of the topic. Some may have become paranoid, believing that to even pay a compliment to someone could be misinterpreted."[15]

Training should lead to greater clarity on exactly what constitutes harassment, not greater confusion. What good results from forcing employees to endure hours of training that only results in misunderstanding the fundamentals of sexual harassment and reluctance to interact with opposite-sex employees?

BE HONEST: TRAINING IS OFFERED TO COVER LEGAL
LIABILITY NOT TO HELP EMPLOYEES

One of the reasons that the message about sexual harassment is not getting through to employees is because the training is aimed at limiting legal liability, and it's not focused on the best way to create a harassment-free workplace. Employees aren't stupid, and they can differentiate between sexual harassment training designed out of a desire to improve workplace relations and instruction designed to meet legal requirements. Interestingly, researchers have confirmed that the intentions of the organization play an important role in the effectiveness of sexual harassment training.[16] The training is less effective when the employees feel that the training is merely provided to meet legal requirements. However, when employees feel that the organization's goal is to genuinely improve the quality of life in the work environment, they are more likely to respond positively to sexual harassment training.

When an organization offers sexual harassment training for legal reasons, but feigns a genuine interest in decreasing sexual harassment, repercussions may be greatest. Instead, a frankness regarding motives may be the best move to help dispel resentment regarding forced participation in the training. Recall how Alexander McPherson resented his university's motives for requiring participation in sexual harassment training sessions. When asked what his university could do to make sexual harassment training more palatable for him, McPherson replied, "Well, if they would call it what it really is. If they had simply made it absolutely clear that the reason you're taking this is not that you are involved in sexual harassment in any way, but you must do this in order to protect the university from lawsuits. If they had just made that clear, so everyone understood—I wouldn't have objected at all." In other words, McPherson felt the university should not pretend to be genuinely interested in making the workplace more hospitable when their motives were purely legal. From his perspective, if the organization had been up front about their legal motives, he would not have resisted participating in training.

SEXUAL HARASSMENT TRAINING ON CAMPUS

I've spent a good deal of time on university campuses, in one role or another, and sexual harassment training on the university campus has problems too. Campus training and warnings can fall into the overzealous category, overstating what constitutes harassing behavior. Some warn that a professor's praise of a promising student should set off warning bells that sexual harassment may be afoot. Over twenty years ago, in their book on sexual harassment on campus, *The Lecherous Professor,* Billie Wright Dziech and Linda Weiner provided a list of warning signs to identify a lecherous professor at your university.[17] One of the warning signs is "excessive flattery and praise of the student." Apparently, according to the authors, both students with low self-esteem and those with high aspirations succumb to this praise trick. Professors tell students about their exceptional abilities "to get psychological access to them."[18] The following, one of their suggestions, exemplifies the overidentification of sexual harassment:

> If a student is having a personal relationship with a professor and is sure that sexual harassment has nothing to do with her situation, she should think again. One type of sexual harasser has a pattern of making a student believe she is intellectually or physically gifted, "special" somehow. Because he recognizes her good qualities or traits that others may not see, she is attracted to that recognition.[19]

This advice sounds similar to the advice given to the students at Rohit's university who were told they should be wary both of professors who dress nicely and those who dress casually. Interviews I've conducted with professors suggest the environment hasn't changed much. Recall the male professor whose human resources department advised him against having lunch with female colleagues. Other male professors are reluctant to meet with female students.

In my own experience it seems that students should value the encouragement of their professors. During my college years at Vassar, as a math and computer science major, my classes were taught almost exclusively by male professors. I also socialized with my male professors, playing squash matches against them or joining them for dinner. It was during these off-campus one-on-one meetings that I got to know them, and they got to know me. I learned about opportunities that I wouldn't have been aware of otherwise.

One of the male professors with whom I socialized went out of his way to highly recommend me for my first job at Morgan Stanley; another wrote me a glowing recommendation that was instrumental in gaining acceptance to graduate school at MIT. I am forever indebted to these professors, without whose help and encouragement my career trajectory may have been quite different. I wonder, though, how I may have behaved differently around these professors, if I were hypersensitive to sexual harassment. Would I have refused the dinners or squash matches? Or if these professors had feared sexual harassment charges and limited their socializing to male students, how would my experience have changed?

Would the male students have had sole access to the benefits associated with socializing with these male professors? Sexual harassment training should offer a balanced perspective. In addition to warning prospective harassers and victims, training should also mention the benefits of close mentor relationships. Scaring undergraduates and professors away from these relationships may result in more harm than good.

EVEN YOUNGER—SEXUAL HARASSMENT TRAINING IN ELEMENTARY SCHOOL?

Sexual harassment training at the university level could use improvement, but some have suggested we roll out sexual harassment training for high school and even younger students. You might be surprised to find out that a six-year-old boy was found in violation of his school's sexual harassment policy when two of his fingers reached under a female classmate's waistband to touch the skin of her back. The principal suspended the boy from school for three days for violating the school's sexual harassment policy. In a newspaper interview the boy's mom said he is too young to understand what the word sexual means.[20]

In Massachusetts, a first-grade boy was charged with sexual harassment for kicking a fellow first-grade boy in the groin during a fight (he said the other kid started it),[21] and when a nine-year-old in North Carolina was suspended for calling his teacher "cute," the principal labeled the behavior sexual harassment.[22] Although experts fortunately concur that these examples do not represent acts of sexual harassment, the label persists.

Just recently, seventeen-year-old Sam McNair's hopes for attending college next year came crashing down. Bad grades? Drugs? Weapons? No, McNair hugged his teacher and received a one-year suspension for sexual harassment.[23] His alleged harassing hug was captured on surveillance video (you can search for "Sam McNair hug" on YouTube.com). McNair's mom says they are a family of huggers, and McNair insists he was just trying to brighten the teacher's day.

Recently, calls for sexual harassment prevention training to begin in high schools or middle schools are gaining strength. Just as Title VII of the Civil Rights Act protects the workplace, courts have found that sexual harassment at school is prohibited by Title IX of the Education Amendments of 1972. Title IX provides that "No person in the United States shall, on the basis of sex, be excluded from participation in, be denied the benefits of, or be subjected to discrimination under any educational program or activity receiving Federal financial assistance." Although Title IX is typically invoked in connection with equality in men's and women's school sports activities, more recently it has been used to ensure that a school provides an environment that is free from sexual harassment.

There's no question that we want our kids and their teachers to have a harassment-free environment. Kids shouldn't be permitted to kick their classmates in the groin, and teachers who don't wish to be hugged shouldn't have to endure embraces from their students. So what's the problem? It's the sexual harassment label that has been assigned to these behaviors that is problematic. Sexual harassment is a term that has its origins in the workplace, and I have two primary concerns about using the label "sexual harassment" and offering sexual harassment training in schools.

First, high schools and elementary schools are different from the workplace. Using the same label to describe different behaviors will only add to the confusion about sexual harassment as students transition to employees. Take, for example, relationships between students. Peer dating is acceptable and even encouraged in schools (for example, students often are encouraged to have a date accompany them to their school-sanctioned prom), and consensual making out on some high school campuses is commonplace. Obviously, this wouldn't be cool at work. In the workplace, issues of kicking a coworker in the groin or posting locker room photos on social media don't come up all that often (at least not in my own experience). There's enough confusion surrounding sexual harassment, and that confusion adds to the sex partition. Let's not add to this confusion. What happens at school should have a different label from what happens at work.

My second concern emerges from my own research. Sexual harassment training at the high school level may have the same repercussions as it does for older employees, segregating the sexes and potentially altering perceptions of female students. Recently calls for sexual harassment training in high schools and middle schools have increased. But what will be the reaction to this training? Will boys be afraid to interact with their female peers at school? Will they think the sexual harassment training is provided for girls who can't fend for themselves?

Providing a unique label such as "sexual bullying" will allow educators to clearly define what is acceptable and what is not on the school campus. Sexual bullying should not be minimized. Because of the victims' young age, some sexual bullying at school may have even greater repercussions for the victim than sexual harassment at work. Referring to the behavior as bullying, and not sexual harassment, helps solve the second problem as well. Bullying is not perceived as just a girl's issue.

In order to address the much less frequent, but more severe, teacher-student sexual harassment in high school and elementary school, sexual harassment training should be provided to teachers. Students, in turn, should be aware of grievance procedures.

AWARENESS IS THE FIRST STEP

Whether in elementary school, high school, university, or a Fortune 500 company, overzealous efforts at reducing harassment are contributing to the sex partition. And, what's worse, it isn't even clear that these training efforts actually reduce harassing behavior. In some states legislation requires employers to provide hours of sexual harassment training, but often we're not using that time as effectively as we could. At the very least, we should ensure that the training actually reduces sexual harassment. However, I believe we should set the bar even higher. I'm confident that we can develop training methods that reduce sexual harassment and encourage cross-sex friendships at the same time.

6

SEXUALLY HARASSED

Welcome sexual harassment is an oxymoron.

—Richard Posner, jurist[1]

If Alexandra Marchuk's allegations are true, she had a tough start to her law career at the law firm Faruqi & Faruqi, LLP (F&F) in New York City. Marchuk, a recent law school graduate, accepted a job at the law firm as a full-time litigation associate. According to Marchuk's legal complaint,[2] here's how her first couple of weeks played out:

Day 1:   Marchuk discovered that she would be working exclusively for Juan Monteverde, a partner in the law firm, at his request.

Day 3:   Marchuk attended a hearing with Monteverde in Delaware, "but it quickly became clear that her primary role was not as an attorney, but as Mr. Monteverde's female companion." Marchuk claimed she was not asked to participate in the hearing, and that Monteverde did not discuss the case with her. However, he did drink heavily on the trip back to New York and, upon arriving back in New York, asked Marchuk to join him at a bar to continue drinking. At the bar, "Monteverde aggressively grabbed and kissed Ms. Marchuk and attempted to fondle her breasts. Ms. Marchuk physically rebuffed Mr. Monteverde's advances." He then allegedly asked her to return to the office for sex, but she declined and headed home alone.

Day 4:   Monteverde took Marchuk to lunch and told her that he wanted her to be his mistress. Although he was married himself, he claimed that he married his wife only to obtain a green card. Marchuk declined.

Still on Day 4:   Monteverde stopped by Marchuk's office, closed her door, and asked her to go out with him that night. Although she said no, he responded, "OK, not to-night." It seems he was not going be deterred.

Day 5:   Monteverde again asked Marchuk to go out for dinner or drinks after work, and again, she declined.

Day 8:   Monteverde told Marchuk she needed to accompany him to a hearing in Delaware, because the judge in the case was partial to good-looking female lawyers. He told her "to wear her hair down, wear a low-cut shirt, and to try to look as alluring as possible during the hearing." Marchuk was getting the idea that perhaps Monteverde did not value her legal ability.

Day 9:   Marchuk complained about Monteverde's behavior to a female partner in the law firm. Recounting tales of Monteverde's behavior, Marchuk emphasized how it had all been unwelcome. The female partner told Marchuk that everyone knew Monteverde behaved inappropriately, and it was best if she didn't complain about it to any other senior partners. Marchuk got the message that if she complained to the other partners she would be labeled a troublemaker.

The lewd comments, sexual banter, and unwanted invitations for sex con-tinued, and Marchuk feared being alone in the office with Monteverde. Fur-thermore, Monteverde allegedly penalized Marchuk anytime she interacted or worked with other male lawyers. Finally, three months into her employment, at a year-end holiday party Monteverde told her she was not going to receive a year-end bonus (upon hiring, she was told that dependent upon performance, she would be eligible for a significant year-end bonus), and implied her employ-ment was on shaky ground. "Under the influence of alcohol and desperate to re-pair what Mr. Monteverde said was her tattered standing at F&F, Ms. Marchuk acceded to Mr. Monteverde's pleas and walked back to F&F's offices with him. After entering his office, Mr. Monteverde pushed Ms. Marchuk to the floor and quickly, forcefully, and painfully had sex with her." The next day, Marchuk consulted an employment lawyer and resigned from F&F.

Only Marchuk and Monteverde know what transpired when they were alone. Yet, sexual harassment, like that which Marchuk alleged, is much more frequently targeted at women than men. And sexual harassment is perhaps the most egregious component of the sex partition. After all, what could drive you away from a positive working relationship with your boss more than incessant requests for sexual relations and persistent lewd and degrading comments, not to mention sexual assault? In her complaint, Marchuk stated that although she "had no romantic interest in Mr. Monteverde and was offended by his sexist behavior, she admired him professionally for his success and highly valued his opinion of her legal ability." Like any new employee, she wanted to learn from and impress her new boss. But Monteverde's alleged behavior made any kind of working relationship impossible for Marchuk. She was even reprimanded by Monteverde for attempting to befriend other employees.[3]

Indeed the wedge driven between the sexes by sexually harassing behavior is far more severe than the barrier caused by fears of sexual harassment allegations. It is because of situations like Marchuk's that we have sexual harassment training in the first place. And it's because of this type of behavior that we need to get it right! All situations are not as egregious as hers, but any excessive, unwanted sexual attention can be troublesome and can result in employees withdrawing or even leaving their employment. Not surprisingly, a summary of forty-nine independent studies on sexual harassment indicated that those who endured sexual harassment at work were less healthy and less happy at work.[4] For victims of harassment, their performance was impacted, their self-esteem took a hit, and they were more likely to be depressed and anxious.

It is important to note that sexual harassment had the same impact on male and female victims. In other words, men who are harassed at work are just as likely to suffer these symptoms as women who suffer harassment. However, since women tend to experience harassment more than men, it is more likely that women suffer these repercussions.

Sadly, for those who suffer sexual harassment, filing charges does not typically alleviate the situation. In fact, just the opposite occurs. Those who keep quiet typically have better outcomes than those who actually file charges.[5] Look at the reaction Marchuk allegedly received upon reporting harassment at her law firm. Victims who file charges often suffer retaliation (despite the fact that retaliation is illegal) and report more unhappiness at work, depression, and anxiety as a result of their reporting. Although reporting sexual harassment may help instigate change in the organization, the consequences for the individual can be daunting.

WHY EMPLOYEES TOLERATE HARASSMENT

Needless to say, employees can be conflicted about how to react to sexual harassment. Not wanting to rock the boat, many employees tolerate the harassment and profess that they are not bothered by harassing behavior and dialogue. This strategy may have short-term benefits, such as not having to endure an investigation and its repercussions. However, not only can this strategy diminish one's self-esteem but also it perpetuates a culture where sexual harassment is considered acceptable. By ignoring or tolerating the behavior, little change is likely to occur.

In lieu of filing charges, many employees simply avoid contact with a lecherous manager or forgo mentoring from a creepy exec. While avoiding harassment, they miss out on valuable opportunities. Usually these opportunities are, in turn, bestowed upon those who tolerate the sexual harassment or same-sex employees.

No one should have to choose between tolerating harassment and being excluded from important colleague networks. Unfortunately, Dr. Francis Conley had to make this decision. She was torn between tolerating sexual harassment and being accepted as one of the boys or blowing the whistle and being ostracized. Conley was a tenured full professor of neurosurgery at Stanford and the first woman to hold this title at any university in the United States. After twenty-three years as a tenured professor, Conley resigned when her colleague Gerry Silverberg was promoted to department chair. What was her beef with Silverberg? Conley claims he sexually harassed her. In a revealing exposé of her life as a female neurosurgeon, *Walking Out on the Boys*, Conley describes an environment where she tolerated harassment for years prior to speaking up:

> I was well acquainted with raucous laughter erupting at my expense over jokes, nuances, antics, guesses about how good I was in bed. One survived in this masculine world by being one of the boys, and for all intents and purposes, I had become one of them. . . . Frequently offended, I dared not offend, for fear of banishment from the only professional camaraderie I had ever known. Not wanting to lose my quasi membership in the surgeon's club, I had never done anything to stop behavior that was repulsive to me and ultimately damaging to my self-respect and dignity. Instead I had developed a fine art of repartee. I, too, could be insulting, using dirty language to turn their faces red. Deflecting put-downs with humor, I earned the reputation of being able to fend for myself, and had developed tremendous pride in having that ability.
>
> Inherently, I knew sexist behavior was wrong, but thought I was above it and had been able to keep it from hurting *my* career. Now . . . I realized I might well have damaged the professional lives of others, because my own inaction, over the years, was as responsible as any other factor for perpetuating the sexist climate medical students found abhorrent and were now fighting.[6]

One can certainly understand Conley's reluctance to speak out. She wanted to break through the sex partition to be accepted as one of the boys in her workplace. She realized that this link with her male coworkers was key to her own success, and she feared she would lose their acceptance if she complained about their behavior.

Conley was caught in a no-win situation. If she complained about the hostile environment in which she worked, she would lose the friendship of her male coworkers, which would damage the career she had worked so hard to establish. If she kept silent, the men would continue with the behavior that she felt "damaged her self-respect and dignity," and future generations of women would encounter the same behavior.

When Conley heard Silverberg was to be promoted to be her department chair, her choice became easier. Conley knew this surgeon would not respect her work, and therefore, she resigned. Conley worked tirelessly to build her groundbreaking career. And now that career was potentially ending, not because of her lack of skills or dedication, but because of issues surrounding relations between men and women in the workplace.

Throughout her book, Conley details how the sex partition impacted her career and the careers of other female surgeons. The struggles that she and others encountered building friendships with the men that surrounded them were substantial. She describes the struggles with cross-sex mentorships and how, typically, male mentorships were all that was available:

> With same-gender mentorships, marvelous nonthreatening intimacy between two people can develop, evolving into a lifelong partnership of having shared something very special. Unfortunately, a close mentor relation between a man and a woman, especially if the woman is younger and the one being mentored, is often fragile, as societal assumptions work to turn the relationship into something it is not.[7]

Ironically, while Conley thrived on the intellectual challenges and grueling schedule of a career in neurosurgery, her primary setbacks resulted from difficulties gaining acceptance as one of the boys and confronting sexual harassment at Stanford. Fortunately, Conley's efforts to change the environment were not in vain. Due to an investigation spurred on by Conley's resignation, Silverberg was removed from the department chair position, and Conley was able to return to Stanford and resume the career she loved. Most importantly, her resignation began a dialogue about sexism and sexual harassment in her department.

However, Conley's career was never the same, because her whistle-blowing cast her as an outsider in the ol' boys' network. She finally came to the realization that she would never truly "belong" in this environment. Although Conley continued to practice neurosurgery, she never resumed her research aimed at curing malignant brain tumors. Sexism and sexual harassment created a barrier between her and inclusion in the male-dominated profession she loved.

Conley is not alone. Many women report having to choose between endur-
ing harassment and holding back a career they love. Feminist author Naomi
Wolf recently described how a sexually harassing professor she had in college brought an end to her poetry writing. According to Wolf, male students
regularly socialized with this male professor, and Wolf valued his feedback and
wanted to hang out with him like the male students did. The story, which Wolf
published in *New York* magazine, describes the unwanted attention from her
professor many years ago. To be fair, she wasn't filing lawsuits or charges (the
statute of limitations had expired); she claimed she was coming forward with
this story to ensure that Yale currently had appropriate policies in place to deal
with such things.

Evidently, while a senior at Yale, Wolf registered for an independent-study
poetry course with the much revered literature professor. The semester was
almost over and the professor had not yet met with Wolf regarding her poetry.
Wolf claims:

> When I saw him on campus, he would promise to go over my poetry manuscript
> "over a glass of Amontillado." I'd heard that some faculty met with students at
> Mory's, and that [the professor] drank often with his male students there. I also
> knew that there was an atmosphere at Yale in which female students were ex-
> pected to be sociable with male professors. I had discussed with my friends the
> pressure to be charming but still seen as serious.[8]

According to Wolf, the professor invited himself to dinner at her house (she
lived with one of his graduate editorial assistants and his girlfriend). The four
had dinner and drank several glasses of wine, and then the two roommates de-
parted, leaving Wolf and the professor alone together.

Then, Wolf alleges, "The next thing I knew, his heavy, boneless hand was
hot on my thigh." Wolf says she turned away from him and vomited in the sink.
He then told her, "You're a deeply troubled girl," and left. They never met
again that semester and, as a result of this incident, Wolf says she never wrote
poetry again.

If Wolf's version of the events is correct, then the sex partition had no impact on the male students' relationships with the professor, as Wolf reported he
often had drinks with male students to discuss their work. Wolf felt pressured
to be social as well. Yet her efforts to be social and imbibe with the professor
backfired. Clearly, Wolf was not able to socialize with him in the same way the
male students could.

Just like Wolf, many employees and students who suffer harassment often must make a difficult choice, particularly if the harasser is someone who can offer them mentoring or sponsorship. Tolerating the unwelcome harassment in order to retain the benefits of the relationship with the harasser is an option, but over time this can take a toll on one's self-esteem. Other choices involve either avoiding or reporting the harassing employee. Of course, along with other unwelcome consequences, this would put an end to the valuable mentoring.

These harassed employees find themselves in a no-win situation, and it is for these employees that sexual harassment training is provided, and why it is so important that organizations get it right. Marchuk, Conley, Wolf, and all women who are harassed deserve a workplace that is free of harassment. It's essential we make sure sexual harassment training is not two hours of wasted time, not fulfilling legal requirements, but two hours that empower employees, help them understand exactly what harassment is, and actually instigate change in the work environment. In a later chapter, I provide concrete suggestions for improving sexual harassment training while minimizing the unintended effects on friendships.

III

SEX, ROMANCE, AND GOLF: MORE ELEMENTS OF THE SEX PARTITION

7

THE BUSINESS TRIP

A man and a man at a bar at a hotel during a work trip, that looks like mentoring, and it is mentoring. A man and a woman at a bar at a hotel on a work trip, that doesn't look like mentoring to anyone.

—Sheryl Sandberg, COO of Facebook[1]

"When I was younger and traveled more for business, I got hit on by just about every man I traveled with. This is not uncommon among women I know," blogs columnist, author, and entrepreneur Penelope Trunk.[2] Like many women, Penelope's business trips were often derailed by amorous traveling companions. Intrigued to hear more, I spoke to Penelope about her experiences traveling with cross-sex companions. On one such trip, her boss made the moves on her, she told me:

> I was traveling with my boss. We were in the hotel lobby, and first he told me about how he used to date someone who looked just like me, and then how he never felt with anyone the way he felt with me. So many men I have worked with have said that—that's a line they use when they're bored at home. Then my boss says we should just spend the night drinking together, 'cause we didn't have a lot to do the next day.

Penelope directly asked her boss if he was trying to sleep with her. When he confirmed, she made it clear that the attraction was not reciprocated. As happens repeatedly on business trips, Penelope's boss placed her in a no-win situation. She was not remotely interested in an affair with her boss but, then again, shooting down the boss doesn't typically fast-track an employee's career. Her best option, and the one she ultimately pursued, was a transfer. When I asked her about the repercussions for declining her boss's advances, she reported:

> He just didn't try as hard. Men who are trying to have sex with you try extra hard at work to get along with you. They tell you how great you are, and how smart you are, and how they understand your work better than anyone else. And if you reject them, they can go one of two routes. They can either be pissy, or they can just try harder, as if they like the challenge. After [my boss] got pissy, I told a superior that I needed to be transferred because my boss was incompetent. So I got transferred. If I said that I need to be transferred because my boss hit on me, then they have to take it to HR, and that was just not going to get me anywhere. I think, in general, if women are going to get upset that they're hit on by men, then they just shouldn't go to work.

Luckily Penelope was granted the transfer. Resuming a normal work life with a boss who bears romantic or sexual interest is challenging for anyone, particularly if the boss is coping with rejection. Despite this, many women fear approaching their human resources departments and, instead of reporting such behavior, continue to live and work in uncomfortable situations. Penelope avoided the messy investigation that would have ensued by reporting her boss's behavior and instead cited the manager's incompetence as grounds for her transfer request.

Although repulsed by her boss, Penelope Trunk was more tempted by travel companions on other business trips, and she blogs about how the business trip setting is particularly prone to romance:

> Now I can see why affairs happen so often on business trips. . . . If you're married with children, a business trip is like an escape to Disneyland. There are no kids to feed and bathe. There's no husband for annoying talks about checkbook balances and the next day's school lunch. There is only freedom and fun. And what does anyone want to do with freedom and fun except have sex? I wish I could tell you that I'm too busy with my great career and big ideas to think about a little one-night stand. But, really, I was consumed with the idea.[3]

Why are business trips such fertile grounds for hooking up? Trunk told me that the initial attraction to traveling companions often developed naturally from close working relationships:

> If you're working really well with someone, you become attracted to them. You're working with them eight hours a day, you're getting cool stuff done,

you're both intellectually stimulated about the same things, and you have shared goals. That's attractive.

Trunk is not alone. For cross-sex travelers, the temptation to hook up on a business trip is relatively common. A 2011 *Newsweek*/Dailybeast.com poll indicated that 21 percent of married men want to cheat while traveling on business, and a much larger percentage of single travelers most likely desire a hook-up on their getaways. It's not hard to understand why the lure is so great. After conducting business, traveling coworkers may dine together, enjoy a cocktail to celebrate a business deal, or treat clients to a local entertainment venue. Afterwards, the colleagues typically return to the same hotel. Hundreds or thousands of miles from home, sometimes in exotic locales or resorts, temptations to engage in a tryst with cross-sex coworkers are often irresistible. However, if both parties are not equally enthralled, awkward and uncomfortable situations can ensue. And even if both traveling companions are interested in hooking up, they must face each other at the home office once the business trip ends. Same-sex travel companions need not fear such complications. They can travel together, drink until they're drunk, and share a hotel room without any concern about sexual attraction or its repercussions.

In order to further uncover the issues that confront cross-sex travel companions, I collected anecdotes from over fifty employees who had traveled with an opposite-sex coworker. (See Appendix B for more details on the participants.) Not surprisingly, most described some awkwardness in dealing with their cross-sex travel companions. The work aspects of the trips were fine. It was the additional activities outside of work that often left employees feeling uncomfortable. At the home office, when the typical workday ends, coworkers are not necessarily expected to hang out together. However, in an unfamiliar city where the business travelers may not have friends or family, are they expected to socialize after the day's work is completed? The workers in my study ate, drank, went sightseeing, and attended movies with their travel companions. One pair even soaked in the hotel hot tub together.

These extracurricular activities were awkward for a variety of reasons. From unrequited sexual interest to having difficulty being taken seriously, outings with cross-sex coworkers can be difficult. For Liana, an auto parts industry employee, an outing with her colleagues left her feeling like an outsider. Liana was the only woman among her male colleagues attending a conference far from home. She didn't typically hang out with her colleagues after work, but since they were out of town she decided to give it a try. On this particular night, her male colleagues chose Hooters as the evening's destination. The Hooters chain of restaurants is, of course, known for sexy young female waitresses who wear revealing outfits. Ironically, it wasn't the waitresses or their revealing outfits that disturbed Liana. Instead, as she described, "The biggest problem was the men didn't take me seriously."

Although some women might be offended by dining in the Hooters environment, Liana described it as "mildly uncomfortable." The bigger issue for her was the difficulty women face being taken seriously at Hooters. While male employees can establish bonds at Hooters that extend back to the home office, it's harder to imagine Liana's colleagues concluding, "I want to give that assignment to Liana—she really impressed me at Hooters." Instead, she described being "hit on" by male conference attendees or mistaken for a colleague's wife.

Why even attend the Hooters outing then? It seems like it would be easier, and certainly more pleasant, to relax in a hotel room. Unfortunately, women trying to break down the sex partition and establish bonds with their male coworkers typically find themselves in a double bind. If they decline invitations to socialize, they risk missing out on valuable time with coworkers and possibly more senior employees. However, when they choose to attend male-oriented outings, women may feel that they are not taken seriously.

I found myself in a situation similar to Liana's on a business trip to Tokyo. My male coworkers were heading out to a hostess bar in the evening. At a Japanese hostess bar, female hostesses light cigarettes, pour drinks, and flirt with the almost exclusively male guests. In this particular bar, only Western-looking, English-speaking women were employed as hostesses, and topless women performed pole dances for more entertainment. I could have remained in the hotel, but fearing I'd miss out on networking opportunities, and having nothing else to do, I chose to join them. I was happy to be included. Despite my efforts to fit in with the boys, it was an awkward evening. The bar staff mistook me for a hostess, and my colleagues had to explain I didn't work there. The bar staff apologized profusely and assigned me my very own woman for the evening. Much like Liana, I felt it was hard to be taken seriously.

DOES ALCOHOL LEAD TO SEX?

Liana's other complaint was that she had been propositioned by other men at the conference. By far the most common complaints of cross-sex business travelers involved issues of sexual interest. Unrequited sexual or romantic interest in a travel companion creates uncomfortable situations, and mutual interest in hooking up has its own set of problems. Bill, an accountant, described how his female boss got a little too friendly after she had too much to drink:

I had to go on a business trip with my boss from work for a conference in Boston. The company paid for separate rooms and our dinner at night. We had dinner and drinks, but it was very awkward, because my boss got drunk and got very touchy with me. I quickly asked for the bill, and we left. I immediately told her I would see her in the morning, and that I had to use the bathroom bad. The next morning, I just acted like nothing happened, but it was awkward after that.

Of course it was awkward. It's hard to imagine a scenario where declining or avoiding a manager's advances wouldn't become awkward.

Bill suggested his boss's inebriated state influenced her decision to put the moves on him, and alcohol seemed to play a prominent role in the after-hours activities of many of the business travelers. Imbibing, they reported, generally increased flirting and touching with their travel companions.

It's well-documented that alcohol does indeed increase flirtation and attraction. Often labeled the "beer goggles effect," the more alcohol consumed, the more attractive people start to look.[4] (Evidence of this effect comes from an interesting study where researchers showed photos of faces to student drinkers in a campus pub. The higher the student's blood alcohol level, the higher attractiveness ratings they gave to the photos. Both men and women in the study succumbed to the effects of beer goggles.) The lesson from this research: Drinking on the business trip can lead to situations you might later regret.

Not only can alcohol make a traveling companion seem more attractive, but it also can reduce sexual inhibitions.[5] It's not hard to understand why a few drinks can lead to wandering hands and flirty innuendo. Many employees ran into situations where, after a few drinks, interactions began to cross the line from professional to romantic. For example, Alan, who had a few drinks with a colleague, described how "the inclusion of alcohol definitely increased physical contact, but nothing crossed the line." Robert described a similar experience imbibing with a female colleague: "We drank quite a bit of alcohol after the day's events, and we got a little friendly, flirting and touching each other."

What happens when employees cross that line? Several of the employees ended up sleeping with their traveling companions, but even when both parties consent, complications can arise. Remember, the two employees typically must see one another on a regular basis back at the home office. If one colleague is interested in pursuing a relationship and the other is not, run-ins at the water cooler can get uncomfortable. Sexual harassment allegations can even result, particularly if one party feels that they were pressured into sex. Even if both parties are on the same page, rumors and allegations of favoritism from other employees can ensue.

WHAT WILL OUR COWORKERS THINK?

Sometimes, even when there is no attraction between cross-sex travelers, suspicious coworkers can start negative rumors. When I traveled for business with my boss, it never occurred to me that my coworkers might think we were up to anything more than business. In reality, on business trips I was usually suffering from jet lag and made a habit of returning to my hotel room early. But, sure enough, rumors started. On one trip my boss forgot to bring his disposable contact lenses. When I saw him sporting an old pair of glasses, and asked him why, he told me he had left his lenses at home. I asked his prescription, and it turns out we had the same contact lens prescription. I lent him some of my disposable lenses and all was well. I'm not sure how the boys back at the home office found out about the incident, but they were convinced that the only way to discover a shared contact lens prescription is if you're dressing together in the same hotel room. My coworkers thought that the fact that my boss and I knew each other's contact lens prescription was concrete evidence we had slept together. I'm not sure I ever convinced them otherwise.

This behavior is not uncommon, as colleagues often question motivations when an opposite-sex colleague is chosen to travel with the boss. If a man chooses to travel with another man, his motivations are rarely questioned, but when a man chooses to travel with a woman, it can open up a can of worms.

Sheryl Sandberg, COO of Facebook, and her mentor, former treasury secretary Larry Summers, once found themselves in an awkward situation on a business trip. Alone together in a hotel room, working late into the night, they realized others may think there was more going on than just work. Sandberg recounted the story for *60 Minutes Overtime*:

> We were in his [Larry Summers's] suite in the living room part of a hotel room, working on a speech, and we finished, and it was 3:00 a.m. We looked at each other, I don't even think we said anything, but we both knew—this is not good. We talked about it for a minute, and well, there's nothing to do but leave. That happens to women and men, and it doesn't happen to men and men. If I had been a man, no one would have noticed or cared.[6]

Sandberg is correct. These concerns don't impact men traveling with other men, or women traveling with other women. It's when a woman and man are in a hotel room together, the rumor mill gains momentum.

A similar concern regarding coworker misinterpretation emerged in an interview Holly English conducted for her book *Gender on Trial*. A male law partner reported his worry about what his coworkers thought when he chose to travel with an attractive blonde:

> You may go out of your way to make clear why [a female] is going traveling with you. I had to go to Chicago to take depositions. One of our female associates was working on the case with me. We went, and I do recall feeling that I had to make sure that people understood that she was there as a part of the prosecution of the case. Whether I said anything differently because she was frankly an attractive blonde as opposed to a young male associate, I'm not sure. It was in my head. I felt a little uneasy because we had to meet the night before the depositions to review, and the only place we had available to meet was in the hotel room. It would have been easier if it was a guy.[7]

Clearly concerned with what other people thought about his relationship with his travel companion, he wanted to make it perfectly clear why he had selected this particular woman. She was included on the trip because she was needed on the case, and not because he desired her companionship for other reasons.

ARE THEY CUTE?

The same lawyer also mentioned that he felt the attractiveness of his traveling companion may have made their business trip seem more suspect to fellow employees. When traveling with a colleague deemed unattractive, many employees report less awkwardness. Not surprisingly, less attractive traveling companions eased the temptation for travelers. Employees were not sexually interested in less attractive travel companions, and there was little concern that their less attractive companions would hit on them. Penelope Trunk bluntly told me that no one should fear unattractive men: "It's not likely that you'll get hit on by a gross man. Gross men don't have a sense of entitlement where they hit on women at work."

I'm sure that unattractive people, particularly after a few drinks, also hit on coworkers. Nonetheless, attractive traveling partners are perceived as more of a threat. James, a male healthcare worker, described how the fact that his traveling companion wasn't his type made his trip fun:

> I recently went on a trip with a female colleague who was twice my age. She was very nice and we were both new to the company. There was no attraction because

she was very overweight—overweight as in very obese. We hung out one night and got all sorts of drunk. We weren't uncomfortable and we even got an opportunity to talk trash about our boss and other coworkers.

Sadly, these employees imply that to really be able to relax with a cross-sex coworker on a business trip, he or she must be deemed unattractive.

WEARING A RING

Relationship status was also important to the travelers, and a ring on one's finger seemed to reduce the likelihood that coworkers would make a move. Having their own special someone waiting at home also kept some employees on their best behavior. Melissa, a healthcare professional, was attracted to her travel colleague, but consideration of her husband at home held her back:

I was on a weeklong business trip with some colleagues. There was attraction with one of the men on the trip. We did hang out after we completed our business there. After the rest of the group went to bed, the man I was attracted to asked to walk me to my room. I know he wanted me to invite him in, but I just said good-night. We never spoke of it again. Part of me wanted to invite him in for sex, but I just couldn't cheat on my husband.

While consideration of a spouse can limit the likelihood of hooking up on a business trip, spouses left at home can also cause friction between traveling coworkers. Understandably, these spouses can experience jealousy when their husband or wife is traveling with an opposite sex coworker. Omar, a male healthcare worker, had to modify his business trip because of a female colleague's jealous spouse. To appease the husband at home, Omar and his female colleague made sure they were always accompanied by others on their business trip. Now that Omar is married himself, he has an even greater appreciation for the feelings of the spouse at home. He reports, "Now that I am married to the love of my life, I would be very cautious about doing anything outside of work with an opposite-sex coworker—even on a business trip."

Omar's concern regarding his wife's jealousy keeps him from socializing with opposite-sex colleagues outside of work. While his loyalty and respect for his wife are admirable, Omar's female colleagues and subordinates suffer from fewer opportunities to network with him. Both Omar and his female colleagues are hindered by having fewer networking possibilities.

WE JUST HAVE NOTHING IN COMMON

While most of the issues on these business trips surrounded sexual or romantic interest, a few travelers just found they had nothing in common with their companions. Some mentioned having to spend considerable time with their travel partner, and having little to say to them. One male telemarketer complained, "The most awkward part of the trip was the lack of stuff we had in common," and a female lawyer carped, "Sometimes I didn't know what to say, so we talked just about work." Even mundane activities can be perceived as unpleasant with a cross-sex companion. Jane, an assistant to the director of her organization, described how being cramped with her boss on the airplane was uncomfortable. She recalls, "The plane ride seemed like it would take forever, and I felt like we were just sitting too close together."

Certainly concerns related to different interests or lack of conversational topics can also impact same-sex pairs. However, a lack of common interests has been documented as an issue facing cross-sex friends, and in a situation where two people are forced to spend significant time together, these differences can be magnified.

STAYING OUT OF TROUBLE

So what are cross-sex travelers to do? Several travelers offered suggestions for escaping their cross-sex companion. Recall Bill's strategy—he excused himself for the evening from his drunk and overamorous boss by telling her of his urgent need to use the bathroom. Another woman pretended to be asleep on the long car ride home to avoid interacting with her colleague. Simpler strategies such as retiring to a hotel room as soon as the workday ended were also implemented. Jonathan, a male telecommunications professional who had been hit on by female coworkers on business trips, advises avoiding end-of-day happy hours and "to stay in groups or just go back to your room." Cathy, a saleswoman, applied a similar strategy when her traveling companion "asked me every night after work if I wanted to go to the bar, and a strip club, believe it or not. That was a little weird. I stayed in."

Unfortunately, turning down a colleague's invitation for dinner or drinks is not always easy, particularly when it's clear you have nothing better to do. Janice, a grocery store manager, describes how declining her male colleague was so awkward that she would prefer to travel exclusively with women in the future:

I was on a business trip with a male colleague for an overnight stay and a two-day food show. I found it to be extremely uncomfortable. The male colleague was quite a bit older than I, so I felt no attraction at all, but he wanted to be together the whole time. He wanted to have drinks together after the day of business activities, and I didn't want to. It was awkward for me to try to say no and avoid him without causing bad feelings. It was really hard to relax and enjoy myself. I hated the experience, and I would try not to go on a business trip with a male colleague again.

While avoiding contact after work may solve some problems, after-work gatherings may also offer the greatest networking potential. Getting to know the boss or a coworker over dinner can be invaluable. When the next high-profile project comes along, that same coworker or senior employee may feel more comfortable handing off to someone that can be trusted. This level of trust can often be developed hanging out after hours on a business trip. Those who feel uncomfortable hanging out after hours may forgo valuable networking opportunities.

In lieu of avoiding interactions altogether, several employees suggested going out in groups instead of one-on-one. Laurie, a government worker, describes how she and her female colleagues remained in groups to avoid a lecherous coworker:

There was one man who became a problem. There were a total of twenty of us, and it was not until later when we exchanged stories we realized there was a trend. He would show up at a female's room and offer a neck massage. He would call on the phone to see if you wanted to take a side trip on the weekend with him. As the week progressed it became more uncomfortable. He was the only man we had this type of problem with. So we always went out to eat as a group. We hung out as a group and even spent the weekend in groups.

Consorting in groups may be practical when there are several employees traveling simultaneously. However, when coworkers travel in pairs, they are often forced to interact one-on-one. While one-on-one interactions have the most potential to blossom into mentorships, they can also be the most awkward for cross-sex travelers.

So, once again, the double bind. Avoiding contact with the cross-sex traveler can minimize awkward situations, but it also minimizes networking potential. So what are cross-sex traveling companions to do? Open and honest communication can go a long way to break through awkward circumstances. Here are a few suggestions for navigating cross-sex business travel:

- Talk about and clarify any potential misunderstandings. Take Sheryl Sandberg's situation in Lawrence Summers's hotel room at 3:00 a.m. If she slinked back to her room and never mentioned it, rumors might begin to fly. Openly talking about the discomfort she felt as a woman leaving her male boss's hotel room at 3:00 a.m. helps dispel rumors, and it also helps raise awareness of the awkwardness that cross-sex traveling companions can encounter.
- Tell amorous traveling companions if they're making you feel uncomfortable. If directly confronting flirty behavior is difficult, something like, "Sometimes I feel like business travel seems awkward with a man/woman, do you ever feel that way?" might help initiate a valuable discussion.
- Speak up if the group chooses an outing that is demeaning to women (or men)—they may not even realize it.
- Go out in groups, if possible.
- Don't drink too much alcohol.
- State plans for later in the evening that create a need for you to be back in your hotel room *alone* at a certain time. Share this with your traveling companion: "I'm happy to have dinner with you, but I need to be back in my room by 9:30 for a phone call with my partner/spouse/child/mom/friend."
- If possible, get hotel rooms on separate floors. Several travelers mentioned the proximity of their rooms was related to the likelihood they would hook up. In general, the closer the rooms, the greater the difficulty in resisting temptation.

It is important to note that not all employees have issues traveling with cross-sex coworkers. A few reported to me that they traveled comfortably with cross-sex companions and felt their business trip was a positive experience. However, the majority reported some discomfort with their cross-sex travel companion.

The male lawyer who was quoted earlier summed up much of the discomfort and awkwardness experienced by many cross-sex travelers when he said, "It would have been easier if it was a guy." Indeed that encapsulates many of the obstacles that make up the sex partition. It's not that the obstacles are insurmountable, and no one is suggesting that men and women can't have successful business trips together. Instead, trips with the opposite sex are sometimes more complicated. Given a choice, many would prefer same-sex companions. And, once again, when preference is given to same-sex colleagues, women tend to bear greater disadvantage.

8

WORKPLACE ROMANCE

My own university is thankfully less prohibitive about student-professor couplings: You may still hook up with students, you just can't harass them into it. (How long before hiring committees at these few remaining enclaves of romantic license begin using this as a recruiting tool? "Yes the winters are bad, but the students are friendly.")

—Laura Kipnis, professor and author[1]

B ill Gates, David Letterman, David Petraeus, and Bill Clinton all succumbed to the temptation of romantic involvement with a woman at work. President Obama and wife, Michelle, started dating when they were both lawyers at the same Chicago law firm, and other celebrities and executives engaging in workplace romances regularly provide fodder for popular media outlets. Despite the prevalence of these relationships, workplace romance can be a headache for the organization. So fraught with complications are these relationships, organizations often attempt to regulate them, discouraging or forbidding employees from romantic fraternization. In fact, the taboo on workplace romance is so great that senior male managers choose to steer clear of work-related interactions to avoid perceptions that they're pursuing a relationship. Recall that 64 percent of senior men are reluctant to have a one-on-one meeting with a junior woman.[2] These men most likely fear sexual harassment charges and fear that the relationship will be perceived by others as romantic.

Not only is this an issue for senior executives, there is also evidence that many rank-and-file employees go out of their way to avoid any perception that they are involved in a romantic relationship at work.[3] Often encouraged by workplace policies that ban or discourage workplace romance, these employees avoid lunches, drinks, dinner, social outings, and even one-on-one business meetings with cross-sex coworkers. Regrettably, in avoiding any perception they are in a relationship, they are missing out on potentially valuable friendships with the opposite sex.

Wariness regarding workplace romance is understandable, especially since the repercussions resulting from participation in workplace romance can be severe. High-level executive careers toppled by workplace romance and covered by the media add to these fears. Awareness of the fate of these execs would leave anyone cautious in their cross-sex interactions. Take the case of Richard M. Schulze and Brian J. Dunn, the previous chairman and chief executive of Best Buy. Schulze had started Best Buy in 1966 as a small music retailer and expanded it into a nationwide electronics chain. Dunn joined Best Buy in 1985. Both were jobless in spring 2012 as a result of Dunn's alleged workplace romance with a twenty-nine-year-old female subordinate that reportedly "negatively impacted the work environment."[4] Dunn was ousted for participating in the relationship and Schulze for knowing about it and not reporting it.

A Best Buy investigation found that Dunn showed favoritism to his subordinate sweetheart, which damaged employee morale. Interestingly, the *New York Times* reported that the female subordinate claimed their relationship was nothing more than a "close friendship that was not romantic or otherwise improper."[5] Unfortunately, readers of the *New York Times* get the following facts: Very senior-level executive lost his high-level job because of an alleged romance with a junior woman that may have been nothing more than a close friendship. The sex partition gains strength.

Another high-profile executive, Gary Friedman, the former chairman and co-chief executive of Restoration Hardware, suffered a similar fate. The *New York Times* praised his work for the retailer: "He joined Restoration Hardware in 2001 when it was near bankruptcy and is widely credited with turning it into one of the nation's most successful high-end furniture retailers."[6] What brought an end to this success story? Workplace romance. Friedman stepped down from his position after evidence surfaced regarding an intimate relationship he had (and was still having at the time of his departure) with a twenty-six-year-old female employee. Although the female employee informed company investigators that her relationship with Friedman was consensual, Restoration Hardware was in the process of launching a stock offering and the board was concerned about the appearance of the relationship to potential investors.

Managers ousted for canoodling with coworkers are relatively common, though no official statistics are available on the frequency of such firings. In a *New York Times* interview an executive vice president of an outplacement firm reported that each year his own company handled about a dozen cases in which a manager had been pushed out after an affair with a subordinate.[7] If just one firm handles this many cases, job loss due to an affair must be relatively common.

When high-level managers lose their jobs because of workplace romance, organizations are sending a strong message. Workplace romance is dangerous. To keep organizational execs happy, employees may avoid anything that could even be misconstrued as a workplace romance. One foolproof method to avoid misperceptions that you're participating in a workplace romance is to limit interactions with cross-sex coworkers. Again, the sex partition gains strength.

EFFECTS ON THE SEX PARTITION

The taboos surrounding workplace romance serve to suppress interactions between men and women in the organization. Workplace romance is so taboo that employees go out of their way to keep all interactions purely professional with opposite-sex employees. While this is admirable, it can get in the way of cross-sex friendship development. The same standard doesn't apply with same-sex friendships. Sarah, a brand manager for a marketing firm, describes how she felt when she found herself in a romantic restaurant with a male manager in her firm:

> I had only been with the company a few days, and I had the need to purchase a car. I didn't own a car, and in Los Angeles you need one. So I found a model that I liked, and I was mentioning it to some of my colleagues who were more senior than me—a couple of levels above me. They were only five or six years older than me, but they were at the brand manager, director level. [I told them] I need to buy this car, and my director said, "I'm a great negotiator—I would be happy to take you out there, and help you buy it." I never bought a car by myself before, so I took him up on it. I felt good about having somebody else there.
>
> It was totally normal to go buy a car with him, but then afterwards, we were going to get a bite to eat. And the restaurant that he selected, that happened to be right nearby, was an Italian place, and when we went inside it was all candlelit and intimate. All of a sudden it didn't feel like a work dynamic anymore. It was awkward when the two of us stumbled in and the next thing we know we find

ourselves sitting across a candlelit table, and he's my director. It was just an awkward situation. I didn't know what to make of it. . . . If it had been another woman I wouldn't have thought twice about it. I wouldn't have been uncomfortable at all if it had been a woman.

Sarah went out of her way to keep her interactions with her director on a purely professional level in the future. Interestingly, she points out that if her negotiating partner had been female, the situation in the candlelit restaurant wouldn't have been remotely uncomfortable. In fact, had she negotiated and then dined with a senior female executive, a valuable mentorship and friendship might have blossomed. But because the interaction was cross sex, their future contact became more stiff and formal.

Anxiety surrounding what other coworkers are thinking can also lead to more conservative behavior around cross-sex friends. Marianne, a female recruiter, described her apprehensions about being observed with a male coworker and suggested that the size of an organization may impact this concern:

When I go out with my one male friend I always wonder what people are thinking. . . . You can really shoot yourself in the foot if you're forging personal relationships that go beyond friendships with members of the opposite sex. Sometimes I do feel it's a little bit different here, because it's a smaller audience. And what you're doing here is even more closely scrutinized than it would be within a larger organization.[8]

Dan, a management consultant, also believed his coworkers thought his cross-sex friendship was something more:

My good friend, the one that I walk around with at lunch, she got engaged a couple of years ago, and this guy saw us walking around together, saw that she was engaged, and assumed that I was who she was engaged to. So, I think people have probably wondered whether there was any kind of romantic relationship going on, because we hung out so much. Although that was the only time anyone ever said something about it, it was obvious that was what they thought.[9]

Sometimes, when others perceive you're having an affair, there can be dire consequences. Take the case of Gerry Marzorati and Megan Liberman. In 2010 Gerry Marzorati stepped down as editor of the *New York Times Magazine*. One reason given for the end of his reign was his promotion of Megan Liberman to deputy editor, an unpopular choice with his staffers. Marzorati defended his choice. "I promoted a young woman, a really smart woman and an ambitious

woman, and ambitious women make people uncomfortable," he told reporters.[10] Yet the *New York Observer* described how Marzorati and Liberman were
"close allies" and "were often seen together," insinuating there was more to
their relationship than work.[11]

We don't know if these two were involved in an affair, but if a man had been
promoted to the role, it's unlikely that a reporter would comment that the two
men "were often seen together." However, when a woman who socializes with
her male boss gets promoted, the promotion is often attributed to sex with the
boss. Sometimes these perceptions are grounded in reality, but more often they
are not. Only a very small percentage of women get promoted as a result of affairs with the boss. In a study of these affairs, Sylvia Ann Hewlett and colleagues
found that of those who admitted to sleeping with the boss, only 12 percent acknowledged they were promoted as a result of the affair.[12] Despite this relatively
small percentage, it's enough to perpetuate the image of women sleeping their
way to the top. Third parties also speculate about the advantages of sleeping
with a superior. Thirty-seven percent of women and 33 percent of men who
knew a coworker who was sexually involved with the boss also believed the
coworker was promoted as a result of the relationship.[13]

Hewlett and her colleagues describe how this perception puts women
in a double bind. If women develop the much-needed close relationships
(not sexual) with senior men, they are perceived as sleeping their way to the
top. However, if they choose the alternative, working hard and avoiding any
potentially incriminating encounters with senior men, they miss out on the
networking that is critical for career success. In their focus groups, these
authors found female employees shared stories of hurtful office gossip and
social isolation because of false perceptions of affairs with senior men. They
describe that the women "felt that the whispering intensified as they moved
up the ranks. As one female in financial services put it, 'If I'd had sex with as
many people that rumors said I've had it with, I would never have had time
to do the actual work of getting the promotions.' One beleaguered manager
told a senior executive, 'I just want to put up a big sign that says, I'M NOT
SLEEPING WITH ANYONE!'"[14]

In fact, women may go out of their way to avoid accusations that they're
sleeping their way to the top. Recall the statistic that almost two-thirds of senior
men are reluctant to have a one-on-one meeting with a junior woman? Well, it
turns out that half of junior women are just as reluctant to have a one-on-one
meeting with a senior man.[15] Most likely these women want to ensure that their
coworkers understand that they're not sleeping their way to the top.

LOVE IN THE CUBICLE—WORKPLACE ROMANCE IS COMMON

If workplace romances were uncommon, workers would be less concerned that their friendly gestures would be misinterpreted as romantic overtures. However, the prevalence of these romances keeps them prominently in the minds of employees. With long workdays and little free time, the workplace provides a unique opportunity for workers to meet potential dating partners. The most recent surveys conducted by a job search website indicate that between 40 percent and 60 percent of employees have engaged in a workplace romance at some point in their career, and almost one in five reports participating in at least two workplace romances in his or her career.[16] If there is no office romance blossoming in your office, simply turn to the tabloids where stories of famous or infamous workplace fraternization are plentiful. Below are just a few high-profile workplace romances that have made headlines:

- David Letterman and staffers: Talk-show host David Letterman admitted to having affairs with several female staffers (while in a relationship with Regina Lasko whom he recently married). Rumors spread that he had a secret bedroom above his set in the Ed Sullivan Theater, reserved for workplace liaisons. Letterman revealed his secret affairs after a blackmailer demanded $2 million to keep quiet about the relationships.
- Former president Bill Clinton and Monica Lewinsky: Clinton, who was married at the time, had an affair with Lewinsky who was then a twenty-two-year-old White House intern.
- Brad Pitt and Angelina Jolie: Many Hollywood couples meet on set. One of the most famous of these couples, Brad Pitt and Angelina Jolie, met on the set of *Mr. and Mrs. Smith* in 2005.
- Bill and Melinda Gates: Melinda Gates, a Microsoft employee, met Microsoft founder Bill Gates while seated near him at a work dinner.
- John Edwards and Rielle Hunter: North Carolina senator John Edwards had an affair with Rielle Hunter, a videographer who worked on his presidential campaign.
- President and Michelle Obama: Michelle was assigned to mentor Barack, who was a new summer associate at the Chicago law firm where she was employed. In his book *The Audacity of Hope*, Obama reports that Michelle repeatedly turned him down for a date, but he finally "wore her down."[17]
- Chelsea Handler and Ted Harbert: Workplace romances can be particularly sticky when they're hierarchical in nature. Ted Harbert, president

and CEO of E! Entertainment, dated Chelsea Handler while her late-night show ran on his network. In other words, he was her boss.

This is certainly not an exhaustive list of famous workplace romances, but it illustrates how workplace romances can run the gamut from happy endings and long-term marriages to those that end in blackmail or impeachment.

Why are workplace romances so prevalent? More women are entering fields that fifty years ago were dominated by men, resulting in the two sexes working side by side more than ever before. According to U.S. Department of Labor statistics, women currently make up 47 percent of the labor force, whereas in 1960 they made up only 32.3 percent of the workforce.[18] The increased representation of women in the workforce naturally increases the opportunity for sparks to fly between men and women at work.

Indeed, social psychologists have found that mere exposure to someone can increase our attraction to them. Aptly labeled the "mere exposure effect," several interesting experimental studies demonstrate its effect. In one revealing study, college students were shown photos of faces. Participants saw the photos of some faces up to twenty-five times, while other faces were only shown once or twice. The more the participants had seen a photo of a particular face, the more they reported liking it. In other words, mere exposure to the photographs increased attraction to it.[19]

I think it's fascinating that just seeing someone more often makes you like them more. It's why we start to like a song after hearing it over and over, and it's why we can fall for our coworkers. In another study of the mere exposure effect participants had short, face-to-face contact with one another. They were paired together for less than thirty-five seconds and weren't allowed to speak to one another. Participants were paired together either one, two, five, or ten times. Once again, mere exposure led to attraction, with subjects reporting that they preferred those they had seen more often to those they had seen less frequently.[20] Repeated exposure to the same coworkers day after day has a similar effect and will naturally increase attraction toward them.

Similarity also breeds attraction, and our coworkers share similar experiences and attitudes.[21] Coworkers at a homeless shelter may share similar philosophies about helping the poor, those who teach at an elementary school may share a love of small children, and employees working together on a presidential campaign may share similar political attitudes. Regardless of the organizational goals, individuals who show up at the same office for work each day often share many of the same experiences. These common interests and shared experiences contribute to greater attraction.

Another appeal of dating coworkers is that they've already been vetted. Unlike someone you may meet at a bar or on a website, it's unlikely that the coworker in the next cubicle is an axe murderer. You know that this person is responsible enough to both land and maintain a job with your organization, and you know how they get along with others. There are few other venues for meeting potential dating partners where you can uncover such valuable information.

With mere exposure, similarity, and dependability working in their favor, it is inevitable that attraction will develop between coworkers. It's what happens

Workplace Romance Statistics

- Between 40 percent and 60 percent of employees have engaged in a workplace romance at some point in their career.
- Almost one in five employees reports participating in at least two workplace romances in his or her career.
- 67 percent of employers cite the possibility of retaliation or conflict between coworkers when a relationship ends as a reason to have policies against workplace romance.
- 7 percent of employees report having switched jobs because of a workplace romance.
- 38 percent of workers know of a coworker who gained a professional advantage because of a romantic relationship.
- 31 percent of workers report feeling uncomfortable because of a coworker's romantic relationship.
- About one in five human resource professionals and employees report that sexual harassment claims occurred in his or her organization as a direct result of workplace romances.
- 77 percent of human resources employees feel that the potential for sexual harassment claims was a good reason to prohibit or discourage workplace romance.
- 70 percent of employees believe that openly dating a coworker could jeopardize their job security or job advancement.
- 68 percent of employees feel that workplace relationships can lead to conflict at work.
- 61 percent of employees feel workplace romance presents a distraction.
- 25 percent of organizations have a workplace-romance policy.
- 35 percent try to hide the fact they're involved in an office romance.

Statistics from Careerbuilder.com, 2011; Parks, 2006; Spherion, 2011; Vault.com, 2011.

after the attraction blossoms that is problematic for the organization and the sex partition. In order to avoid these problems, sometimes it's easier to avoid social interactions with opposite-sex employees altogether.

WHAT'S THE PROBLEM WITH CANOODLING A COWORKER?

It's not all bad. Workplace romance can lead to increased productivity from happy workers who are eager to get to work to see their romantic partner. However, the downsides for the organization are often perceived to outweigh any benefits.

If the couple breaks up (and the majority do), the organization must deal with the repercussions of ex-lovers negotiating daily business with each other. Turnover is costly for organizations, and romantic relationships, either good or bad, can also drive workers to seek employment elsewhere. Why find a new job? Employees involved in a relationship who feel that their organization disapproves of romantic relationships may try to find new work. Other times, a desire to avoid an ex can motivate workers to make a change.

From the organization's perspective, the greatest headache associated with workplace romance occurs when allegations of sexual harassment surface. But, if workplace romance is consensual, welcome, and mutually desired, then how can it result in sexual harassment charges? Romantic interest is not always reciprocated, and relentlessly pursuing a date with an uninterested coworker could be perceived as harassment. Sometimes, out of revenge, a disillusioned romantic partner charges his or her ex with sexual harassment. In other cases sexual harassment charges are not brought by either of the ex-lovers, but instead are brought by a third party who alleges favoritism by the romantic couple.

Many don't realize that sexual harassment charges can be filed by coworkers who are not involved in a romance but who feel that an office romance is resulting in favoritism. In the California Supreme Court case that first decided this issue, Miller v. Department of Corrections, Edna Miller and Frances Mackey were Department of Corrections employees.[22] They alleged that the prison warden, Lewis Kuykendall, was having consensual relationships with three female prison employees (his secretary and two other female subordinates). They further alleged that transfers and promotions were provided to these three women because of their relationship with the boss. Although Miller and Mackey were not themselves subjected to any sexual behavior by Kuykendall, they claimed that the warden's sexual relationships created an environment in which the only way for women to advance their careers was to have sex with their supervisor.

The court ruled in favor of Miller, sending a strong message to employers that sexual favoritism is discriminatory and can be penalized.

Even if sexual harassment charges are not filed, office morale can take a hit when employees feel that a romance is resulting in favoritism or unfair treatment. As a result, organizations often go to great lengths to discourage workplace romance.

SHHHHH! LET'S KEEP OUR ROMANCE A SECRET

I'll admit I've had a few of my own workplace romances. And like most, I tried to keep them secret for as long as possible. My workplace did not have any explicit policies prohibiting workplace romance, but it just seemed inappropriate or somehow unprofessional to date a coworker. I'm not alone—a good number of those participating in workplace romance do try to keep them quiet. A recent online survey indicates that just over a third of employees report attempting to keep their workplace romance a secret.[23]

One of my own workplace relationships was uncovered when text messages sent via company beepers (before cell phone texting was common) were reviewed by management. Who knew they would review such a thing? Like me, relationship partners typically fail in their attempt at keeping their romance quiet, and coworkers ultimately uncover the romance despite the secrecy surrounding it.[24]

Office policies and culture are not all to blame for the high levels of secrecy surrounding workplace relationships. Those in extramarital affairs, for example, are never going to go public with their relationship. Yet organizational policies and cultures that discourage office romance certainly add to the secrecy that typically envelops these relationships.

Ironically, this secrecy that surrounds workplace romance can be even more problematic than the relationship itself—both for the organization and the sex partition. From the organization's perspective, when workplace romances are out in the open, then supervisors can keep an eye on the couple. They can ensure that professionalism is maintained in the office and that no favoritism results from the romance.

With regard to the sex partition, the secretive nature of these relationships leaves employees having to "out" their coworkers who are romantically involved, and it increases general suspicion regarding workplace romance. If employees were open about their romantic relationships at work, coworkers would not need to resort to playing detective to spot colleague romances. However, when secrecy is the norm, employees often look for cues to tip them off to a budding romance between their workmates. They scrutinize all cross-sex pairs to figure out which duos might be up to more than work. Unfortunately, the cues that signal a romance are often the same as those that would indicate a cross-sex friendship.

One study examined just what the cues were that prompted employees to label a work relationship as romantic (see figure 8.1).[25] The most common response, given by 78 percent of the employees, was that they had seen the co-worker couple together outside of work. Other common giveaways to budding romance included observing the couple spending an unusual amount of work time chatting (57 percent), having long discussions behind closed doors (42 percent), and attending business trips together (33 percent).

Take a closer look at these cues used to identify romantic relationships. Aren't they the exact same cues that would be used to identify friendships? It's not like these folks are spotted emerging from a dark supply closet with their zippers down. Instead, they are being identified as having a relationship merely because they were observed outside of work together. Business trips and long discussions could certainly be work related. However, it's the cross-sex nature of these relationships that makes them suspect. If two same-sex colleagues were observed spending time at work chatting, having discussions behind closed doors, or traveling on business, the default assumption would be that they were hashing out a work problem or taking care of a needy client. However, when the pair is male-female, thoughts often turn to the possibility of a romantic interest between the coworkers. Cross-sex coworkers then try to avoid these situations to steer clear of rumors.

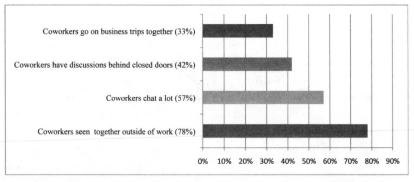

Figure 8.1. Cues Employees Use to Determine If Coworkers Are Romantically In-volved (Data from Quinn, 1977).

POLICING WORKPLACE ROMANCE

With all the issues that can arise from workplace romances, it's understandable that organizations strive to eliminate them. However, often their efforts have unintended consequences for the sex partition, leaving employees avoiding any inkling of impropriety with cross-sex coworkers. Is there a better way for organizations to address the concerns surrounding workplace relationships while minimizing the impact on the sex partition?

Cultural anthropologist and writer Margaret Mead suggested that only the complete eradication of workplace romance would allow both sexes to work productively together. She argued that taboos on workplace romance were needed so that men and women could work together and establish friendships at work. "A taboo enjoins. We need one that says clearly and unequivocally, 'You don't make passes at or sleep with the people you work with.'"[26] With these taboos in place she believed that men and women working together would become more like brothers and sisters in an environment where "sex is set aside in favor of mutual concern, shared interests, and, it seems to me, a new sense of friendship."[27]

Mead has a point. If romantic relationships were completely eradicated from the workplace, then there would be no fear that a friendship would be misconstrued as a romantic relationship. If, indeed, such a taboo existed, where romantic relationships at work were perceived as equally appalling as, say, incestuous relationships, then perhaps cross-sex friendships would be more likely to blossom. Just as brothers and sisters can pal around without anyone questioning whether they're sleeping together, male and female coworkers could also establish friendships without worrying what others are thinking.

Unfortunately, Mead's solution is impossible to implement. While there are currently taboos against workplace romance, they are not nearly as commonly accepted as other societal taboos. Therefore, despite the taboos, workplace romances are plentiful. Unfortunately, it is this toxic combination, the taboos against workplace romance in conjunction with a high prevalence of coworker relationships, that create barriers between men and women at work. Those involved in workplace romances often strive to keep them secret, and those not in romances keep the opposite sex at a distance to avoid any suggestion of impropriety.

Since it's futile to try to eliminate workplace romance, the only solution is to attempt to reduce or eliminate the taboo on workplace romance. If workplace romance was openly accepted in organizations then there would be less need for secrecy. Ideally, employees who are romantically involved would disclose their relationship to the organization, and the organization could ensure that no favoritism permeates the workplace. While not every employee will be willing to disclose his or her relationship (the married executive who sneaks off for an extramarital fling with his or her assistant would probably prefer to keep it quiet regardless of the workplace policy), a general openness regarding these relationships would aid in reducing concerns about cross-sex interactions.

Actual organizational policies addressing workplace romance run the gamut from no policies to strictly forbidding any fraternization. Although it may seem illegal for your organization to dictate who you can date outside of work, legal challenges to nonfraternization rules have generally been rejected by both state and federal courts.[28] In other words, your organization can legally tell you who you can and can't date.

As an alternative to formal written policies on workplace romance, many organizations opt for unwritten understandings. Some of these informal policies allow coworkers to date, but ask them to use good judgment and common sense to avoid "sticky situations."[29] Other workplaces require those involved in a relationship to sign a consensual relationship agreement (also sometimes referred to as a "love contract"). These agreements shield the employer from any liability should the relationship go sour. The pair typically must vow that their relationship is voluntary and consensual, and that they will not exhibit any favoritism as a result of their relationship. The agreement also usually allows management to provide a second pair of eyes on the relationship to reduce the likelihood of impropriety.

Consensual relationship agreements may not be the most romantic way to start a workplace romance, but they are a step in the right direction for the organization. By encouraging the disclosure of relationships, instead of promoting secrecy, they may help reduce gossip and rumors about cross-sex friends who are not dating.

ROMANCE ON CAMPUS

Different types of organizations have different issues with regard to workplace romance. At universities, where student-professor relationships are hierarchical by nature, it's clearly not desirable for a professor to have grading or supervisory power over a student with whom they are romantically involved. As a result many universities ban *all* sexual or romantic relationships between students and professors.

As an example, the University of California (UC) system banned professor-student relationships in cases where the professor has teaching or supervisory responsibility over the student, and also where the student is interested in a subject within the professor's expertise.[30] Prohibiting supervising or grading a romantic partner seems understandable, but banning a professor from dating someone with interest in his or her area of expertise is a little murky. In other words, at UC, professors are only permitted to date students who aren't interested in their work. Penalties for violating the rule range from written censure to dismissal.

The larger issue with these policies is they discourage professors from appearing as if they are dating students. Recall the male professor who described that he avoided dinners, drinks, and late-night meetings with female students. The taboo on professor-student relationships is so great that it can limit the interactions between students and professors of the opposite sex.

FORBIDDEN LOVE

Not only do bans on workplace romance discourage friendships between men and women but also they may ultimately backfire, having the reverse effect of what was intended. That is, they may ultimately increase the likelihood of attraction between coworkers. We tend to have an attraction to things that are forbidden.[31] Basically, there are certain freedoms to which most people just feel entitled. Take away one of these freedoms and people become motivated to reestablish it. This explains why we sometimes desire something more after we think we may have lost it. With regard to workplace romance, forbidding love at work may make it more desirable.

Forbidden love has had a rich history, from classic literature to contemporary film. Romeo and Juliet may have had less passion for one another if their relationship was embraced by their families. This enhanced attractiveness of forbidden love has been confirmed by researchers. Young, unmarried couples in one study described how much their parents disapproved and interfered with their relationship. Not surprisingly, those couples who had interfering parents reported more love for each other and were more seriously considering marriage than those who did not.[32] Thus the act of interfering with romance can actually make the romance stronger. Organizations should be aware that an unintended consequence of forbidding workplace romance is the possibility it could make coworker coupling more desirable.

FRIENDS OR LOVERS?

So how does someone decide whether to pursue a romantic relationship at work? Researcher Lisa Mainiero found that when deciding whether to initiate a workplace romance employees typically weigh the risks.[33] These risks ranged from career risks, such as losing the respect of coworkers, to risks that a marriage partner will uncover the relationship. However, I claim these are the same risks that are associated with the *perception* that someone is in a romantic relationship. Unfortunately, the consequences are often the same regardless of whether one is participating in an actual romantic relationship or just perceived to be participating in one by their coworkers. Therefore, employees may weigh these same risks when deciding whether to initiate a cross-sex friendship. Reducing the potential risks for employees by eliminating severe punishments for workplace romance will increase the likelihood that employees will cross the gender line when seeking friendship.

9

JEALOUSY, MARRIAGE, AND AFFAIRS

I love being married. It's so great to find that one special per-
son that you want to annoy for the rest of your life.

—Rita Rudner, comic[1]

Dental assistant Melissa Nelson worked for her employer, dentist James Knight, for ten years, and Knight reported that Nelson was one of the best dental assistants he ever had. Then Knight fired Nelson. Why? It turns out, Nelson lost her job because her boss's wife decided Nelson "was a big threat" to their marriage.[2] Evidently, Knight found Nelson to be an "irresistible attraction" and feared he might try to initiate an affair with her if she continued her employment. Ultimately, it was Knight's wife who had enough and ordered her husband to fire Nelson. Nelson had done nothing wrong. She considered Knight a friend and father figure and denies ever flirting with him or seeking any type of romantic or sexual relationship with him. She was fired because she was attractive, and her boss's wife thought she was a threat.

Nelson sued for sex discrimination, and her case went all the way to the Iowa Supreme Court. After all, Nelson claimed, if she had been a man, she would still be employed. Knight countered that Nelson was not fired because of her gender; indeed, he hired another woman to replace her. Instead, he claimed, she was fired because she represented a threat to his marriage. In July 2013, the all-male Iowa Supreme Court sided with Knight, ruling that no sex discrimination had occurred.[3]

While most responses to spousal jealousy are not this extreme, married workers clearly carry an extra burden when it comes to cross-sex friendship development. In addition to the taboo on perceived extramarital encounters at work, these employees also must ensure their cross-sex friendships are not misperceived by their spouses at home. Significant others provide one more reason to avoid unnecessary interactions with cross-sex coworkers.

Say, for example, a married man is meeting a male coworker for drinks once a week. His wife has a weekly dinner date after playing tennis with a female coworker. The spouses encourage one another to attend these outings. Similarly, late-night text messages to their same-sex friends may go unnoticed. Now switch the sexes. If the married man regularly meets a female friend for drinks, or the married woman regularly meets a male friend for a tennis date or dinner, the relationship suddenly becomes more scrutinized. Even the nightly texts may raise questions. One male employee in a research study summed it up this way, "Friends with women? You've got to be kidding. It's nothing but trouble for anybody that cares about his marriage."[4]

In general, researchers have found that cross-sex friendship is more challenging for married folks. Not only do those who are married have fewer cross-sex friends[5] but also those cross-sex friendships that do exist tend to be characterized by more superficial interactions.[6] I asked employees who were involved in a romantic relationship how they would feel if their spouse enjoyed an occasional beer after work with an opposite-sex work friend. The most common response as to their reaction was "It depends," and it depended on several factors. In general, the more frequent the outings, the more concern. Those who felt included in the friendship, or knew the friend well, were less threatened than those who felt excluded or were not acquainted with the friend.

Brittany, an IT consultant, suggested that her jealousy would depend on whether her spouse initiated the friendship before or after he was in a relationship with her: "I guess depending on how close and how frequently they went out, I might start to get a little uneasy. It depends if it's somebody he became close with after we were engaged in a relationship. If it was somebody he knew before he met me, that would be a little different, but if it was somebody he met afterwards, it might get a little funny. Especially if I didn't know her well." Other researchers have also found that cross-sex friendships that predate the marriage are not an issue for the spouse.[7] Thus, the initiation of new cross-sex friendships may present a more thorny issue for married individuals than the maintenance of these relationships.

Once again, looks play a role. Several of those I spoke with suggested that the attractiveness of the spouse's cross-sex friend was relevant. Becky, a finance professional, admitted, "I would probably be a little bit concerned. I think it would depend on the person. I know this is going to sound really terrible, but it would depend on what she looked like and how old she was."

EXTRAMARITAL AFFAIRS

Whether out of jealousy or fear that their spouse will engage in an extramarital affair, spouses can put the kibosh on their husband or wife's friendships with cross-sex coworkers. Many organizations dislike extramarital affairs almost as much as spouses do. Organizations frown on workplace romance, but the punishments are often more extreme when the workplace romance constitutes an extramarital affair. Job loss resulting from extramarital work affairs turns up in the media with surprising frequency. One of the best-known cases of a career-ending affair is that of former air force lieutenant Kelly Flinn. Flinn was the first female B-52 pilot in the United States Air Force. Not married herself, Flinn had a relationship with Marc Zigo, a civilian soccer coach at her base, who was married but told Flinn he was separated and filing for divorce. Flinn was discharged (she was permitted to resign with a general discharge instead of facing court-martial) for committing adultery, for lying about it, and for not ending the relationship when ordered to do so by her commander. Flinn had broken the gender barrier and was clearly a valuable asset to the military. Yet her career was brought down by an affair with a married man who she didn't even realize was still married.[8]

The civilian workforce also offers tales of career-ending extramarital affairs. Harry Stonecipher, president and CEO of Boeing, was credited with the resurgence of Boeing. However, in 2005, when news broke of his extramarital affair with a coworker, he was fired for violating Boeing's code of conduct. The relationship was consensual and the woman did not report directly to Stonecipher.[9]

Steve Phillips was fired from his ESPN hosting position when he confessed to an extramarital affair with a twenty-two-year-old coworker, Brooke Hundley. The network reported that Phillips's "ability to be an effective representative for ESPN has been significantly and irreparably damaged, and it became evident it was time to part ways."[10] (Firing was only one of Phillips's problems resulting from this relationship—Hundley penned a note to Phillips's wife describing the affair and a birthmark on Phillips crotch, then she crashed her car into Phillips's house. Phillips's wife filed for divorce.)

Mainstream media often seizes upon the salacious details of these career-ending extramarital affairs. Recent victim, CIA director General David Petraeus, grabbed headlines when he resigned because of an extramarital affair with his biographer. As CIA director, his extramarital affair was particularly risky because it brought the potential for high-level blackmail. Congressional representatives also have a history of doomed careers following extramarital affairs. In the last five years, Senator John Ensign resigned after an extramarital affair he tried to keep quiet, Representative Mark Souder resigned after an extramarital affair with a staffer (ironically the pair filmed an abstinence-in-education video together), and married Representative Chris Lee resigned after allegedly e-mailing photos of himself bare-chested to a woman he met on Craigslist. As I write this, another scandal emerges. The *Washington Post* referred to a videotaped kiss between married representative Vance McAllister and a staffer as "Smoochgate" and questioned whether the congressman's career could recover.[11]

Although high-profile employees' extramarital affairs grab headlines, you don't need to be a senior executive to suffer this fate. Laural Allen and Samuel Johnson lost their jobs at a Walmart store because of their relationship. Allen, who was separated from her husband at the time, worked with Johnson at a local Walmart. When the store manager learned that they were dating, he fired them both. Walmart claimed that its prohibition of extramarital dating stemmed from its strongly held belief in the family unit.[12] As part of this case, the question was raised as to whether a workplace can legally demand employees follow rules regarding who they can and cannot date. New York State's attorney general sued Walmart for discrimination, because, he claimed, the law states that workers can do whatever "legal recreational activities" they want after work hours. In other words, these two workers should be permitted to do whatever they wish in their free time (including dating whoever they want to), as long as it's legal. The appellate division of the state Supreme Court ruled once again in favor of Walmart by stating that dating is not a "recreational activity."[13]

What do these career-ending extramarital affairs have to do with cross-sex friendship and the sex partition? So fraught with danger are these relationships that married employees have additional incentive to avoid any perception that they may be involved in an extramarital affair at work. Same-sex friendships are preferred, and cross-sex friends suffer the consequences.

DOES YOUR HUSBAND OR WIFE HAVE AN OFFICE SPOUSE?

If spouses are jealous of cross-sex friends at work, they most likely wouldn't be too happy about their real-life spouse having a "work spouse." In lieu of being called "friends," close cross-sex friends at work are often referred to as "office wives," "office husbands," or "office spouses."

In *Psychology Today*, work spouse was defined as "a person at work with whom you have a special relationship in which you share confidences, loyalties, experiences, and a degree of honesty and openness."[14] The definition sounds a lot like the definition of a good friend to me. Furthermore, authors of a recent study on work spouses concluded that "the lines between one's work and one's personal life are becoming blurred, with work spouses serving as confidantes on extremely personal issues and wielding considerable influence over each other's decisions and purchases."[15] Work spouses are very common, with 32 percent of workers reporting currently having a work spouse,[16] and 65 percent reporting having a work spouse at some point in their lives.[17]

In reality, work spouses are nothing like real husbands and wives. True spousal relationships are based on a lifetime commitment and typically involve sexual relations. "Work spouses" are neither committed for a lifetime, nor are they sexually intimate. Work spouses are just close friends. By referring to these close cross-sex work friendships as "spousal," we merely create more barriers to them.

I certainly would be more jealous if my husband labeled his female work friend "a work wife" than if he merely referred to her as a work friend. The terms "office wife" and "work wife" take the purely platonic cross-sex friendship at work and make it sound like something illicit. It implies there is something more to these friendships than just friendships—something that should be hidden from one's actual spouse. Indeed, 22 percent of married people say their real spouse does not know about their work spouse.[18]

Certainly the media adds to this suggestion that work spouses have a touch of romance. For example, the *Wall Street Journal* ran an article with the headline "Does Your Work Wife Get a Valentine? Some Co-Workers Want to Acknowledge a Deep Yet Platonic Bond on the Romantic Holiday."[19] (In case you can't figure this one out on your own, they concluded that organizations, wary of sexual harassment issues, frown on Valentine's Day gift-giving to office spouses, and that real spouses may not understand the giving of a valentine to an office spouse.) The suggestion here is that a man and a woman can't have a close friendship without a little romance or attraction.

Along this same line, popular media ask questions such as whether a work spouse's appearance is important, and whether a work spouse is similar in appearance to one's real spouse. Once again, analyzing the physical appearance of the work friend and comparing the appearance of the work friend to one's actual spouse implies physical attraction in these relationships. (Okay, if you must know—results indicated that 38 percent were similar in personality to their real spouse, and 52 percent said they were complete opposites. Eight percent said their work spouses were similar in appearance to their real spouse and 52 percent said they were opposite. Forty percent of men and 22 percent of women felt the appearance of their office spouse was important to them.)[20]

Chad McBride, who studies work spouse relationships, has found that less than 30 percent of employees used the term "work spouse" to describe their own friendships at work, but instead these labels are assigned by their other coworkers. "There's a level of discomfort about it [the label 'work spouse'] because it makes it sound like something salacious is going on when there's not," says McBride.[21]

What's most disturbing about the label of "office wife" or "office husband" is that labels can be self-fulfilling. Social psychologists have repeatedly found that the labels we assign to things, the words that we use, actually shape how we perceive things. The classic example of this effect of labeling comes from a study of teachers and students. In this classic study by Robert Rosenthal and Lenore Jacobson, teachers were told their pupils had completed an intelligence test over the summer and were told which of their students performed well and which did not. In other words, the teachers were told which students were "smart." In reality, the students were given randomly assigned test scores, and so those labeled "smart" had not actually performed better than others. Nonetheless, it turns out the label of "smart" was self-fulfilling. The teachers treated the children they thought were smarter differently, and by the end of the year, the children who were randomly labeled "smart" actually performed better in school.[22]

We label someone smart, and we treat them as if they are intelligent. If we label someone as our work spouse, and the term "spouse" implies romance or physical attraction, we will be more likely to be physically attracted to that person. Indeed, 13 percent of work spouses reported having some sort of romantic hookup that "crossed the line" with their work spouse.[23] Nearly all of them reported regretting it.

For those not wanting to cross that line, the esteemed pop psychologist Dr. Phil offers some advice on "How to keep boundaries with a work spouse." He suggests, "Don't be alone with a person of the opposite sex separate from your job. Romantic relationships come out of recreational activities."[24] I guess Dr. Phil doesn't think that cross-sex friendships are very important. Perhaps that's because he's male.

In general, the use of the terms "office spouse," "office wife," and "office husband" add to the barriers that impede cross-sex friendship at work. They promote spousal jealousy (from the actual spouse), and they imply that close cross-sex friends at work are more than just friends. Although many of the obstacles to cross-sex friendship at work are difficult to overcome, this one is easier to break down. Merely referring to close cross-sex friends at work as "friends" in lieu of "spouses" will help promote healthier and longer lasting relationships.

Getting rid of the office spouse label is an easy fix, but other issues surrounding spouses, marriage, and friendships at work are harder to tackle. Including your spouse (and by "spouse," I'm referring to your real spouse, not your office spouse) in your work life and introducing him or her to your work friends (of both sexes) can dramatically reduce suspicion and jealousy.

Hiding or minimizing your cross-sex friendships at work can only get you in trouble. Recall the dentist, Knight, who fired his assistant, Nelson, because his wife was jealous. The last straw for Knight's wife was finding text messages between Nelson and Knight. What were the text messages about? Mostly about innocuous matters like updates on their kids' activities. (To be fair, Knight allegedly once texted Nelson that her shirt was too tight.) But Nelson claims she never flirted or sought any type of intimate relationship with Knight.

What if Knight had shared the text messages with his wife all along? "Hey honey, I just got a text that Nelson's boy just won his soccer tournament." It might have reduced his wife's suspicions just enough. It might also have kept him from sending the text about Nelson's shirt. At least Knight's wife wouldn't have had the shock of discovering the texting on her own.

Attempts to hide or minimize your cross-sex friendships at work only create more problems down the road. Openness and honesty regarding your friendships with the opposite sex can allow these relationships to grow with less suspicion.

10

ROMANTIC AND SEXUAL ATTRACTION

Between men and women there is no friendship possible. There is passion, enmity, worship, love, but no friendship.

—Oscar Wilde, writer[1]

Organizations and spouses aren't all to blame when it comes to the impact of romance on cross-sex friendships. It's true that policies on workplace romance make cross-sex friendships at work more difficult, but even without these policies, romantic and sexual attraction can plague friendships between men and women. In the film *When Harry Met Sally,* Harry Burns and Sally Albright share the drive to New York City after graduating from college in Chicago. During the drive, Harry tells Sally that no man would ever be friends with a woman without wanting to sleep with her.

Harry: You realize of course that we could never be friends.

Sally: Why not?

Harry: What I'm saying is—and this is not a come-on in any way, shape or form—is that men and women can't be friends because the sex part always gets in the way.

Sally: That's not true. I have a number of men friends, and there is no sex involved.

Harry: No, you don't.

Sally: Yes, I do.

Harry: No, you don't.

Sally: Yes, I do.

Harry: You only think you do.

Sally: You say I'm having sex with these men without my knowledge?

Harry: No, what I'm saying is they all want to have sex with you.

Sally: They do not.

Harry: Do too.

Sally: They do not.

Harry: Do too.

Sally: How do you know?

Harry: Because no man can be friends with a woman that he finds attractive. He always wants to have sex with her.

Sally: So, you're saying that a man can be friends with a woman he finds unattractive?

Harry: No. You pretty much want to nail them, too.

Sally: What if they don't want to have sex with you?

Harry: Doesn't matter because the sex thing is already out there so the friendship is ultimately doomed, and that is the end of the story.

Sally: Well, I guess we're not going to be friends then.

Harry: I guess not.

Sally: That's too bad. You were the only person I knew in New York.[2]

Was Harry correct—can men and women be friends without sex getting in the way? In order to answer this very question, researchers talked to eighty-eight pairs of cross-sex friends.[3] The pairs of friends were separated, guaranteed anonymity and confidentiality, and then questioned about their romantic interest in their friend. As suggested by the fictional Harry Burns, men were much more attracted to their female friends than vice versa. Indeed, men desired to date their friend regardless of their own relationship status (women who were currently in a relationship were less likely to desire romance with their friend). The men were also more likely to overestimate how attractive they were to their female friends.

So Harry's question persists: Can women and men be friends without sex getting in the way? Studies reveal they can—between 35 percent and 72 percent of cross-sex friendships are truly platonic.[4] However, these numbers may underestimate the problem of sexual attraction in cross-sex friendships. By interviewing or surveying individuals who are already in cross-sex friendships, these numbers only included individuals who were able to overcome sexual attraction and become friends.

It's important to understand this statistical anomaly better, so stick with me here. Say that Harry Burns was correct, and that men and women could never be friends if one friend was sexually attracted to the other. Then surveys of cross-sex friends that ask, "Are you sexually attracted to your cross-sex friend?" would find that zero percent of cross-sex friends were attracted to one another. Why? If sexual attraction keeps friendships from forming then all cross-sex friendships that exist must not have any sexual attraction. This zero percent would certainly not indicate that sexual attraction was not a problem for cross-sex friends. Indeed, just the opposite would be true. It would indicate sexual attraction is an insurmountable barrier for cross-sex friends. Unfortunately, we have no statistics on the number of cross-sex friendships that never formed because sexual attraction got in the way.

In reality, some friends can maintain a cross-sex friendship despite physical attraction. However, when one friend is interested in more than a friendship, then the friendship is typically doomed. The friend who is not interested often backs off from the friendship. Laurie, a technology consultant, described how she ended a workplace friendship when romantic interest surfaced:

> I just stopped being friends with him. Usually I just would either try to bring up the fact that I have a boyfriend in casual conversation so the other person gets the message that I'm not interested, or really try to be less friendly than I might normally be. Or I just stop being friends with them at all.[5]

Laurie struggled to make sure her own friendliness toward male coworkers was not misinterpreted as romantic or sexual interest. Misinterpretation of friendliness is a common issue between men and women and can result in uncomfortable situations for the friends.

THAT'S NOT WHAT I MEANT—
THE ROLE OF MISINTERPRETATION

When someone is attracted to you, sometimes they search for signals that you feel the same way. Often they find these signals even where they don't exist. I used to swim laps at a local pool to stay in shape. I arrived at the pool one day to find a dozen roses waiting for me at the pool office. The roses were from an anonymous admirer and were addressed to the woman in the yellow and black swimsuit who arrived each day at 9:00 a.m. That was clearly me. In the note accompanying the roses, my admirer revealed that he knew I was interested in him because of the way I tugged on my ear each time I emerged from the pool. He apparently interpreted this ear tugging as a sign of interest in what he had to say. In reality, I tugged on my ear when I emerged from the pool to get the water out of my ears—not to send a signal of romantic interest.

Misinterpretations aren't usually this extreme, but men are more likely than women to misperceive friendliness as sexual interest. Men, in general, tend to think about sex more than women, and so they're more likely to see sexual interest when it's not there. (Men typically think about sex nineteen times a day, while sex crosses women's minds about ten times a day.)[6]

Sometimes organizations set up their employees for misinterpretation. When Safeway began enforcing its "superior service" initiative, employees were required to be friendly to shoppers. Seems like a reasonable request. Employees were told to "anticipate customers' needs, be courteous, escort them to items they cannot find, make selling suggestions, thank them by name if they pay by check or credit card, and offer to carry out their groceries."[7] The policy was enforced by the use of undercover shoppers, and employees were warned that those who didn't conform to the policy could be subject to remedial training, disciplinary letters, and termination. What happened? Thirteen workers filed grievances indicating that they were propositioned by shoppers who misinterpreted their friendly behavior for flirtation. Twelve of these thirteen employees were women. In particular, the women wanted to have the option to avoid eye contact and to refuse to walk a man to his car at night. These women realized that men were more likely to misinterpret friendliness as sexual interest.

I talked to a supermarket cashier, Brenda, who told me similar policies were in place at her store, and the use of undercover shoppers to police these policies continued until just last year. During that time, she was not only required to smile, thank customers by name, and offer to carry groceries out to the car, but her store went even further. Within the last five years, she told me, she was encouraged to ask how a customer's day or weekend was going, and question him or her about his or her plans for the weekend. Brenda described how male customers frequently misinterpreted these friendly gestures:

> They ask you to be friendly, and I think men sometimes just take that the wrong way. I try to treat all my customers the same, but I think men's perceptions are just different than women's sometimes. I'm more uncomfortable dealing with men in the grocery store than women. I never said anything, 'cause I thought I'd lose my job. But it just got a little too personal for me. I'd say, "So, did you have a good weekend?" and they'd say, "Well it would have been better if you were there." Why do I have to ask them what their weekend was like, and what they were doing? That's none of my business. I've even had a gentleman wait for me in the parking lot. After I thanked him by name and all that in the store, when I got off, he was outside, in his car, waiting for me.

The waiting customer asked for Brenda's phone number and wanted to know if she would go out with him some time. Fearing that he might be a sexual predator or that he would say something negative about her to store management, she politely provided an incorrect phone number.

These female supermarket employees had to decide between being reprimanded at work or misinterpreted by male customers. Male employees didn't have this problem, and female employees didn't have this problem with female customers. It was the male customers who were most likely to misinterpret female friendliness.

If some men misinterpret service-with-a-smile as flirtation, one can imagine what happens when women try to befriend a man at work. Not surprisingly, the likelihood of misinterpretation is pretty high. About 67 percent of us have had our friendliness misinterpreted on at least one occasion, although significantly more women than men reported experiencing this type of misperception.[8] Research confirms what the supermarket employees learned: that a smile or eye contact is misinterpreted as sexual interest by men much more frequently than by women.[9]

When it comes to cross-sex friendships, unfortunately, in the majority of cases, the friendships can't survive after one friend misinterprets friendliness as sexual interest. Of those who reported a misinterpretation of their friendliness, only 32 percent reported that they were able to remain friends.[10]

In the workplace, misinterpretation can be particularly tricky. In a piece she wrote for the *New Republic*, Marin Cogan described how journalists must express interest in their sources, and this professional interest can be misinterpreted for romantic interest. According to Cogan, "The problem, in part, is that the rituals of cultivating sources—initiating contact, inviting them out for coffee or a drink, showing intense interest in their every word—can often mimic the rituals of courtship. . . . A source may invite you to meet at the bar around the corner from your apartment. If you agree, he might offer to pay for the drinks and walk you home."[11] It gets uncomfortable when her professional interest in them is misinterpreted. So uncomfortable is this situation that some female reporters may choose not to call back a source who presumed romantic interest. Male journalists do not face these issues interviewing in the predominantly male political sphere. However, when misinterpretation results for the female reporter, she must decide whether to forgo the source, and possibly set back her career, or endure unwanted flirtations and signals of romantic interest.

Lisa, a television sports reporter I spoke to, reported a similar issue. Instead of meeting her sources for coffee, Lisa tracked hers down in locker rooms. Reporting for a top-twenty-five television station, she covered well-known sports teams in her region. Not surprisingly, Lisa was hit on by professional athletes who misconstrued her interest in them. From subtle encouragement to meet up for dinner to more blatant invitations to hotel rooms, Lisa was forced to explain to the athletes that her relationship with them was purely a professional one. She explained:

> There's an epidemic of athletes having affairs and having girlfriends in differ-
> ent cities, and it's frankly just a part of their life. So, sometimes they base their
> interactions on exploring whether you're willing to go there with them. It made
> it challenging for me as a woman. I once heard a newspaper reporter I know talk
> to a player about getting together for a beer some time. I could never do that
> cause if I ever did that—if I even joked about meeting a player outside of the work
> environment for any reason—it would be inappropriate, given that I'm a woman.

The problem may be greater for female journalists and reporters, but, really, many women have a similar issue at work. Whether it's a professional athlete or a potential mentor, there's a reasonable chance that asking an opposite-sex coworker to join you for coffee or beer would be misinterpreted.

Another example of how men and women can view the same situation quite differently comes from the television world. In covering conservative talk-show host Bill O'Reilly's sexual harassment case, the *New York Observer* interviewed television news anchors and producers. (To fill you in on the case, a female producer of O'Reilly's Fox TV talk show, *The O'Reilly Factor*, charged O'Reilly with sexual harassment. She alleged that he talked to her about using a vibrator and about his sexual fantasies that involved her. They settled out of court.) The *Observer* wanted to determine if this type of behavior was common in television.

The difference in perceptions between the male and female television em-ployees was stunning. Reading the different perceptions of the office vibe, I couldn't help but think how difficult it would be to establish a platonic cross-sex friendship in this environment. A man described in the *Observer* as a "promi-nent on-air host" depicted the television news world this way:

> At the producing level it's all young women, 99 percent of whom have no chance
> of being on TV, and they like powerful men. Each host has around him lots of
> good-looking unmarried women. Women are excited by power, let's be totally
> clear. The temptation to have sex with your staff is overwhelming. . . . You can't
> imagine how sexually out of control it is.[12]

The women in this environment were also interviewed to get their perspec-tive. The women didn't exactly see eye to eye with the producer. They didn't report how sexually excited they were by the powerful men at work. Instead, the women complained of unwanted touching and groping, unwanted invitations to return to hotel rooms, clunky and incessant sexual innuendo, unwelcome shoulder rubs, and shameless requests for dates. They also reported requests for three-way orgies and oral sex, all by powerful male executives and well-known male on-air personalities.[13] It seems that the men were viewing their interactions with women through a sexual lens. As a result of the misinterpretation, it doesn't seem like an environment where the women could comfortably hope to develop a rewarding mentor relationship with a senior male executive.

Several research groups have watched this misinterpretation unfold right in their labs.[14] In one study, the researchers simulated a speed-dating setting. Male-female pairs were asked to talk about a neutral topic for three minutes in a room by themselves after which they were separated. Once separated, the pair completed a survey about their own sexual interest in their partner and their perceptions of their conversation partner's sexual interest. After the survey was completed, they moved on to another "speed meeting" partner and repeated the process.[15]

Not surprisingly, men were more likely to think that their female conversation partners were more sexually interested than they actually were. This bias was even greater when it came to attractive women. Men were even more likely to perceive that attractive women were sexually interested in them. Women, on the other hand, actually demonstrated an under-perception bias. In general, women thought their conversation partners were less sexually interested than they actually were. The more attractive the woman, the less likely she was to think her conversation partner was sexually interested in her.[16]

It's tough to develop friendships when potential friends interpret things differently from the way you do. However, misinterpretation doesn't just come from our friends or potential friends. From a young age we avoid cross-sex friendships out of fear that someone else, a third party, will think we're dating our friend.

WHAT WILL EVERYONE THINK?

Although friendly conversations with cross-sex coworkers can sometimes lead to misinterpretation by one of the conversation partners, other coworkers may also think there's more than a friendship blossoming. In elementary school were you ever teased because of a friendship with an opposite-sex playmate? My ten-year-old son's friends are almost exclusively male. That's not unusual. Starting in the elementary school years, children avoid cross-sex friendships because they fear their friends will think they're dating their cross-sex friend, or that they "like" or "love" their cross-sex friend. Indeed, those boys who befriend girls and those girls who befriend boys are subject to intense teasing about the nature of the friendship.[17] In one study, some elementary school boys revealed that they secretly "liked" one girl in particular. However, the boys were hesitant to spend time with this girl or to talk to her, because they feared that they would be teased by their peers. Furthermore, the boys did not share their feelings about this girl with anyone, but if the secret got out, the "couple" was often made the brunt of their friends' jokes.[18]

Even in the rare situations where children have a cross-sex friend (not someone they "like," but an actual friend of the opposite sex), they tend not to reveal the friendship at school. Although they may acknowledge the friend at school, they will restrict their play to same-sex friends while in public. Only in the privacy of their own home will they feel comfortable enough to play with the cross-sex friend. The stigma associated with cross-sex friendships is too great for the children to risk demonstrating their cross-sex friendship in public.

There is one situation where children comfortably interact with cross-sex peers at school, and that is when the interaction is directed by a teacher or other adult. If the teacher instructs a group of children to work together, then the danger that peers will think they, themselves, have sought out the opposite-sex partners is relieved. Without the chance their interaction will be perceived as "liking" the other, the mixed-sex groups can work together comfortably.[19]

So, eventually, as we age, our friends stop teasing us about spending time with the opposite sex, and we can pursue these friendships without fear of ridicule. Or do they? At the other end of the age spectrum, research indicates the elderly seem just as concerned about their cross-sex friendships as the elementary-age children. Much as the children felt that interaction with the opposite sex indicated "liking" or "loving," interviews with unmarried, elderly women revealed these women felt a friendship with a man was the same as a romantic, dating relationship. These older women perceived all male friends as courting them.[20]

The elderly women exhibited the same fear of peer ridicule as the elementary school children. Just like the children, these women went to great lengths to hide their male friendships to eliminate any suggestion that they were behaving "improperly." One woman described her behavior when a male friend came to visit: "I don't let him in my apartment. It wouldn't be proper. People would talk."[21] Another woman refused to name her male friend in the interview, because she feared other people would discover her relationship. Finally, another interviewee said she would not go out in her hometown with her male friend because "people would get the wrong idea."[22]

Clearly concerns about what others think about our cross-sex friendships haunt us throughout our lives. Having these social norms ingrained at such a young age, it's no wonder men and women at work have difficulty forming friendships. However, one lesson from the children may give hope for adults. Recall the children were willing to work or play with opposite-sex children when instructed by the teacher. The direction of the teacher removed any fear that the children were seeking out the opposite-sex playmate on their own. In the workplace, if networking or mentor programs are mandatory, it may remove some of the stigma associated with interacting with the opposite sex.

FRIENDS WITH BENEFITS

Cross-sex friends who want more than a platonic relationship, but not a romantic relationship, have one more option. Friends with benefits (FWB) relationships, which have garnered much media attention lately, are relationships between cross-sex friends where the friends have sex but don't consider their relationship romantic.[23] Unlike hookups or one-night-stand sexual encounters, FWB relationships are more stable friendships, where the friends see each other regularly. Although many think of "friends with benefits" as a relatively new type of cross-sex friendship, the idea has been around for a while. For example, in the 1980s the term "flovers" was coined for friendships with sex.[24]

FWB relationships have gained attention recently because of their presence in popular media. In one episode of the television show *Seinfeld*, friends Jerry and Elaine decide to have a purely physical relationship based upon a set of ground rules. However, as their FWB relationship progresses, they experience difficulties maintaining their original friendship. More recently, the plots of two films also tackled this topic. In the 2011 film *Friends with Benefits*, characters Jamie and Dylan believe adding sex to their relationship will not lead to complications. As with Jerry and Elaine, this pair also experienced difficulties maintaining their friendship and begin to develop deep mutual feelings for each other. Characters portrayed by Natalie Portman and Ashton Kutcher ran into the same problem in the 2010 film *No Strings Attached*.

These relationships break with the traditionally accepted notion that women link sex and love, and that women typically desire sex only when they are in love. (Men, by contrast, are generally thought to have no problem separating the two and are perceived to enjoy sex without love.) Previously, researchers have found that for men the release of sexual tension is the most common reason for initiating sex, but for women the "most important reason was to receive love, intimacy, and holding."[25] These research findings support the cliché that "men give love to get sex, while women give sex to get love."[26]

However, in friends-with-benefits relationships, both participants are interested in sex without love. Indeed, most research on hookups and friends with benefits suggests that women are regularly engaging in sex without love.[27] Nonetheless, there is some evidence that women are more interested in the friends aspect of the relationship (the emotional connection), and men are more interested in the benefits (or sexual) aspect of the relationship.[28]

Although no studies to date have assessed the prevalence of this type of relationship in the workplace, one study reported that a whopping 60 percent of college students had participated in an FWB relationship.[29] This number seems rather inflated, and the actual percentage is probably much lower, as indicated by another study finding 16 percent of college students reported participating in an FWB relationship.[30]

So how do friends-with-benefits relationships impact the sex partition? Certainly, these relationships defy those who claim that friendship and sexuality cannot coexist. In this sense, the FWB relationship breaks down one barrier to cross-sex friendships. That is, the friends no longer must decide between sex and friendship, they can have both.

Reality, however, suggests that these relationships can be problematic. Friendship researcher Donald O'Meara describes how having sex can impact friendships: "With each increasingly intimate physical act, the dyad probably finds it more difficult to maintain a clearly defined friendship identity."[31] Just as the recent film characters have had trouble adjusting to this friendship, so do actual participants in these relationships. FWBs report their biggest concerns are that sex would harm the friendship or create unreciprocated desires for a more romantic relationship.[32] Other problems result when one friend in the FWB relationship becomes involved in a romantic relationship with someone new. When this occurs, the FWB relationship will likely end.

While sex in friendship has most likely been occurring for a long time, only recently has data been collected on the high prevalence of these relationships, particularly among college students. Although no historical prevalence data is available, it seems likely that friends-with-benefits relationships are becoming more common. Most of the research on these relationships has focused on college students, so the prevalence of these relationships among older individuals is also unknown. However, if college students commonly engage in these relationships, then it's not unlikely that they would continue to pursue FWB relationships with their cross-sex friends after graduation.

Within the workplace, it is hard to imagine a distinction between a romantic and a FWB relationship. It's almost comical to imagine a conversation between a human resources manager and a superior-subordinate pair engaged in a friends-with-benefits relationship. One can imagine their explanation that no favoritism exists in their relationship, because although the pair is indeed engaging in sex, they are merely friends. Will friends with benefits be asked to sign consensual relationship agreements? Although it is not yet clear how these relationships will function in the workplace, certainly a workplace culture that is intolerant of workplace romance is not going to embrace FWB situations.

FWB relationships are just one more complication added to the already complex interactions between men and women. And they represent another complication that same-sex heterosexual friends need not address. If we expect men and women to work together productively, we can't continue to ignore these issues of romantic and sexual attraction. Instead, we need to provide tools for employees to deal with these issues. Specific suggestions for addressing these issues are provided in later chapters.

11

BIRDS OF A FEATHER

The one thing that unites all human beings, regardless of age, gender, religion, economic status, or ethnic background, is that, deep down inside, we all believe we are above-average drivers.

—Dave Barry, author[1]

During World War II, Winston Churchill described how a misunderstanding emerged between American and British military officers.[2] The British had an urgent issue they needed to discuss with the Americans and told the Americans they needed to "table it." By "table it," the Brits meant they wanted to discuss the issue immediately—they wanted to bring it to the table. The Americans agreed this was an important issue to discuss, but to the Americans, the term "table it" meant to defer the issue or leave it on the table. Churchill described how a lengthy argument between the two parties ensued before both realized they wanted exactly the same thing.

Different languages, cultures, and etiquette often result in difficulties and misunderstandings when we try to conduct business internationally. Fortunately, a multitude of seminars and university courses offer assistance to those conducting business abroad. When exchanging business cards in Japan, business travelers are advised that they should read the card before putting it away to avoid insulting their colleague. Those visiting China are advised that overly strong handshakes are considered offensive. In Russia, firmer handshakes are the norm, and business travelers might be told to expect to consume some alcohol while conducting business with their colleagues.

Despite the enormous efforts we make to bridge cultural differences, little attempt is made to bridge gender differences in the workplace. Just as our international business associates aren't really that different from us, differences between men and women are small, but important. As with our foreign counterparts, different communication styles and different interests can drive a wedge between the sexes. And, as with our international counterparts, greater understanding of our cross-sex colleagues would go a long way to bridging these gaps. Unfortunately, a lack of understanding regarding our cross-gender coworkers can lead to a preference for same-sex coworkers.

Not surprisingly, most gender differences have their roots in childhood, and I see them every day in my own home. My husband has a warning that he often shouts to me. "Kim, bend your knees!" he cautions, as my hockey-player son comes barreling into the kitchen attempting to check me into the refrigerator. Other than playing ice hockey, my son loves to wrestle and roughhouse with his friends (and occasionally his parents), and his make-believe games usually involve weapons, fighting, and destruction. These games are quite different from the games I enjoyed with my girlfriends in elementary school. I can't recall ever checking my parents or tackling my friends. These gender-specific play styles and interests we adopt at an early age impact our expectations for friendships throughout our lives.

Consistent with my experience at home, researchers studying young children have found several key gender differences in play styles. Primarily, young boys tend to play in larger groups than girls, and their play tends to be rougher. Often termed "rough-and-tumble play," boys' play is often characterized by pushing, pulling, hitting, chasing, and wrestling (typically without hurting one another).[3] Preferring to play outside, boys' play style often emphasizes competitiveness—these boys are striving to achieve and maintain dominance over their male playmates.[4] Checking someone into the refrigerator is a prime example of rough-and-tumble type play.

Most girls don't like boys' rough style of play and will even withdraw from it. Playing in smaller groups, girls typically form close relationships with just one or two other girls.[5] While boys' friendships tend to be centered on common interests, girls' friendships tend to be characterized by the sharing of confidences. Gender researcher Vicki Helgeson summarizes these gender differences: "Boys view friendship as instrumental: A friend is someone with whom you do things. Girls view friendship as more emotional: A friend is someone with whom you connect."[6]

It is important to note that these gender differences in play styles don't apply to all girls and boys, but, instead, they represent statistically significant tendencies. Statistically speaking, men are taller than women, but that doesn't mean that all men are taller than all women. Similarly, some girls may enjoy rough-and-tumble play and some boys may not. However, in general, boys are more likely than girls to adopt this rougher style.

So averse are girls to boys' typical play style, girls sometimes just stop playing when boys are involved.[7] In one study, very young children (average age of two years and nine months old) who were previously unacquainted paired up with either a same-sex or cross-sex play partner and the pair were given toys. The researchers then measured the amount of time a child spent simply standing passively watching their young partner play with the toys. Within the girl-girl pairs, the girls were rarely passive, and both girls actively played with the toys. Boy-girl pairs were another story. In these mixed-sex pairs, the girl frequently stood aside and let the young boy monopolize the toys. It's not that these girls were more passive than the boys (indeed, they were more social than the boys when with another girl), but when paired with a boy the girls became more passive.

Although these differences in play styles and preferences for same-sex play partners start at an early age, they tend to increase in strength over time. By age five, this preference for same-sex playmates is stronger for boys than girls. By age six and a half, children spend eleven times more play time with same-sex than with opposite-sex playmates.[8] Why? One reason is that boys who play with girls are perceived as feminine, and boys generally don't tolerate feminine behavior in other boys. Girls do not feel the same need to reject masculinity and tend to be more accepting of masculine behaviors in other girls.[9]

When my son was a toddler he had a doll that he liked to carry around. The doll was aptly named "Baby" and was permanently dressed in pink pajamas with white polka dots. Reactions from other parents ranged from shocked looks to giggles when they saw him carrying Baby. Occasionally, a parent or shop owner would tell me how fabulous it was that I let my son play with a doll. Clearly, a boy with a doll was perceived as unusual, and this lack of tolerance for anything feminine in boys forces the genders further apart.

Adults aren't entirely to blame for the segregation of boys and girls, as the preference to play with one's own sex is not unique to humans. Even nonhuman primates exhibit a preference for same-sex playmates, indicating that there's probably more than socialization influencing playmate choices.[10]

One particularly perplexing aspect of the toddler preference for same-sex playmates is that many three-year-olds have not yet established gender constancy.[11] That is, children of this age don't fully understand that their biological sex will remain constant throughout their lifetime. They often think their biological sex could change if they adopt characteristics of the opposite sex (e.g., wearing a dress for boys or getting a buzz haircut for girls). So even though they logically think they could become the other sex at some point, they still have a preference for same-sex playmates.

Not only do young boys and girls have different play styles, but also, stemming from these differences, boys and girls typically develop different conversational styles.[12] For boys, communication is used to convey or establish dominance over other boys. As a result boys' conversations are often characterized by interruptions, threats, and topping one another's stories. Girls, on the other hand, strive to cultivate connection with one another. They're more likely to take turns when speaking and to agree with their friends. While boys are more likely to order someone to do something ("Get over here!"), girls are more prone to polite suggestion ("Could you please come over here?").[13]

DO THINGS CHANGE AFTER WE GROW UP?

Not surprisingly, as we age, we maintain many of the same communication and interaction styles developed as children. The same issues that encourage boys and girls to play separately result in a preference for same-sex friendships in adulthood. As adults, men's and women's friendships are remarkably similar to their childhood friendships, resulting in yet another barrier for male and female employees desiring to establish cross-sex friendships. Often described as "side-by-side" relationships, men's friendships are typically focused on some outside activity.[14] Much like young boys, these male-male friendships are often action oriented as opposed to person oriented and typically involve less communication than women's friendships.[15]

My brother, Tom, has become a good buddy to my son, who's now ten. The pair can play Wiffle ball or video games for hours, and Uncle Tom is a regular at Little League baseball games. At last Saturday's Little League baseball game, Tom asked what grade his nephew was in. Given the amount of time they spend together, I was a little surprised by this gap in his knowledge. "You don't know what grade he's in?" I asked. "Hey, I know his batting average and his ERA [earned run average]," he replied. In other words, he knew all the important stuff. This selective knowledge is evidently typical in male friendships. In his book *Buddy System: Understanding Male Friendships,* Geoffrey Greif summarizes:

> Guys are interesting—they can watch the Super Bowl together every year yet not know how many children the other guy has, that he just broke up with his girlfriend, or where he works. They will get a great sense of the other guy's football

knowledge, though. Does he grasp the nuances of the salary cap, no-huddle offense, and the challenges that a coach faces?[16]

What about women's friendships? Female friendships are often described as "face-to-face" as opposed to "side-by-side," because the female partners are oriented toward getting to know one another on a personal level.[17] As a result, female friendships are typically characterized by more self-disclosure, affection, and compliments than men's friendships.[18] Unlike men, women will almost certainly know where their girlfriends work and whether they have just endured a breakup. They are less likely, however, to have a sense of their girlfriend's football knowledge.

GOLF VS. SHOPPING

Although gender preferences established in childhood tend to permeate our adult friendships, coworkers always have at least one interest in common—their work. Therefore, coworkers who are employed in the same department or who have comparable jobs often share similarities that ease their interactions.[19] While this commonality may help some initiate cross-sex friendships at work, others may find it difficult to launch the friendship beyond the work domain. Common interests (outside of the work at hand) are often needed to initiate a friendship, and cross-sex friends may struggle to find shared interests.

We know that men typically structure their friendships around activities, but what are these activities? Greif reports that sport was the most common activity shared by male friends. Eighty percent of the men he interviewed said they participate in or watch sports with their friends. By contrast, none of the women said they participated in sports with their friends (although a few said they exercise with friends).

Sports unite men of all different backgrounds. Not only does it provide a shared activity for established friends but also sports talk can help men maintain a conversation and avoid awkward silences. In my own interviews, Michael, a lawyer, described how sports helped him initiate conversations with other men:

> Obviously, guys tend to like sports, right, so it's easier, you have something in common. You can swing a bat, and you hit 70 percent of the time if you bring up something about sports with a guy, but the ratio is probably lower with a woman.

Sports is often a form of communication for men. At my son's hockey practice, the parents (mostly dads) stand around quietly after the kids hit the ice. Then, one will break the silence with a comment about a questionable play in an NHL (professional hockey) game the previous night. A passionate discussion of the ins and outs of the previous night's game will ensue. The dads hold a diverse set of jobs and have roots all around the world, but the hockey discussion bonds the accountant, the music agent, the finance guy, the animator, the physicist, and the landscaper. All of a sudden, they have a common ground. They're friends.

So women just need to study the sports section of their local newspaper, and then they can become full-fledged members of the old boys' club, right? Unfortunately, it's not quite that easy. Although an interest in sports bonds men, it isn't clear if it's something that can necessarily be shared with women. What happens when a woman's sports knowledge is equal to or better than a man's? Would a debate about a controversial call during Monday's night's game ensue? It may not. Men often interact with each other in a competitive way, but defeating a woman with sports talk may not hold the same glory. After a lifetime of competing with same-sex friends, men may be uncomfortable competing with women.

Sports talk is not only a shared hobby or a shared topic of conversation, but for many men sports is integrated into conversation about other topics. Recall that Michael reported, "You swing a bat" to imply give it a try? Sports analogies permeate conversation in the workplace. A senior male executive once told me, "You'll have to punt," in response to a work problem.

Clearly, punting referred to football, and I knew it had to do with kicking. (In my defense, this was before my UCLA days, and I had only attended school at Vassar and MIT. Vassar didn't even have a football team, and MIT was no football powerhouse.) I could have asked, but I wanted to be considered one of the boys and was sure my confusion regarding punting was not cool. A coworker translated, and I was all set until a few months later another manager told me to "Throw a Hail Mary." The sports talk continued. By the end of my tenure as a trader (I retired to pursue gender research after I "hit a home run" trading equities), I had encountered the following sports expressions in everyday business.

Hit a home run	(a great success)
Punt	(concede)
Left at the starting gate	(slow to respond)
Throw a Hail Mary	(last ditch effort with little chance of success)
Do an end run	(go around the normal process)
Go to the bullpen	(bring in someone new)
It's a slam dunk	(it's a sure thing)
Batting a thousand	(getting everything correct)

Despite women representing almost half of the U.S. workforce, expressions relating to women's interests have not yet permeated the workplace. One wonders if women will ever confuse men in the workplace with their own jargon. "Don't turn it into a chignon," could indicate not to complicate a situation (a chignon is a complicated, time-consuming updo for hair). For now, it is typically the women in the office that can be left puzzled by the meaning of an expression. Although clearly a small issue, and certainly not insurmountable, it illustrates how sports permeates workplace communication.

If sports is the common link that binds men, what do women prefer to do with their friends? Perhaps not surprisingly, women like to talk and shop. Greif's survey found talking was the most common shared activity between female friends (65 percent of women reported enjoying talking with their friends), and shopping was number two (60 percent of women reported shopping with their female friends). Although some men said that they, too, talk to their male friends, they mostly talked about sports and women. None of the men went shopping with friends except occasionally to look at cars. Women also mentioned laughing and crying together with their friends, and not surprisingly, none of the men reported sharing a good cry with their male friend. These gender differences make cross-sex interactions less predictable and lead to a preference for same-sex conversations.

Does all this really impact women's careers? Francine Katz claimed it did. Katz, the top female executive at Anheuser Busch, took her former employer to trial in 2014. Alleging that the King of Beers paid her less than her male counterparts, Katz described an environment where she was excluded from male-only corporate jets and men's hunting and golf outings. However, Katz also testified that former CEO August Busch III avoided discussing a serious environmental issue with her because he feared that the discussion would make her cry. It seems unlikely another woman would have avoided discussing this issue with her for that reason. (Interestingly, Katz also testified that she had never cried while on the job at Anheuser Busch.) Again, these gender differences lead to a preference for same-sex interactions.[20]

Basically, sharing news about the purchase of a fabulous new pair of pumps with a male colleague will probably not be the start of a great new friendship. Sharing news of a Major League Baseball pitcher's no-hitter with a female colleague may be equally ineffective. As a result of different interests, cross-sex friends may just have less to talk about than same-sex friends. Interestingly, women who tend to exhibit masculine personality traits and men who behave in a feminine way may have an advantage in this area. Friendship researcher Heidi Reeder found that masculine women and feminine men had an easier time establishing cross-sex friendships.[21] Why? The most likely explanation is masculine women and feminine men have more in common with the opposite sex, find them more similar to themselves, and have more comfortable interactions with them.

Once again, it's critical to note that these barriers are not insurmountable, and many men and women can find shared interests to discuss and similar communication styles. However, they contribute to the barriers that make up the sex partition, causing cross-sex friendship formation to become more challenging.

WHY CAN'T YOU UNDERSTAND ME?

Even if men and women can find common ground for discussion, gender differences in conversational styles can also create a barrier to cross-sex friendships. In her books on gender differences in communication, Deborah Tannen describes several gender differences in communication style that are commonplace at work.[22] An example of such differences lies in responses to "troubles talk." When a problem is discussed with a female friend, the friend most likely responds by sharing a similar problem or by offering sympathy. However, when troubles are shared with a male friend, he is more likely to respond by giving advice, telling a joke, changing the subject, or remaining silent.

The problem for cross-sex friends is not in the response itself, but the interpretation of that response. Men looking for a solution to a problem and garnering sympathy instead may feel that the response is condescending. Similarly, a woman who expects sympathy in response to her problem may feel that the offer of a solution is condescending and minimizes her feelings. That is, the offer of a solution may carry the suggestion that the woman would not have been able to solve the problem on her own. These different styles lead men and women to seek out same-sex friends when it's time to discuss problems.

Humor is yet one more example of how communication differences can drive a wedge between the sexes.[23] Men act funny by teasing, while women prefer to express themselves with more self-deprecating humor. This becomes problematic because women often take men's teasing personally, and men can believe women's self-disparaging remarks to be true. Women get angry at the men, and the men question the women's competence.

In *Business Networking and Sex: Not What You Think*, Ivan Misner, Hazel Walker, and Frank De Raffele describe how gender differences in networking strategies can also leave cross-sex coworkers confused.[24] When women meet new contacts, they try to establish a relationship first. Only after a relationship is established, do women turn the focus to business. Men, by contrast, feel it's better to focus on business first and build a relationship later. The authors don't suggest that either strategy is optimal. However, problems can clearly arise when women try to network with other men. The strategies clash as women seek to build a relationship, while the men are trying to get down to business. Women may be left thinking the men aren't interested in establishing a work-ing relationship with them, and men may think the women aren't sufficiently focused on the business at hand.

Misinterpretation across gender lines stemming from differences in con-versational norms abound. On a case by case basis these gender differences may seem trivial. An occasional misinterpreted joke or gesture can certainly be overlooked. However, in the long run, these differences make communication with same-sex coworkers more comfortable and predictable than conversations with cross-sex coworkers and, therefore, lead to a preference for same-sex com-munication.

NONVERBAL CUES

Misunderstanding doesn't only result from verbal communication between the sexes, but sometimes women's nonverbal cues can be misinterpreted by men. I experienced this after graduate school, when I interviewed with several Wall Street trading groups. One of my job offers from an investment bank came with a warning. The head of the equity division at this bank told me that he didn't want to hire me, but his employees convinced him I was the one for the job. Why did he dislike me? Apparently, I had nodded my head too frequently when he was talking to me during my job interview. He interpreted that to mean I lacked confidence. If we hire you, he told me, you'll have to stop the head nodding.

Seriously? Who knew that head nodding or lack thereof was such a critical component of landing a job. The division head who interviewed me was one of those people who liked to hear himself talk, and he was going on and on about something during my interview. I nodded to indicate that I was paying atten-tion, interested, and not falling asleep. Clearly, this signal was lost on him, and it almost cost me the job offer. Since then, I've learned that women do nod their heads more than men, and the executive was correct, it can be interpreted as an act of submission.[25] I didn't accept the job offer. I figured if the manager had such a negative reaction to my head nodding, I'd most likely have a hard time connecting with him.

With regard to the sex partition, I don't think a woman would have judged my potential as a trader by my head nodding. But this manager wasn't used to seeing this nonverbal behavior among his male employees, so to him, my head nodding seemed strange. And, if it weren't for other supporters, it would have cost me the job offer.

Head nodding isn't the only gender difference in nonverbal behavior. Men typically take up more space than women, another indicator of confidence. Understanding these differences can only help us navigate them more effectively.

WHO'S WATCHING THE KIDS?

Regardless of different conversational styles or interests, developing friendships at work requires a substantial investment of time, and here again, women may be at a disadvantage. Attending extracurricular work functions or just hanging out at the water cooler chatting for a few extra minutes at the end of the day is instrumental in friendship development. Those who are rushed to get home from the office often do not have the extra time to cultivate important new relationships with their colleagues or superiors.

Why are women so rushed? Women typically bear the burden for a disproportionate share of household tasks and child care. Frequently labeled the "second shift," women often assume these household duties after a full day at their job outside the home. A recent study indicates that 35 percent of full-time female employees assume 100 percent of the housework, and 60 percent do at least 75 percent of housework.[26] With regard to child care, 28 percent of full-time working mothers assume 100 percent responsibility for child care, and 56 percent assume at least 75 percent of the responsibility.

In other words, women are assuming responsibility for the majority of the household chores and child care. These additional responsibilities leave women without a lot of free time to develop new friendships or mentor/sponsor relationships. One survey found that 68 percent of moms said they would like to network with colleagues but cannot find the time.[27]

In addition to the reduction of time for friends, the differentiated roles in child rearing also construct a barrier to cross-sex friendship. With women typically undertaking a larger role in child rearing than men, it is one more interest that women typically share with each other and less with other men.

I recently heard that new moms can be left out of networking sessions for yet another reason. Colleagues sometimes don't ask a new mom to join them because they want to be understanding. In efforts to respect the demands on her time, they don't want to impose any additional pressure on new moms to socialize. While the colleagues' intentions are thoughtful, the new mom feels even more excluded from networking opportunities.

Lisa, a television sports reporter for a top-twenty-five television station, wasn't sure exactly why, but becoming a mom drastically changed her experience at work. She told me that when she returned to her job after her maternity leave, she received no support at work and eventually lost her job. Her male boss no longer had her back, and she no longer garnered respect from her male subordinate, the number two sports reporter, who ultimately usurped her job. Basically her two most important working relationships had begun to fall apart, and the only aspect that had changed was her status as a mom. Although the attacks were subtle, Lisa only needed a few days back at work after maternity leave before she realized everything had changed. Small errors that would have previously gone unnoticed were now a bigger issue. She explained, "After being there for thirteen years, and being a star employee, and having built up so much good will, I just didn't get any support when I got back from my maternity leave. I'm not talking about support, like I need time off for this or that. I'm just talking about support to do my job as I had always done it before. I felt like I came back to a situation where all of a sudden the game was set so I was going to fail. Suddenly I went from being a star employee to being a target."

Lest you think that Lisa slacked off at work because of her newly acquired motherhood duties, that's not her style. While thirty-eight weeks pregnant, Lisa logged eighteen-hour days. She continued broadcasting right up until delivery, even completing an 11:00 p.m. news show while in the beginning stages of labor. When she returned from her maternity leave, she told me she sensed the change in these coworkers almost immediately, but that didn't deter her. "I always put up a fight. I thought, I am going to be the best damn, hardest-working employee they've ever seen. I'm not going to give them any reason to get rid of me." Although her hard work landed her two national awards for the best sportscaster in her state, things continued downhill for her in the office. Two years after returning from maternity leave, she was told her contract was not renewed. Who got her job? Her male subordinate. It is interesting to note that her male subordinate who took over her job had befriended her male boss when they worked together in another market. It's all about having friends at work, and when you don't have them, you can't do your job.

When I asked Lisa why she thought becoming a mom changed things with these male coworkers, she couldn't provide an answer. Her subordinate did admit to her that he resented Lisa's maternity leave—he had to cover for her and received no extra compensation for his trouble. Whether the cold shoulder was due to resentment related to her maternity leave or just the fact she was now a mom, there was one thing about which Lisa was certain: The working relationships with these male coworkers had dramatically changed. "Without question, in my heart, I feel like the fact I left to have a child ended my TV career."

If having children alienates women from their coworkers, then at least childless women should be able to establish large work networks. Unfortunately, it turns out that childless women have their own set of issues resulting from their choice not to become a mom. Researcher Caroline Gatrell has explained, "Women who explicitly choose career over kids are often vilified at work and face enormously unjust treatment. Bosses believe they are cold, odd, and somehow emotionally deficient in an almost dangerous way that leads to them being excluded from promotions that would place them in charge of others."[28] Other researchers concur that childless women feel out of the loop when it comes to being included in networking events.[29]

Once again women find themselves in a no-win situation. Those with children and those without are penalized when it comes to their networks. Men, by contrast, are far less affected by issues surrounding kids. Those with children typically bear less responsibility for child care than their wives, and those without children are not spurned by their colleagues.

HAVING FRIENDS IN HIGH PLACES

Yet another difficulty establishing cross-sex friendships stems from power differentials at work. We all want powerful friends, especially at work. Why? We want to gain something from our friendship, and powerful friends can help us out. Friendships tend to be exchange oriented, and if we provide benefits to our friends, we expect something in return. To be fair, our family relationships and a few close friendships may be characterized as more communal relationships, or relationships where we give without expecting anything in return. But, as greedy as it sounds, the remainder of our friendships are typically exchange oriented.[30] In these relationships, some type of repayment is expected for the benefits we provide to our friends.

In an exchange relationship, we naturally desire the highest-status friends possible in order to obtain the greatest benefits. In the workplace, if men typically hold more power and resources, they have less incentive for establishing exchange relationships with women. Unfortunately, this creates a circular problem for women. Women's difficulty establishing friendships with men results in having less power at work. As a result of their less powerful positions, their desirability as friends decreases further.

WE'RE NOT THAT DIFFERENT

Regardless of whether we're talking about power differences, communication differences, differences in friendship style, or different interests, understanding these gender differences can help us to understand our cross-sex coworkers a little better. However, we must be careful not to overly exaggerate these differences. After all, the most striking lack of knowledge about the opposite sex is how similar the two sexes really are.

That may sound like a contradiction. Gender differences exist and these do contribute to the sex partition. However, biological differences aside, men and women are far more similar than they are different. Unfortunately, stereotypes of men and women tend to exaggerate differences, and these stereotypes also work to keep the sexes apart. In other words, we tend to perceive men and women as much more different than they actually are. Take, for example, perceptions of male and female managers.

Women in management often must behave counter to the traditional feminine stereotypes. You can't always be nice and polite when running a company or managing a work group. However, we notice it more when women behave in these characteristically unfeminine ways. When a male boss reprimands an employee, he's doing his job. When a woman does it, she can be labeled "bitchy." Despite the abundant research evidence that men and women have very similar management styles and are equally effective in the management role, these stereotypes persist. Busting myths like "men make better bosses" or "female leaders are bitchy" is an important step in bringing the sexes together.

Despite overwhelming evidence that women and men make equally good leaders, my own research (with coauthor Janet Lever) indicates that twice as many people would prefer to work for a man than a woman.[31] Why this preference? In one word—stereotypes. Female managers in our study were described as too:

Emotional
Moody
Catty
Gossipy
Bitchy
Backstabbing
Dramatic
Jealous
Petty

Indeed, these were the nine most popular adjectives used to describe why people didn't want to work for a woman. Not surprisingly, none of these adjectives were used to describe male bosses. Those who didn't want to work for male bosses described male leaders as too self-centered and competitive. They had too much "male ego" and were too "power hungry." Male and female leaders essentially behave in a very similar manner, yet are described quite differently. Increasing awareness of how men and women are similar is also important in bringing the sexes together.

A new movement to eradicate these harmful stereotypes, started by Sheryl Sandberg, suggests we ban the term "bossy" when describing young girls. An assertive young boy is often labeled a leader, while a similar young girl can be labeled "bossy." When the young girl grows up and goes to work, the label may change from "bossy" to "bitchy." If we can change perceptions in children, then perhaps future generations of female leaders will gain more acceptance.

Although subtle, the gender differences and perceived differences outlined in this chapter create real obstacles to cross-sex friendships at work. One almost cost me a job offer. Funny how we make efforts to teach employees how foreigners might misinterpret their behavior but completely ignore how gender differences (or perceived differences) might contribute to misunderstandings between men and women in the workplace every day. Just as we teach employees about the pitfalls of conducting business cross-culturally, we need to educate our employees about gender differences. Greater understanding of the sexes will help reduce the likelihood of misunderstandings and increase our appreciation for our cross-sex coworkers.

⑫

MORE PARTITIONS: SAME-SEX FRIENDSHIPS, AGE, RACE, AND SEXUAL ORIENTATION

One's friends are that part of the human race with which one can be human.

—George Santayana, philosopher and writer[1]

Imagine you're a young female employee in a male-dominated workplace. You're ambitious, hardworking, and have aspirations of reaching the C-suite. So what's the best strategy to befriend senior managers and boost your career? Even the top levels of male-dominated corporations are not completely female free, and there are often at least a few women at the senior levels of management who could serve as friends or mentors. Perhaps you could bypass the sex partition altogether and just seek out other women to befriend. Unfortunately, the small numbers of senior women may not be the only problem you'd encounter in your attempts to establish same-sex friendships. Research suggests that another issue, competitiveness between women, may complicate your attempts at friendship with female management. Female competitiveness can hinder the development of same-sex friendships between women, particularly when one woman is more senior in the organization.

Competition between women is well-documented,[2] and the term "queen bee syndrome" was coined to describe successful women who undermine the success of other women as a result of competitiveness with these women.[3] Several interesting studies provide evidence for the queen bee syndrome. In one such study, participants read a story about a successful female leader.[4] Half of the participants were given the opportunity to penalize this fictional leader by giving her poor ratings, and the other half were not. Both male and female participants took the opportunity to penalize the successful female character when given the opportunity. However, for the female participants, their own self-confidence received a boost when they were able to penalize the successful woman. The men's self-confidence was not impacted by their ability to penalize the fictional woman. In other words, for women only, those who were able to put down the fictional female felt better about themselves.

More evidence of queen bees comes from a study where faculty members rated the commitment of doctoral students in their department.[5] Although the male faculty members perceived male and female doctoral students as equally committed to their careers, female faculty members perceived the female graduate students as less committed than their male counterparts.

Basically, some women tend to devalue other women to make themselves look better. The interviews in Susan Barash's book *Tripping the Prom Queen* illustrate just how this competitiveness and undermining can play out in the workplace. One of her interviewees, Tori, a forty-five-year-old woman in sales described her experiences with women at work:

> There is this mentality where women are jealous on every level, and then we are competing for clients. If you make money, if you have a good marriage, if you wear nice clothes, if you are younger, and most of all, if you are good at work, the other women sort of hate you. Nothing is said, but it can be felt.[6]

Maureen, a thirty-two-year-old internist gives the perspective of a younger woman trying to establish a connection with her older female boss:

> I see that Lillian, my boss, who is in her fifties, is envious and jealous of me. I think that she keeps important work from me because she is afraid that I will get the credit for doing a good job. She leaves me to figure things out for myself when it would be so much easier for her to simply tell me how she has done it in the past. I know that it wasn't easy to get here and that twenty-two years ago it must have been even rougher. But I am so willing to learn from her and so eager to get the benefits of her expertise. It's a shame it has to be this way.[7]

Instead of banding together, some women seem to be distancing themselves from other women. In my own research, women describe how competitiveness between female employees led them to prefer male management.[8] Some of these women thought that competitiveness between women was particularly harsh in male-dominated environments. Others thought the female competition stemmed from jealousy and was more likely to be directed at attractive women.

Those who report to queen bees may be correct that they'd be better off working for men. Working for queen bees can be so stressful for women that physical and psychological problems can ensue. Women who report to female managers are more likely to show up for work experiencing physical ailments such as headache, stomach ache, neck pain, muscle aches, and suffering more psychological symptoms such as anxiety, trouble sleeping, and difficulty focusing.[9] We don't know for sure that the negative reaction to the female boss is a result of queen bee syndrome, but it's telling that men don't have these issues. Indeed, men's levels of physical and psychological symptoms were the same regardless of whether their boss was female or male.

Why are women so harsh toward other women? Some have suggested that these women are strategizing to escape the bias against female leaders in their organization.[10] Instead of challenging the bias they encounter, they choose to distance themselves from women as a group to improve their own chances for advancement. As a result, these women typically emphasize how different they are from other female employees in the organization. "I'm not like the other women, so you shouldn't discriminate against me." Unfortunately, this strategy can involve criticism of their female colleagues and lack of support for others of their own gender.

Band conductor Emily Moss described to me how, in her experience, female mentors were hard to come by. Band conducting is notoriously male dominated, and Moss had to seek out mentorship from men. She was inspired by her own mentors, and although she enjoys mentoring other women, she finds that isn't the case with all her female colleagues. She described to me:

> I have really had to navigate being a woman in this field on my own, but I love, love, love that I can be that for other up-and-coming women who want to be conductors. Unfortunately, I know some of my female conductor colleagues do not necessarily feel that way. They don't want to be "the female conductor" who has to be a role model for everybody. I think it's they just want to be known as a "conductor," not a "female conductor." They're afraid if they accentuate the "female" and talk about it, then somehow people will judge them differently.

Sad but true. Some women think their best career strategy is to become one of the boys. As a result, they often turn their back on up-and-coming women who need help. One study found that women were reluctant to hire other women into prestigious positions.[11] Why? They're afraid that a poorly performing female will make all women look bad, and they fear that a highly qualified woman will steal the spotlight. Whether good or bad, the female candidate doesn't stand a chance.

As a rule, queen bees typically propose that the forces holding women back are not structural and, instead, are based on women's lack of skills or ambition. Sound familiar? In her book *Lean In*, Sheryl Sandberg claims women just need more confidence, ambition, and commitment to reach parity with men in the workplace. Like many women at the top of their game, Sandberg shares the perspective that women, themselves, are partially to blame for their own lack of progress at work. (Interestingly, research indicates that women who hold one of the top two positions in their organization and who hold an advanced business degree are more likely to suggest that women's inequality stems from a lack of motivation.[12] Sandberg earned an MBA from Harvard Business School and holds the number two—COO—position at Facebook.)

Just relax. I'm certainly not calling Sandberg a queen bee. Sandberg should be lauded for reigniting a discussion on women's lack of advancement in the workplace. She clearly cares about helping women advance, and her book offers great suggestions for both men and women. Her "lean in" circles encourage women to network and help other women. But we need to keep her opinions of what holds women back in perspective. There may be psychological phenomena that led Sandberg to analyze the performance of other women differently than she would other men. Even if men and women are equally reluctant to "lean in," Sandberg may have been more likely to notice this deficiency in women.

In fairness to high-level female execs, these women have every reason to think the current system is just. Since their own hard work and motivation paid off, it makes sense that they'd believe a similar strategy should land every hardworking woman a spot in the C-suite. Unfortunately, many qualified women who have been repeatedly denied promotion don't share the same view. Unfortunately, disparaging the motivation and commitment of female colleagues also exacerbates the sex partition by making it more difficult for these colleagues to develop mentor relationships at work. After all, who wants to serve as a mentor for an unmotivated and uncommitted employee?

Nowhere is women's lack of support for other women more evident than when you ask women which gender they prefer to work for. As I mentioned previously, my own research revealed women's (and men's) preference to work for male bosses.[13] So strong is this preference that we couldn't find any category of women who preferred female leadership. Those women who currently report to a woman, women who currently report to a man, women who have never reported to a woman, women who have never reported to a man, women who were employed in female-dominated workplaces, and women in male-dominated workplaces—they all want to report to a man. Most shockingly, even women who were managers themselves stated a preference for male management. That's right, of female managers who had a preference for the gender of their boss, 75 percent preferred to work for a man, and only 25 percent preferred to work for a woman. Got that? Three-quarters of female managers say they prefer male managers to female managers. How can women expect to get ahead if women don't want to work with their own gender?

Women clearly need to step up and start supporting their own. If the sex partition challenges friendships between men and women, we can't create any more barriers for women at work. In fact, women should be going out of their way to help other women. Although this book has focused on obstacles to cross-sex friendship, it seems we can't even take same-sex friendships for granted.

So if the queen bee syndrome challenges friendships between women, and the sex partition makes it more difficult for women to befriend men, what's an ambitious female employee to do? Fortunately all women do not succumb to the queen bee syndrome, just as all cross-sex friendships are not hindered by the sex partition. There are many female managers who are fabulous mentors to junior women. I've had a few of my own. By describing the importance of male friendships, I certainly didn't intend to minimize the value of these important same-sex female friendships. Women can help women in the workplace in ways that men cannot. It is essential to establish friendships and network with both genders to achieve your full career potential.

RACE AND THE SEX PARTITION

If barriers to friendship exist between the sexes and between women, what about other groups? Do other groups face similar barriers in establishing friendships? The short answer is yes. In general, people like those who are similar to themselves, and humans have long preferred to socialize with similar others. This preference for similar others is nothing new. Plato wrote in *Phaedrus*, "Similarity begets friendship," and Aristotle noted in *Nichomachean Ethics* that people "love others like themselves." Often labeled "homophily," we just want to associate with others who are like us. Our marriage partners, our close friends, our acquaintances, and our workplace networks most often consist of others who we find similar to ourselves.

Gender is just one of many attributes we use to determine similarity. Race, ethnicity, age, religion, education, and occupation are other attributes that individuals use to determine who is similar.[14] It turns out, the more similar you are to your friend, the happier you'll be with the friendship.[15] In the workplace, homophilous ties tend to be stronger, more intimate, and more sought out in times of stress.[16] It's not hard to figure out why we prefer similar others. Similarity makes communication easier, makes our friends more predictable, and results in us trusting our friends more.[17]

Therefore, gender is not alone in creating obstacles to friendship, and other attributes, such as race, age, and sexual orientation, may also pose barriers to friendships at work. Many have argued that one explanation for the under-representation of minorities in management positions is their exclusion from social networks. Similar to women, racial minorities tend to receive less support from their coworkers. One study examined only managers with high potential (that is, managers who were particularly effective in their organization and with potential for future advancement). It turns out high-potential minorities had fewer high-status people in their networks than high-potential white managers.[18] Furthermore, larger networks provided more support for white managers than for minority managers. Yet another study found that black employees received more support (such as receiving direction, guidance, role modeling, affirmation of ideas) from same-race mentors and sponsors than from similar cross-race relationships.[19] This suggests that racial minorities must overcome a race partition in order to establish cross-race friendships.

The race partition and sex partition share another commonality. Just as the sex partition is exacerbated by sexual harassment training, the race partition may be exacerbated by racial-sensitivity training. Black and white police officers involved in racial-sensitivity training were studied in order to evaluate the training. Shockingly, the white officers became more prejudiced toward blacks *after* the sensitivity training.[20] That is, the training that was designed to improve the communication and relationship between the black and white officers resulted in the white officers having more negative attitudes toward their black coworkers. The researchers suggest that the white officers resented the fact that the program was initiated for the benefit of black officers. Just as men often resent attending sexual harassment training, the white officers resented being required to attend training for the benefit of black officers.

AGE AND THE SEX PARTITION

Race and gender both play a role in friendship development, but what about age? A sixty-nine-year-old retired professor recently explained to me how age can construct its own barriers to friendship between the sexes. Although the potential for sex creates a barrier between men and women, it also binds them. How? Younger women tend to get noticed by male employees. Granted, it's not necessarily for professional reasons, but nonetheless, they get noticed. However, once a woman ages past the mid-fifties, the retired professor claims that women fall completely off the radar of male colleagues. She told me, "Once one is too old to be a serious sex partner for most of the organizational 'male players,' men simply don't notice older women. In recent years, I've had young guys actually bump into me, because I was just so off their radar screen." Men physically bumped into her as if she wasn't there. I'm certainly not advocating that women use their sex appeal to break down the sex partition, but aging women may simply disappear from awareness.

Older women face other barriers as well. The same professor described how older women don't get taken seriously as organizational players. "In the last half dozen years while flying back and forth between two homes several times a month, people would ask me if I was going to see my grandchildren while my partner (who has white hair, a beard, and is in his seventies) was always assumed to be traveling on business." While her husband could establish new business contacts on his flights, it was unlikely her business travel would result in a new contact.

Unfortunately, stereotypes of older women as grandmotherly and not relevant in the workplace persist. We regularly see older men in positions of power, so we have less bias against older men. Hopefully, as we become exposed to older leaders and greater numbers of older women assume positions of power, these stereotypes will diminish. Research indicates that exposure to counter-stereotypic examples leads to a reduction in the use of stereotypes. A Hillary Clinton presidency, for example, would help break down stereotypes of older women by providing an exemplar of an older woman in a position of power.

With regard to the sex partition, older women may face a mixed bag. A male manager may be less likely to fear that an older woman will misinterpret his friendliness as sexual interest. That is, he may feel more comfortable in a one-on-one meeting and on a business trip. However, he may be less likely to notice the older woman or to take her contributions seriously. Therefore, the sex partition is not stronger or weaker for older women, it's just different.

LESBIAN WOMEN, GAY MEN, AND THE SEX PARTITION

The sex partition may not impact all employees in the same way, and gay and lesbian employees may face unique issues in their workplace friendships. The sex partition argument is heterosexist in that many of the barriers that constitute the sex partition assume the friends are heterosexual. Cross-sex friendships between straight women and gay men may suffer fewer obstacles than those between heterosexual men and women. Indeed, one female dot-commer I interviewed mentioned that a gay male work friend was "no threat whatsoever" and that her friendship with him was similar to her same-sex friendships.[21]

Professor and friendship researcher Nicholas Rumens found that some gay men feel that entering into a platonic friendship with straight women was easier for them (relative to straight men) because romantic or sexual interest did not play a role in these friendships.[22] Yet another obstacle is removed for gay men in their friendships with women, in that they consider themselves exempt from accusations of sexual harassment. One gay man told Rumens, "I enjoy a sexual intimacy with the women in the office that comes from having a sexual banter with them. . . . It would be difficult for a straight man to do that."[23] In fact, the gay men he spoke with describe how the ability to talk about sex and flirt without fear of misinterpretation helps them to establish and maintain friendships with women at work.

Although the sex partition may have less impact on the cross-sex friendships of gays and lesbians, these employees may encounter barriers to same-sex friendships. Just as concerns surrounding romantic or sexual interest of the friend impact cross-sex heterosexual friendships, these same concerns may impact same-sex friendships when one friend is gay. In one study of friendships between lesbian women and straight women, the heterosexual women expressed concern that their lesbian friends were going to "cross the sexual line,"[24] and another study found that both male and female heterosexuals thought same-sex homosexuals were sexually interested in them.[25]

In a study of friendships at work, Rumens found that gay men often felt like outsiders in the masculine culture in their organizations. In some ways, this helped them create a bond with the women in the workplace, because they both shared this outsider role. One gay manager acknowledged, "Being a manager here is about being a man in the traditional sense, you know, all balls and bluster . . . so it's nice to get some respite from all those hang ups by hanging out and making friends with the women."[26]

Furthermore, the gay men in Rumens's study reported more difficulties establishing friendships with men in the organization because men were more likely to be homophobic than women. What about closeted gay men? Unfortunately, gay men who feel forced to hide their sexuality at work don't fare much better. Either through "counterfeiting" (pretending to be heterosexual) or through "avoidance" (trying to elude sexual labels altogether), these men try to fit in within their homophobic workplaces. As Woods and Lucas point out in their book *The Corporate Closet: The Professional Lives of Gay Men in America*, in order to maintain their closeted status, gay men avoid establishing any real connections with their colleagues. The need to socialize and become one of the guys is essential to career success, and the gay men they interviewed cited substantial barriers to establishing these important friendships.[27]

Clearly, gay men and women face barriers to friendships in the workplace. The heterosexist nature of this book was not intended to diminish the significance of these barriers in any way. In many ways, the barriers facing gay men at work are similar to those facing women. That is, difficulty establishing friendships with the heterosexual male managers at the top levels of management may inhibit the careers of gay men, much as it does women, in the workplace. More work clearly needs to be done to break down these obstacles.

BREAKING DOWN THE SEX PARTITION: WHAT YOU AND YOUR ORGANIZATION CAN DO

13

BRINGING EMPLOYEES TOGETHER

Sometimes the thing that brings us together also pulls us apart. Sort of like a zipper.

—Jarod Kintz, writer[1]

My team-bonding outing to a paintball park didn't go so well. Although I usually pride myself on my athleticism, one of my employees described how shooting paintballs at me "was like shooting at f-ing Bambi." My coworkers and I dressed in fatigues, wore military-style helmets, carried heavy guns loaded with paintballs, and shot at one another for what seemed like days. In retrospect, I'm not sure how this was supposed to be a team-building experience. I was covered with bruises and was truly angry with my coworkers for physically harming me. I could barely walk for a week.

My company-sponsored golf outings weren't quite so bad. At least I didn't suffer physically afterward. But I was new to golf, and a good number of my male colleagues took golfing *extremely* seriously. I worried that my short drives would slow down my foursomes, but rushing only made things worse. It's not that I expected girlie activities, but something a little more gender neutral might have been nice. Had we headed out for a group dinner, a hike, or a field trip to a local museum, I would have felt much more comfortable.

Even the Morgan Stanley getaway exclusively for female executives was held at a golf resort and came with mandatory golf lessons. Giving Morgan Stanley the benefit of the doubt, the goal was to teach women a skill to help us fit in better with our male colleagues and clients. Let's teach the women to be more like men, so they'll assimilate better. There has to be a better way.

There are steps the organization can take to bring employees together, but they need to proceed with caution, lest they make things worse. Of course organizations should encourage employees to network, and company-sponsored events are a great way to encourage socialization. Sponsoring outings where men and women can socialize together in a nonthreatening environment can help establish bonds that help both employees and the organization. But common sense suggests the activities should be chosen carefully with both genders in mind. For me, shooting paintballs was equivalent to taking the men in the office for mani-pedis. Gender-neutral activities offer the best environment for both sexes to get to know one another.

Social gatherings are a great start, but sometimes such gatherings break down by gender. Women gravitate to other women, and men to other men. There's nothing wrong with everyone doing their own thing, but it doesn't promote cross-sex networking. Activities that force interaction encourage men and women to get to know one another without suspicion.

When done right, team-building activities can be valuable network builders. But once again, organizations need to proceed with caution. The term "team-building exercises" may bring to mind activities like "trust falls," where employees are asked to fall backwards and trust that Jimmy from accounting—who is standing directly behind you—will catch you before you crash to the ground. From blind obstacle course driving to sumo wrestling in fat suits, there are a plethora of companies willing to set up "valuable" team-building opportunities for your work group.

However, I believe the best team-building exercises are the simplest. Creating environments where employees are encouraged to network within the workplace is the best way to get men and women to interact. You probably have heard by now about the many perks offered to the employees at Google. To name a few, this trendsetting organization provides free breakfast, lunch, dinner, and snacks to all its employees. The organization is equally innovative in the methods it utilizes to get employees mingling with one another.

For example, Google researched how to best encourage networking in the cafeteria.[2] They installed long tables, so that employees who don't know one another are forced to chat, and they even established the ideal length of the lunch line. It turns out, waiting three or four minutes in line for your lunch is considered optimal—any longer is a waste of time and any shorter isn't enough time to meet new people.

Although the goal of the Google lunch line is networking of all employees, it's also ideal for cross-sex networking and breaking down the sex partition. There is no danger in the lunch line. No one is going to think John and Judy are up to shenanigans because they were spotted next to each other in the lunch line. It's a safe place for men and women to network.

Further encouraging employees to network, Google implemented TGIF company gatherings on Friday afternoons, where company highlights are discussed and new employees are introduced. The meetings are accompanied by snacks and beer, and employees are encouraged to socialize after the presentation. But as frequently happens with organizational attempts at networking, senior engineers became hard to find at TGIF meetings. Once again, recognizing the importance of having all employees engaged in networking activities, Google took steps to remedy this problem. At one TGIF meeting they handed out thousand-dollar cash bonuses to employees to entice them to attend.[3]

From lunch lines to TGIF meetings, Google makes networking part of its organizational culture. They don't just talk about networking or have an annual dinner, they make changes to the work environment that encourage employees to interact with one another. Networking is an organizational priority at Google, as it has to be if the sex partition is to be dismantled.

Another key element to the success of networking initiatives is that top management must be on board. In business school at MIT, if the professor called on a student who couldn't come up with an immediate answer as to how the particular company we were discussing could get out of its particular mess, there was thankfully an answer that applied to all situations. Whatever the company's problem, and whatever the ultimate fix, the solution always "needed to have the backing of senior management." It was almost comical how frequently that answer was given by flustered MBA students trying to come up with something intelligent to say about the problems of a besieged corporation. But it always worked. The professor would nod positively and move on to his or her next victim.

The success of this pat response was due to its underlying truth. Backing of senior management is needed for the success of almost any organizational initiative. Thus, it's no surprise that backing of senior management is key to the success of networking efforts. It is essential that senior management not only approve of networking solutions but also participate. If networking is deemed an important part of the corporate culture, senior management should not have separate dining rooms or secluded office space. To emphasize the importance of networking at Google, founders Larry Page and Sergey Brin attend the weekly TGIF meetings.

Exhibiting a similar commitment to networking was former eBay CEO Meg Whitman. Whitman didn't work from a cushy office on an executive floor, she worked from a cubicle. Why? The corporate culture was one of open collaboration, and if the CEO didn't conform to this culture then it would send the wrong signal to employees. As a fellow cubicle dweller, Whitman sent the message that *all* employees were supposed to interact with one another. In other words, the networking priority had the backing of senior management.

WOMEN-ONLY ACTIVITIES: THANKS BUT NO THANKS

What about women-only networking activities? In addition to the golf outing with female execs, at Morgan Stanley we occasionally had women's dinners and lunches as a way for female employees to connect. The organizers of these same-sex events should be lauded for recognizing the problem women face establishing networks, but the same-sex nature of these social events raises some questions.

First off, what is suggested by offering such events? As far as I know there were no lunches, dinners, or weekends for male, black, Asian, handicapped, overweight, brunette, or gay employees. Indeed, no other employee category had their own events. Unfortunately, separate events for women reinforce stereotypes that women are different from men in some fundamental (nonbiological) ways. It suggests that women have some difficulty networking that needs to be filled by the organization. Well, that's partly true. They do have trouble networking, but not with other women.

For years scholars have cautioned about isolating women at work, and have instead called for the importance of cross-gender ties. Researcher of social networks in organizations, Professor Daniel Brass describes results of his own work, "Encouraging women to form networks with other women in the same organization may be unnecessary, or, at worst, nonproductive. In terms of acquiring influence, the results of this research suggest that both men and women be encouraged to build contacts with members of the other gender."[4] Harvard Business School professor Rosabeth Moss Kanter suggested that if women's networking events turn into "peripheral social clubs" they can "reinforce stereotypes about women's greater interest in talk than in tasks."[5] Similarly, Professor Herminia Ibarra concludes from her research "that women are likely to benefit from the development of greater ties to their male colleagues."[6] Cross-sex lunches or dinners would provide far greater benefits to women than segregated supping opportunities.

Some organizations go as far as to offer women-only management training programs designed to boost the career potential of female employees. The goals of these programs are, once again, admirable. In addition to imparting managerial skills to the women who participate in these programs, they offer a forum where women can discuss experiences that are unique to women in the workplace. The women may be able to support one another in discussing what it's like to be one of few females in male-dominated management.

However, the same-sex nature of these programs is again problematic.[7] Although research has shown that these programs provide women with some new leadership or management skills, researchers conclude they "serve to exclude and isolate women further from the male-dominated management ranks."[8] A primary career obstacle for female managers lies in their lack of ties with senior male managers, and offering women-only management training perpetuates the isolation instead of offering new networking opportunities. Furthermore, since the programs are made up of women, they don't exactly provide a realistic environment for the women to practice their newfound management skills (there are no men there). And most important, by segregating the women, these programs once again perpetuate stereotypes that men and women are so different they cannot be trained together. Or worse yet, they send a message that women are such poor managers that they need special help.

By contrast, mixed-sex management training programs allow men and women to obtain leadership skills without isolating women from the men in the organization. Often these training programs require participants to break out into small groups to discuss a particular topic. This provides an ideal opportunity for cross-sex networking.

If your organization has women-only events to promote networking, they should be lauded for their good intentions. However, you may want to explain the value of cross-sex networking to the planners of these events. Once they are aware of the sex partition, they may be willing to focus more on cross-sex networking events.

FORMAL MENTORING PROGRAMS

Formal mentoring programs are another avenue for bringing men and women together without fear of misinterpretation. Recall that starting in elementary school, children avoid cross-sex friendships because they fear their friends will think they're dating their cross-sex friend, or that they "like" or "love" their cross-sex friend. However, there was one situation where children comfortably interacted with cross-sex classmates, and that's when the interaction was directed by a teacher or other adult. If the teacher directs boys and girls to work together, then the danger that peers will think they have sought out the opposite-sex partners themselves is relieved. Without the fear their interaction will be perceived as "liking" the other, the mixed-sex pairs can then work together comfortably.

Organizations can learn from these children's behavior. Creating formal mentor programs where mentors are assigned to their protégés eliminates fear that the relationship will be misinterpreted. If Sam is assigned to mentor Sally, he is required to meet with Sally on a regular basis. Others won't question Sam's motives for mentoring Sally or meeting with her, and Sally won't get the wrong idea when he asks to meet with her. Sally need not fear that her coworkers will think she's sleeping her way to the top, or that Sam will get the wrong idea when she asks to meet with him.

Unfortunately, the assigned, formal mentor relationships do not typically have the intensity and level of commitment of more spontaneously created, self-selected mentor relationships.[9] However, formal relationships are a start. Once cross-sex mentor relationships are accepted as a norm in the workplace, the forming of more spontaneous and self-selected cross-sex mentor relationships will be regarded with less suspicion.

BETTER NETWORKS LEAD TO BETTER PRODUCTIVITY

This may seem like a lot for an organization to undertake to help employees establish networks. Fortunately, stronger networks benefit everyone, especially the organization. Certainly any organization desires enhanced productivity, and establishing connections between employees actually results in increased productivity for the organization. It's a win-win situation. However, instead of trying to increase productivity by encouraging networking, organizations often concentrate their efforts on hiring employees with the greatest intelligence, relevant experience, and highest levels of education. These traits, referred to as human capital, undoubtedly can help organizations outperform their competition.

However, organizational leaders may be surprised to learn that social connections are just as important to the organization as human capital. Often referred to as social capital, the social networks or connections within the organization enhance the organization by allowing the strengths of different individuals to be combined. Solving complex problems often requires knowledge and expertise from different specialty areas. Social capital allows for the combining of resources to solve such problems. Individuals or teams that may not have the knowledge to complete their task alone must turn to their network for help. Since the collective knowledge of a network is greater than the knowledge of any individual, bigger networks often translate to more extensive knowledge bases and increased problem-solving skills.[10]

After examining productivity in three organizations, researchers found that social capital was related to productivity in all three organizations, but human capital was related to productivity in only one.[11] In other words, social capital was a better predictor of productivity than human capital.

What does all this mean for the organization? Creating opportunities for networking will not only help break down the sex partition but also will enhance the networks of all employees. These enhanced networks can improve productivity and impact the bottom line for an organization. Team-building exercises and other organizational attempts to bring employees together are well worth the effort.

14

EXPANDING YOUR OWN NETWORK

Behold the turtle: He only makes progress when he sticks his neck out.

—James Bryant Conant, scientist[1]

I've had many great mentors and supportive friends at work and at school. People who have helped me well beyond what was expected. To all of them, I am forever grateful. Personal contacts helped me land my first job on Wall Street, gain admittance to graduate school, and find an agent to help publish this book.

I'm not alone. In general, those with more friends receive more job offers and higher pay. I won't reiterate all the benefits of friendship that I outlined in the first chapter, but friends are clearly a key to success in any professional endeavor.

Unfortunately, if you wait until you need a job, a graduate school, an agent, an introduction, a promotion, or just some information, it's often already too late to establish connections. Building a network takes time, and it's essential to start building up your network before you need it.

For some, networking seems to come naturally. For others, like myself, it takes a concerted effort. And then there's the sex partition, which only adds to difficulties networking. That's no reason to give up. The goal of this chapter is to provide tips on establishing connections at work with both men and women.

Getting started can be daunting, but your network may already be bigger than you realize. Utilizing the network you already have to its full potential can be a great start. Some particularly valuable advice on this topic was given to me by a manager at Morgan Stanley named R0ml (yes, that's a zero in his name—his real name is Robert, but he went by R0ml, pronounced like Rommel). I was a recent college graduate and working as a computer programmer for Morgan Stanley's information technology department. As a hardworking computer programmer, I took my job extremely seriously. I put in long hours and almost always ate lunch while writing computer code at my desk.

R0ml shared his valuable insights with me after I put in a request for a cubicle change. My cubicle was centrally located in what seemed like a major thoroughfare through the office. On their way to the water cooler, the bathroom, the cafeteria, or the elevator, my coworkers would always stop and check in with me. "How's it going, Kim? What are you working on?" I'd politely engage, and then, as quickly as possible, get back to my computer coding.

When a cubicle became available in a less traveled corner location, I made it known that I wanted the isolated corner to become my future home. Without the constant interruptions, I was sure I could significantly increase the amount of computer code that I produced. That's what inspired R0ml to have a talk with me. He explained that squirreling away to write computer code wasn't good for Morgan Stanley or me. He explained the value of talking to my coworkers. Learning about their work projects or their solutions to a particular problem might inspire my own work. "You need to get up from your desk more, talk to people," he advised. Although I thought that eating lunch at my desk exhibited a strong work ethic, he pointed out my desk lunches were yet another missed opportunity to network with my colleagues.

At the time, I thought he just didn't get it. I tried to get R0ml to understand that these conversations with my colleagues were not going to help my work. Learning where Bill rode his bike that weekend or what Bob did at the beach was only keeping me from writing more computer code. How could that information possibly help me with my job? R0ml explained that Bill and Bob both had information that would be valuable to my work; I just needed to find out what it was. I should ask them what they were working on, what problems they encountered, and how they solved them. I also could help them with their work projects, which would benefit the organization as a whole. Furthermore, friendly social connections with colleagues like Bill and Bob could only help me as my career progressed.

My request for the cubicle in the remote corner was denied, but it was many years before I truly appreciated R0ml's guidance. Now I understand the wisdom of his advice. We can learn something from all of our coworkers, not just those we deem worthy of being our mentors or advisors. This brings me to my primary advice on networking:

Treat everyone like a mentor, and you'll be amazed what you can learn from them.
Many self-help blogs and books on mentoring suggest you scout out a potential mentor and pursue that one person. There's nothing wrong with this targeted strategy, except that you may miss out on a lot of potential mentoring. I'm not saying you should give up on connecting with the important exec down the hall, but the exec's assistant may have insights that are equally valuable. Assistants, secretaries, and receptionists see a lot of high-level managers come and go, and often have learned a good deal about what it takes to break through. They know about what's going on in the organization and have the ear of at least one (if not more) important person in your company. Make sure you get to know them, and listen to what they have to say.

Instead of concentrating on building one mentor relationship, focus on cultivating the relationships you already have. Ask people questions and really listen to their answers. Find out what the Bills and Bobs in your organization are working on, who they rely on, what they've learned recently. Assume that everyone you encounter has something valuable for you to learn, and it's your job to discover what that is. I guarantee you'll be amazed by what you discover.

If, like me, you have been squirreled away in your cubicle without seeing the light of day, you need to make networking a priority. It's not as daunting as it may sound. Here are some additional tips you can use to get started adding to your circle of information providers and tapping into those you already have. These tips will help you network while minimizing interference from the sex partition.

It takes work. Be prepared. Making friends and adding to your network is not easy, and it takes effort. To be an effective networker you must make networking a priority.

Water cooler talk and cubicle chats aren't a waste of time. It's counterintuitive (at least for me) that chatting with others instead of doing your work actually makes you more productive, but it's true. You must buy into this to be able to establish a valuable network. Sure, it may be true that you would get more work done today if you forgo water cooler conversations, but you must realize that these chats are a long-term investment. They'll help you down the road. Really. Coworkers, even those you might think are useless, often have valuable information to pass on to you. Unfortunately, that information isn't just going to pour out of them as you walk up to them at the water cooler. It's your job to find out what that information is. You need to ask questions and really listen to the answers. You may be able to help out your coworkers, too, and they'll appreciate your efforts. Those coworkers that chat a lot often have more connections, and they may begin to sing your praises to other people.

Office parties aren't a waste of time either. Do you remain in your cubicle while others share cupcakes to celebrate Brutus's birthday? Just like the water cooler, these are great networking opportunities. The sex partition is minimized in these situations, because no one questions your motivations for being there. After all, it's Brutus's birthday.

Haste makes waste—take your time. If you're always rushing from place to place and task to task, you won't have time to establish new friendships. Once again it may seem counterintuitive. Using time efficiently certainly seems like the best strategy for getting more work done, right? You may accomplish more, but your network will suffer. Leaving a couple extra minutes to get to your meeting provides time to stop and follow up regarding your colleague's kid's soccer game. It also gives you time to take in your surroundings. When you're not counting the seconds until the elevator door opens, you may notice who is riding in the elevator with you and acknowledge them.

Have a positive attitude. No one wants to befriend a sourpuss. If you go to the water cooler with a curmudgeon face, you won't get the same reception as someone with a smile. If you look stressed out and rushed, you'll be less approachable. Be open to starting a conversation.

Be a good coworker. Offering assistance to a coworker and being considerate of others' ideas will be appreciated. Perhaps word will get out that you're a good person to get to know.

Mix up your group outings. As many employees already have realized, one great way to network is to go out after work in groups. Young employees, in particular, often participate in group outings after work. Groups are great, because the sex partition is minimized in the group setting. Although the groups are typically mixed sex, no one questions your motivations for participating in group outings. The only downside of group outings is they tend to be made up of people you already know well. Recall there is often more value in networking with those outside your immediate circle of work friends (the value of weak ties). Also, while these group outings appeal to younger employees, more senior execs may be less likely to participate in group outings. In order to make these outings better networking opportunities, ask group members to bring a friend from another department. Invite senior execs as special guests to your favorite after-work hangout spot. To get the most out of group outings, you'll need to branch out from the regular crowd.

Small groups are good too. Sometimes when groups get too large, it's hard to forge new friendships. One alternative to the large group is to invite a few people you are comfortable with to lunch or after-work drinks and ask them each to bring one other person. Keep the group small enough so that you can get to know the new people. Figure out what you have in common with each new person and talk to them about it. If you can't find anything in common, then find out what they're passionate about and ask them about that.

Follow up. For salespeople, following up often comes naturally—for me, not so much. Yet following up with new friends is a method of establishing a longer lasting friendship. Forwarding a new friend an interview you read with their favorite drummer demonstrates that you're a good listener (you remembered their favorite musician), and that you're interested in a friendship.

Go easy. Don't be overzealous in following up. If you act like your contact is your new BFF, your motives might come into question—particularly if you're following up with an opposite-sex employee. If you're concerned about misinterpretation of your follow-up friendliness, include a disclaimer. Keep follow-ups professional and not too friendly or wordy. For example, "Re: article on drummer you like, see attached" doesn't imply that you're sitting in your office pining away for him or her.

Really listen. Remember each person you're talking to has something valuable to share with you. To find out what this is, you need to be a good listener. The focus of the conversation shouldn't be you. This doesn't mean you can't tell your coworkers anything about yourself or your experience. You should certainly reciprocate with your own helpful information. However, your focus should be on them, on really listening to what they say, and on following up with questions. If you're thinking about what you're going to say next, you're not being a good listener.

Keep it short. You're networking here, not bonding. If you're known for being too much of a talker, coworkers may start to avoid you. Knowing how and when to exit conversation is as important as understanding how to start a conversation.

Include those in other organizations in your network. In addition to networking within your workplace, you should try to include a few people outside your organization in your network. While at first this may seem daunting, staying in touch with coworkers who move to another company is a great way to accomplish this goal. Set up a quarterly lunch with them and find out how things work at their new company. Attending conferences and joining organizations are other great ways to meet people with similar jobs at other organizations. Not only does this give you the opportunity to find out about job openings in other organizations but also it can provide ideas for making valuable contributions to your own organization.

Include your coworkers in your electronic social networks. It may seem silly to get LinkedIn with colleagues you see every day, but LinkedIn is a great way to keep contacts after you (or they) switch organizations. So valuable is LinkedIn to finding a new job, some organizations forbid their employees from having an account or listing their present employment out of fear their employees will be poached. However, of the hundred most connected people on LinkedIn (those people with the most "connections" on the site), only five are women.[2]

Share a laugh with your coworkers. What do you call a monkey that sells potato chips? A chipmunk. Okay, clearly, you'll have to do better than that, but the use of humor brings colleagues together. Humor is an important part of establishing friendships with peers, bosses, and mentors. How does it work? Sharing a laugh with your coworker can improve your coworker's mood, makes your coworker feel like the two of you have things in common, and helps your coworker feel like he or she knows you better.[3] In situations where one of the jokers has higher status in the organization, joking can even make the power differential seem less noticeable.

Recall that having little in common was an obstacle that frequently blocked potential cross-sex friends. Humor can help bridge this gap. Humor researcher Cecily Cooper suggests that when a woman expresses humor with a male colleague, it may jumpstart a friendship because it signals to the man the two are more similar than he may think.[4] Hey, you made me laugh—you're not as alien as I thought you were.

Take the opportunity to bring some levity into your office and you'll be rewarded with better relationships with your colleagues. After all, who would you rather befriend—a sourpuss or someone with a sense of humor who can appreciate the lighter side of things? But proceed with caution. Not all humor is equal, and it's important to keep your humor on the positive side. If a person or group is the brunt of the joke, you may wind up alienating more people than you befriend.

Whether it's the use of humor or a conversation at the water cooler, an advantage of these strategies is that they minimize the impact of the sex partition on your networking efforts. It doesn't seem suspicious that Mary and Bob were seen talking in the elevator, or that Steve and Sue were both at the water cooler at the same time. If you begin to seek networking opportunities in your everyday activities, you'll be surprised at how quickly your network grows.

15

MAKING FRIENDS IN HIGH PLACES

Today, the lines between mentoring and networking are blurring. Welcome to the world of mentworking.

—Beverly Kaye & Julie Winkle Giulioni, authors[1]

Mentor, from Homer's *Odyssey*, served as a teacher and overseer of Odysseus's son while Odysseus was fighting in the Trojan War. Since then, we've adopted the term "mentor" to refer to a person who teaches or guides someone with less experience. I realize I spent the last chapter recommending that you should treat everyone as a mentor, but it's also critical that you add traditional mentors to your network. Those more experienced than you can pass on valuable knowledge and insights that you just can't get from your peers. And you don't only need one mentor. The more mentors you can add to your network, the better.

In the workplace, research indicates those with mentors receive more promotions and more pay than those without mentors.[2] Good mentors also inspire their protégés. From helping protégés set career goals to coaching them through difficult situations, mentors serve as career guides. By providing tips on how best to manage or complete a job task, mentors can enhance your job performance. By providing insight into the corporate culture, they can help you get noticed by other senior managers. Since men typically hold the majority of senior management positions, men are often able to provide greater mentoring benefits to their protégés, and research indicates that those with male mentors earn more money.[3] That's not to say that female mentors are not valuable—there are plenty of fabulous female mentors out there too.

Although sometimes mentor relationships are formally initiated and managed by the organization, more often they develop informally, much like a friendship. It is these more informal mentor relationships that have been shown to provide the greatest career benefits to the mentee.[4] Unfortunately, it's not only up to the mentee to find a mentor; the mentor must play a role as well. In fact, the greater the role the mentor plays in relationship initiation, the greater the benefits from mentoring will be.[5]

You get it. You need to include senior executives in your network, but how do you proceed with this task? My advice for choosing mentors for your network comes from finance portfolio theory. Time and time again, as friends learn about my career on Wall Street, they ask me for investment suggestions. I tell them the secret to successful investing is diversification. What does that mean? It means don't put all your eggs in one basket. Even if you think that Amazon and Google are the greatest companies on the planet, and there's no way they're going to fail, you don't put *all* of your money in Amazon and Google. You diversify. You invest in many, many different companies in several different industries, maybe putting slightly more money into your few favorites. That way, if Jeff Bezos (Amazon's CEO) gets hit by a bus, and no one else can get the company going again, you're still okay. Your portfolio is diversified, and you still have money in some healthcare companies, some technology companies, and some consumer products companies. I can actually mathematically prove to you that diversification is the best investment strategy, but don't fear, I won't do it here.

Your network of senior executives is like an investment portfolio: It must be diversified. I realize those with male connections earn the most money, but that doesn't mean that you only seek out men. Perhaps female mentors have more insights on work and family balance, but do you only choose female mentorship? No, you diversify! You add senior executives from your own organization and from other organizations and other industries to your network. You include both older execs and younger ones in your network. They will all be able to provide a unique perspective that can help you.

So you know you need to diversify your network of senior managers. But you still need to locate these people, and finding a few people that you can count on for career advice can be tricky. Obviously, when choosing senior managers to add to your circle, you want people who have exhibited their ability to succeed. That doesn't necessarily mean you hit up the CEO. It's equally important that your prospective mentors have time to meet with you. An extremely successful mentor who always cancels meetings won't be of much help. A valuable mentor will have achieved success but will also have the time to share his or her insights with you.

The sad truth in corporate America is the higher you move up the corporate ladder, the fewer women you find. No matter how much you want to diversify your selection of mentors, there will probably be more male mentors available than female. For women, that means if you want senior execs in your network, you'll probably have to cross the gender line. Unfortunately, the sex partition makes it more difficult to establish these relationships.

Catalyst, an organization dedicated to studying and advancing women in the workplace, provides evidence of this effect, reporting that only a small portion of senior-level women (23 percent) are satisfied with the availability of mentors in their workplace,[6] and other researchers report similar findings that women have more difficulty than men when it comes to finding mentors and establishing high-quality networks.[7] Fortunately, all hope is not lost. The following suggestions will help you connect with potential mentors, while minimizing the sex partition.

First, once you've found a senior executive you'd like to add to your mentor circle, you'll need to break the ice. To get things rolling, all you need to do is ask. Ask a potential mentor for a meeting to discuss your career. As opposed to lingering around his or her office, a direct request lets your potential mentor know exactly why you want to spend time with him or her. You're not stalking, but you're being perfectly clear. It's not because you want to sleep with or date him or her. You just want career advice.

Another way to let your mentor know that your motives are purely professional is communicating what you want to get out of this relationship. Do you need advice on a specific topic? Do you need help networking? Be specific and, as always, be professional. "My job sucks; what should I do?" doesn't inspire potential mentors. "I know you have one of the largest client lists in the firm, and I was wondering if you had any suggestions as to how I might expand my client list" would be much more likely to be taken seriously.

It's also helpful if potential mentors understand why you chose them. Maybe it's because they were in your position five years ago, and you want to emulate their career. Maybe they have a similar educational background. Maybe you like something about their management style. Once again, specificity is key. It will help them understand that you're not seeking them out because they're cute or they're single. This relationship is purely professional.

It would be great if a close friendship developed with your mentor, but at least in the initial stages, it's best to keep it purely professional. That doesn't mean you can't congratulate your mentor if his or her favorite team just won the Super Bowl, but he or she doesn't need to know about your date last night or why you were arguing with your spouse. Steering clear of personal talk, at least in the initial stages, helps send the message that your motives are all business.

Once you land a mentor, make sure you're a good protégé. Implement your mentor's suggestions and provide your mentor with feedback. Not only will this let your mentor know that you're serious, but also no one will question your motives.

Taking on the role of mentor yourself is a great way to learn how to be a good protégé. You'll learn what's annoying and what inspires you to help your protégé, and you can use this knowledge to win yourself valuable mentors. In doing this, you're helping someone else move up the ranks. It's win-win.

EXUDE CONFIDENCE AND FOLLOW UP WITH RESULTS

My experience on Wall Street provided me with a few more insights on getting the attention of senior executives. My manager and I started our trading group together, and as the group grew, I remained second in command. After the first few years, we were trading a significant amount of money every day. Some days we made a lot of money, other days we lost a lot of money. We had more up days than down and produced a nice annual profit for the firm.

One day, when my boss was out of town, we lost a lot of money (I don't want to provide the exact figures of our loss, but many small businesses don't earn this much in a year). My boss called in some words of advice for me. He told me that, given the loss, the head of our division would probably check in with me. The advice was, "It doesn't really matter what you say to him, just sound confident."

It doesn't matter what I say? Clearly I needed to explain the loss. He explained further that the head of the division doesn't really want to know, nor does he have time to understand, the details of our trading strategy. He just has to be sure that everything is under control, and he's very good at sensing whether things are under control. That's his job. If he senses any fear or uncertainty, then he'll find someone he can trust to come in and oversee things.

At first this sounded like counterintuitive advice. Was it possible that *how* I said something was more important that *what* I said? It turns out, it is. (Research supports the importance of confidence—for example, jurors are more likely to believe confident witnesses.)[8] If you sound confident, people will think you know what you're doing (and hopefully you do).

Like our division head, many managers have, out of necessity, developed the ability to detect weakness. So confidence isn't just important in the trading environment, it works everywhere (I used it to negotiate with my insurance company just yesterday). If you want a senior executive to trust you and include you in his or her inner circle, you must sound confident.

When seeking the advice of a mentor, confidence is equally important. No one wants to spend their valuable time providing suggestions to someone they don't feel is capable of implementing the suggestions. You need to make sure that your potential mentor sees you as someone who can get things done. If you seem overwhelmed by your mentor's suggestions, then the suggestions will cease. If you seem eager to implement the suggestions, the suggestions will keep coming.

Although confidence is critical, all the confidence in the world isn't going to help you if you can't produce results. Confidence allowed my division head to feel comfortable if we lost money over a couple of days, but we still needed to prove ourselves over the long run. Fortunately, we did. Our success spoke for itself. We produced strong results for the firm, and that got us noticed. Senior execs have an incentive to surround themselves with successful people, and to be accepted to their inner circle, you need to have your results speak for themselves.

BEFRIEND THE BOSS

Exuding confidence and producing solid results are great ways to attract the attention of senior executives. However, there's one more senior employee whose attention you get for free—your manager. You should always be sure to befriend your boss. I've always had a good relationship with my managers and can't imagine showing up for work every day working with a boss I didn't consider a friend. Many aren't so lucky. A recent survey revealed that 60 percent of Americans thought they'd do a better job if they got along better with their boss, and they're correct.[9] Buddying up with your boss has its rewards. You may think that managers should treat all of their subordinates equally, but managers typically have a close working relationship with only a few of their underlings. Often referred to as the manager's in-group, these subordinates are typically provided greater responsibility, trust, and access to resources. Not surprisingly, the in-group employees wind up doing a better job at work.[10]

So how can you join your boss's in-group? Just like your friendships outside of work, friendships with the boss are most frequently initiated because of common interests or repeated contact with him or her.[11] Don't stalk the boss, but if you find out he or she is obsessed with polo, it would behoove you to familiarize yourself with the ins and outs of chukkers and polo ponies. If NASCAR is your boss's thing, at least know when the Daytona 500 is held, and what type of cars compete in these races.

One last piece of advice on befriending the boss: Employees are more likely to become friends with the boss if the boss and subordinate have a third friend in common.[12] In other words, you need friends in order to make more friends. Befriend the boss's friends and you're more likely to land in his or her in-group.

SPONSORSHIP VS. MENTORSHIP

Mentor relationships and connections with senior executives are valuable, but some have suggested that sponsor relationships are even more essential to career success. A sponsor differs from a mentor in that a sponsor goes even further to promote the career of his or her protégés, often putting his or her own career on the line for them. While mentors typically assist their protégé directly, sponsors typically advocate for the protégé when the protégé is not present. Sponsors work behind the scenes, often without the knowledge of the protégé, to promote the protégé's interest.[13] For example, a sponsor may nominate the protégé for a promotion or work assignment, or advocate for the protégé in a meeting of senior managers. Sponsors also often introduce their protégés to important connections outside of the company.[14] Any one of these efforts could drastically change the career trajectory of the protégé.

Sponsor relationships are often more visible in the organization, and therefore sponsors must be cautious when advocating for their protégé. In order to ensure that the protégé will fulfill his or her responsibilities in a manner that will reflect well on the sponsor, managers typically only choose to sponsor those that he or she knows well. Once again, a friendship is a necessary prerequisite.

Recently, the Center for Work-Life Policy completed research on the value of sponsorship for executive women and concluded: "If today's female executives find themselves outside the inner sanctum, it's not only because they're removed from the crucial conversations that determine who moves up, but because they have no proxy. Sponsorship corrects that. By providing women the authoritative voice they lack, the backroom access they're often denied, and the advocacy they desperately need, sponsorship truly levels the playing field."[15] Kerrie Peraino, head of diversity at American Express, was quoted expressing a similar sentiment regarding sponsorship: "You can have a strong network, drive strong results, even know all the unwritten rules. But if you aren't sponsored by someone in a position to weigh in on your behalf at the decision-making table when you're not there, you're not getting the next opportunities."[16]

Despite the clear benefits of befriending a sponsor, only 13 percent of female employees at large companies report having sponsors. Men, by contrast, are

46 percent more likely to cultivate these important relationships.[17] Once again, women say it's worth crossing the gender line to find male sponsorship. Men, the female employees claim, make better sponsors because they are better connected both within and outside the company, are more powerful, know how to succeed, and typically have more time to devote to sponsoring.

In her book *Forget a Mentor, Find a Sponsor*, Sylvia Ann Hewlett makes it clear that you don't ask someone to be a sponsor, you have to make them want to be your sponsor. Hewlett explains that sponsorship is a two-way street. In other words, sponsors gain as much from you as you do from them. That's why they're willing to work so hard on your behalf. How can a high-level exec benefit from hanging out with you? As Hewlett explains, "They recognize the incredible benefit to their own careers of building a loyal cadre of outstanding performers who can extend their reach, build their legacy, and burnish their reputation. . . . They need your support and skills. They need you to build their bench strength and complement their expertise."[18] In other words, having talented, loyal employees scattered throughout the organization is a huge asset for a senior executive.

In order to obtain sponsorship, you have to produce results, and potential sponsors need to be aware of those results. If you're not comfortable touting your own accomplishments, find a trusted coworker or manager to do it for you. It's important that word gets out that you're someone who can help senior executives achieve their goals.

WHAT ABOUT THE SEX PARTITION?

What about the sex partition? Although the previous suggestions will help grow your network while minimizing the impact of the sex partition, there's no way to completely avoid it. If you feel the sex partition is impacting your network, that's no reason to give up. There are yet more guidelines that should help minimize the impact of the sex partition on your work relationships.

First and foremost is professionalism. Your appearance, your conversations, and your behavior should all exude professionalism. Avoiding heavy drinking at work gatherings, for example, sends the message that you're not a partier looking for a good time, you're a trusted employee. I would have thought that most of us already know this one, but Hewlett's research found that 73 percent of business leaders rated provocative clothing as the primary appearance issue for aspiring career women.[19] For those who haven't figured this out, plunging necklines and tight-fitting clothing are not appropriate at the office. Once again, they send the wrong message.

Introducing your spouse or significant other to your coworkers and to senior execs also sends the message that your working relationships are purely business. It indicates that your spouse or significant other is a priority in your life. The earlier on in your career that you can introduce them, the better. Some single employees go as far as creating an imaginary love interest that they describe to their coworkers to send the message they're not interested in dating anyone at work. If you don't have a significant other and you're not into imaginary friends, you can at least make sure everyone knows you adhere to a firm policy of not dating coworkers.

It's not that there's something inherently wrong with dating coworkers. However, if you're known as someone who dates coworkers, then you may be labeled a romance seeker. Once you're assigned this label, others may be more likely to perceive you as interested in them, even when you're not. Or when they know you're not interested in them, they may worry about what other employees will think if they see you together. Steering clear of office relationships altogether sends a message of professionalism.

If, despite your professionalism, interactions with a cross-sex coworker or mentor seem awkward, get it out in the open. Does he or she seem nervous around you, or, on the contrary, is he or she becoming a little too friendly? Talk about it with him or her. For example, "Sometimes, I feel like it's awkward when I have a male/female mentor—I worry what others will think or say." Talking about it openly will clarify your relationship and can make the relationship more comfortable for both of you.

If you are a senior manager's favorite then, Hewlett has suggested, you need to point out to other employees why you deserve this position.[20] In other words, if coworkers become suspicious as to why you are landing all the best assignments, make sure they know about all of your recent accomplishments. Hopefully, they will attribute your success to your hard work and not to sex with a senior manager.

If rumors start to fly about you and a coworker or senior manager, there's no time to waste. Rumors need to be halted. If you're suspected of sleeping with your sponsor or mentor, and you're not, you must try to convince your coworkers that you were rewarded based on your merits.

Research garnered from how rumors spread indicates two integral aspects to shutting them down.[21] The first is timeliness. The quicker you detect the rumor, the quicker you're able to quash it. The longer it festers, the more difficult it is to suppress. The best strategy is to jump ahead of rumors that you're sleeping your way to the top. If your mentor works with you, let your coworkers know that he/she is your mentor before rumors start. Tell them what you're working on with your mentor and how frequently you meet. This will help rumors stop before they begin.

The second key to shutting down rumors is to have help eradicating them. Don't try to quash the rumor on your own. Get your friends out there and make sure they correct the misinformation on your behalf. The more agents you have out there to set the rumor straight, the quicker the rumor will cease.

IT TAKES EFFORT, BUT IT'S WORTH IT

If this all sounds like a lot of work, it is. Developing friendships, mentor relationships, and sponsor relationships takes effort. You have to be committed to establishing these relationships in order to make them work. However, it will pay off in the long run. Will sex partition issues get in the way? They might, but it's important to remember that these issues are typically not insurmountable; they just require you to tread more carefully. And when the sex partition seems insurmountable, remember that there isn't only one person in your organization from whom you can benefit. You're diversified. Set your sights on someone else and move on.

16

LET'S BE PERFECTLY CLEAR: NAVIGATING SEXUAL OR ROMANTIC INTEREST AT WORK

State your name, rank, and intention.

—Captain Adelaide Brooke from *Doctor Who*[1]

In the film *Liar, Liar*, Fletcher Reede is devoted to his legal career. Putting his job first, Fletcher often breaks his promises to spend time with his son, Max. When he misses Max's birthday party, Max makes a wish that his father would not be able to lie for an entire day. The wish immediately becomes true, and Fletcher is unable to lie, withhold information, or even mislead. As Fletcher enters his workplace, he's forced to tell each and every employee exactly what he thinks of them. His 100 percent honesty reveals just how often most of us hide our true feelings and intentions at work.

I'm certainly not calling for everyone to adopt this absolute disclosure. However, if everyone was open, honest, and direct about their intentions there could be no misinterpretation at work. No one would fear that friendliness would be misinterpreted as sexual interest, because sexual interest would be stated. No one would wonder if sexual interest was reciprocated, because everything would be out in the open. I realize it's unrealistic to expect this level of 100 percent openness, but a greater degree of honesty would go a long way toward breaking down the sex partition.

In fact, openness and honesty are key to navigating all issues surrounding romantic and sexual interest at work. When it comes to romance at work, there are basically five situations that can become uncomfortable for cross-sex friends. The goal of this chapter is to help you navigate through all five. Although honesty is a big part of getting through these situations, it's not all up to the employees. There are also steps that the organization can take to make navigating these sticky situations a little easier. When it comes to romance at work, the big five are:

1. You have a romantic interest in your coworker, but you don't know if it's reciprocated.
2. You think a colleague may have some romantic or sexual interest in you, and you're not interested.
3. You fear your friendliness toward an opposite-sex coworker will be misinterpreted as sexual interest.
4. You and your coworker have a mutual attraction or are already pursuing a romantic or sexual relationship.
5. You and your coworker are platonic friends but worry about what your coworkers think.

A closer look at each of these situations reveals that they do not necessarily mean doom for your cross-sex friendships.

BROACHING ROMANTIC INTEREST IN A COLLEAGUE

In order to be perceived as professional as possible, it would be best to avoid all romantic entanglements at work. But many of us spend an inordinate amount of time with our coworkers, and attractions are naturally going to develop. If the workplace offered men and women a technique for broaching romantic attraction to their colleagues, it would solve a lot of problems.

I can't believe I have to say this, but if you're interested in a colleague, then leaning in for the kiss, awkward groping, and clunky come-ons are not the way to go. Yet time and time again these are the go-to moves for workers looking to hook up with a colleague. Why? Because misinterpretation of friendliness, hubris, or misplaced self-confidence leaves an impression that the come-on is desired. For ex-San Diego mayor Bob Filner, twenty women felt his alleged sexual advances were unwelcome.[2] One alleged victim of his come-ons, Lisa Curtin, described to KPBS News that Filner "reached over to kiss me, I turned my head, and at that moment, on the side of my face, I got a very wet saliva-filled kiss including feeling his tongue on my cheek."[3] What was Filner's defense? He spoke of the hubris in his behavior, implying he thought his advances would be welcomed by the women he pursued.[4]

Filner is not alone. Recall the allegations against former United States senator Bob Packwood, where a clerical employee alleged that Packwood "walked over to me and pulled me out of the chair, put his arm around me and tried to kiss me. He stuck his tongue in my mouth."[5] Allegations against Herman Cain suggested that he parked the car and then "suddenly reached over and put his hand on my leg, under my skirt and reached for my genitals. He also grabbed my head and brought it towards his crotch."[6] Feminist author Naomi Wolf described her professor's unwelcome moves: "The next thing I knew, his heavy, boneless hand was hot on my thigh."[7] If, instead of these alleged clunky advances, these men had broached their interest in a more professionally acceptable manner, then their offers could have been shot down (or accepted) without repercussions.

Broaching sexual interest in a professional manner sounds like a contradiction in terms. We're taught over and over that sexual interest in a coworker isn't professional. Yet our current policies, which discourage employees from developing romantic or sexual interest in coworkers, simply aren't working. We know organizations can't stop romantic or sexual attraction between employees, and if the sexual attention is perceived as welcome, then all the sexual harassment training in the world won't help. ("I didn't intend to sexually harass, I thought he/she was interested in me.") After all, sexual advances are only harassing if they are unwelcome.

Most people are aware that sexual harassment involves "unwanted" or "unwelcome" sexual attention. That is, consensual sexual attention, or sexual attention that is desired, does not constitute harassment. However, one of the most common questions that I receive regarding sexual harassment involves just this distinction: "How do you know if sexual attention is unwanted unless you try?" That is, the term "unwanted sexual attention" implies the outcome of the attention should be known prior to the advance, but how is this possible? Since men traditionally initiate first dates or make the first move, men are typically at a greater risk of misinterpreting interest. It is the employee who attempts to initiate romance who may end up facing sexual harassment allegations.

Even the EEOC acknowledges the complications involved in determining whether sexual conduct is indeed unwelcome, stating, "Because sexual attraction may often play a role in the day-to-day social exchange between employees, the distinction between invited, uninvited-but-welcome, offensive-but-tolerated, and flatly rejected sexual advances may well be difficult to discern. But this distinction is essential because sexual conduct becomes unlawful only when it is unwelcome."[8]

So how does one broach sexual interest in a professionally acceptable manner? Get consent. Unfortunately, consent isn't always on the minds of employees. An oft-repeated riddle illustrates this point. An equity trader posed the riddle to me and a trader in my group named Davilyn at a work dinner. "What is the difference between rape and seduction?" Being a salesman himself, the answer he was looking for was "salesmanship." Davilyn gave a better answer. She stood up in the crowded restaurant and shouted, "CONSENT!" Davilyn was obviously correct. However, the misinformed salesman was shocked. Despite the fact that he had been posing that riddle to all his clients for years, no one had ever answered him that way before. Consent was clearly not on his radar.

We need to be sure consent is on everyone's radar. You must get the okay, prior to diving in. (By the way, obtaining consent is also a good idea for your romantic relationships outside of the workplace.) "Can I kiss you?" would have saved Bob Filner a lot of headaches. But do employees know how to obtain consent? Sadly, many don't.

What if we had a universally accepted signal of sexual or romantic interest? Employees would have to signal their interest and gain acceptance before asking for dates or sex or kisses or anything romantic or sexual in nature. In other words, organizations could actually teach people how to broach such interactions and obtain consent. Instead of the current paradigm of pretending romantic attraction at work doesn't happen, organizations could offer their employees some useful skills. In lieu of having employees go in for the awkward grope, the uncomfortable kiss, or the unwanted touch, employees could have a professionally accepted way to garner preapproval. In other words, organizations could teach their employees how to obtain consent.

If you're like most people, you're probably asking, "Seriously? Do employees really need that? Men and women have been pursuing one another since the dawn of time; why offer lessons on it now?" My answer is many people don't need it. Maybe even most people don't need it. Think of it like sexual harassment training. Most people can figure out how to interact with coworkers without harassing them—even without attending sexual harassment training. The training is nonetheless necessary for the minority who can't figure it out on their own. It is these few that cause a disproportionate share of the harassment problems. Since we don't know in advance which employees are likely to sexually harass, we must offer sexual harassment training to everyone.

Similarly, some men and women may be able to effectively judge whether their romantic interest is reciprocated and can obtain consent on their own. However, we need to have some professional guidelines for those who are not good at this. Learning a professional manner for obtaining consent would help those who see signs of sexual interest when they are not there. Since we don't know which people need this help, the professional manner of obtaining consent must be used by everyone.

Such signals of sexual interest aimed at obtaining consent certainly appear in other contexts. Former Idaho senator Larry Craig recently brought the foot-tapping-in-the-bathroom-stall signal into the spotlight. Apparently, foot tapping in a public men's bathroom signals a desire for anonymous gay sex.[9] Those who are in a bathroom stall and want to signal their interest, first tap their feet. If the person in the next stall also taps their foot, it is a signal that the interest is reciprocated. Next, typically, one of the interested parties will stick their hand underneath the stall or pass a note on a paper. After both parties consent, and it's safe, they move on to sexual contact in the space beneath the partition between stalls. In case you missed it in the news, Senator Craig was arrested for allegedly signaling his interest in a public bathroom in the Minneapolis–St. Paul International Airport in June 2007. Why did this foot tapping evolve as a signal of interest? Because the alternatives, such as exposing your arousal in a public bathroom, can get you in trouble if others in the bathroom aren't keen on having a restroom sexual encounter with you.

More recently, Governor Brown instituted the "yes means yes" law in California. Under this legislation, California universities that receive public funding require that, prior to engaging in sexual activity, students obtain "affirmative, conscious and voluntary agreement." This law aims to make obtaining consent the norm on college campuses.[10]

An analogous situation occurs in the workplace. Leaning in for the kiss, a grope, a hand on the thigh, or even lingering around someone's desk or cubicle can get you in trouble if the target is not receptive. A recognized signal of interest that it is either confirmed or rejected by the prospective partner could help avoid any unwanted physical come-ons.

So what would be an appropriate method of signaling interest and obtaining consent? First, the method would have to be officially sanctioned by the organization and presented to employees, to ensure it would be universally recognized. It need not be as subtle as foot tapping, and probably should not be subtle at all (the problem with foot tapping is one could accidently provide consent). As suggested by the "yes means yes" law, a verbal acknowledgment is all that's needed. A simple script, "Are you okay taking our relationship outside of the professional realm?" that requires a simple yes or no answer would suffice. If that's too corny, something more lighthearted and humorous could be implemented, as long as all employees were familiar with the phrase or word. "Kangaroo?" "No, thanks."

If the signal is rejected, then the employee must accept this conclusion and cannot repeat the invitation. A response of "no" would have to mean no. If the allegations against them were true, then Bob Filner, Herman Cain, and Bob Packwood would have benefited from the use of a script. Individuals could no longer suggest that provocative dress was a signal of consent or that a coworker was sending signals suggesting sexual interest. Interest would have to be confirmed. It's important to note that the script should not only be used before groping or kissing a coworker but also before asking a coworker on a date.

The script has obvious flaws. For example, there is no hard evidence that an employee used the script, and so one could claim consent was obtained, when in fact it was not. Similarly, one could consent when given the script and then later deny ever having consented. Organizations could demand that written consent be obtained to establish a record, but that does eliminate some of the romance. So while not eliminating all problems, this solution would certainly help eliminate one. That is, it would eliminate awkward situations where one believes their sexual advances are desired, but they're not.

Most important, the script would allow men and women to interact with less fear. Friendliness would be less likely to be misinterpreted as sexual interest (he didn't say "kangaroo"), and fears of clunky advances would be reduced. This is an easy lesson that could be taught during sexual harassment training and would both reduce the likelihood of sexual harassment charges and break down the sex partition.

Consent needs to become the policy when it comes to workplace romance. It needs to be the obvious precursor to any romantic entanglements at work. "I thought it was welcome" could never again be an acceptable justification for grabbing, groping, kissing, or any other come-on. If you're interested in a coworker, obtain consent first. It's not hard, you just have to ask, and it could save lots of headaches.

A COWORKER IS ROMANTICALLY INTERESTED IN YOU

The second potentially awkward situation at work occurs when a coworker is interested in you, and you don't feel the same way. Finding yourself on the receiving end of unwanted romantic or sexual interest can be extremely challenging. If your organization has not implemented a script, or the enamored employee has chosen not to use it, you're in an uncomfortable position. If it's your boss that has the hots for you, you must tread even more carefully.

Once again, directly addressing the situation is the best response. "Are you flirting with me? Because you're making me uncomfortable." Unfortunately, disclosing your lack of romantic interest may be difficult, especially if you're not

100 percent sure their interest is romantic or sexual. What if you tell someone you're not interested, to find out they're not interested in you?

It's tough to come out and directly confront your amorous colleague, but your disapproval of his or her behavior doesn't have to be harsh or malicious. The most important thing is that this person knows his or her behavior is making you uncomfortable. Try, "I'm sure you're just joking around when you say things like that, but it makes me really uncomfortable, so please don't do that anymore." It gets the message across loud and clear, but it gives the amorous employee an out. "Oh, yeah, I was just kidding."

If it's the environment that's making you uncomfortable, then talk about it. Recall that Sarah felt awkward when her colleague invited her to lunch at a romantic restaurant, and she wondered whether her colleague was aware of the restaurant's romantic ambiance before they walked in. She was only interested in a friendship with this man but thought he might have been interested in more.

Sarah could have let her coworker know that the whole lunch made her uncomfortable. Indicating, "I'm sure you didn't know that this was such a romantic restaurant. It actually makes me uncomfortable to be in a restaurant like this with a male coworker. I'm sure you didn't realize what it was like, but let's just eat quickly and get back to work." Her intentions were made perfectly clear—this is a business lunch, not a romantic one.

If the direct approach doesn't work, you can always implement what I call the third-grade strategy. Recall in third grade, if you "liked" or didn't "like" a boy or girl in your class, you'd have a friend do your bidding for you. When all else fails, the third-grade approach still works. Have a trusted colleague send the message for you.

Finally, and most important, if the behavior is making you uncomfortable and your efforts at discouraging the behavior are being ignored, then head to a trusted manager or your human resources department. You have every right to be safe and comfortable at work, and those who don't take no for an answer should be reprimanded.

WILL YOUR FRIENDLINESS BE MISINTERPRETED AS SEXUAL INTEREST?

Recall the fictional anecdote that opened this book about the woman who declined the invitation from a senior colleague. Joe, a senior partner, invited Anita to grab a beer to discuss her long-distance-running training regimen. Anita was thrown off by this invitation. She didn't know if it was a date and certainly didn't want to send the wrong message to Joe. She was also concerned about what her coworkers and her spouse would think when they found out she was imbibing with a senior manager in the firm. Anita declined the invitation.

What if Joe had added to his invitation for a beer, "Don't worry, it's not a date. I really just need some suggestions on my training. I'd suggest we get coffee during the day, but it's tough for me to get free time during work hours." Would it have made a difference? It might have just been enough to make Anita comfortable with the situation. Openness and honesty about your lack of intentions are just as important as openness about your romantic feelings.

Since men are more likely to misinterpret women's friendliness as sexual interest, the burden of this disclosure typically falls on women. This doesn't have to be an awkward, serious "Sit down we need to talk. I'm afraid you might be misinterpreting my friendliness" type of conversation. Just be honest and recognize how your friend might misinterpret your actions.

Let's say, like romantic restaurant visitor Sarah, her colleague also wasn't interested in anything more than a friendship. He could have said, "I had no idea it was this kind of restaurant. You probably think I'm trying to hit on you or something, but I'm not, and I really didn't know this was a romantic restaurant when I suggested we come in here." Clearly stating his intentions, he would have put Sarah at ease, and perhaps a great friendship would have blossomed. Recognizing how a colleague might misread a situation and clarifying your intentions are critical in these situations.

YOU'RE ALREADY CANOODLING WITH A COWORKER

In the fourth type of sticky romantic situation, you and a coworker are already engaged in a romantic or sexual relationship. First and foremost, for the sake of your colleagues, don't keep it a secret. I won't reiterate all the problems involved with secrecy in workplace romance (see chapter 8), but secrecy increases suspicion of all romantic relationships. On the other hand, your coworkers don't need to know the details of your love life either. Once they know the two of you are an item, keep it professional in the office.

The other guidance here is really common sense. If you maintain a professional demeanor, your relationship shouldn't pose a problem. I don't need to tell you that coworkers won't think it's cool if you show favoritism or give preferential treatment to your lover. Displays of affection at work are equally inappropriate. Continuing last night's argument in your cubicle will be deemed unprofessional.

Maintaining professionalism at the end of the relationship is also key. It may be hard to reestablish a healthy working relationship after the romantic liaison ends, but it is critical to demonstrate professionalism through every stage of the relationship, particularly the last one.

For good reason, most organizations frown on subordinate-superior relationships. If you're dating your boss or your direct report, one of you should probably work on getting a transfer. If your organization frowns on workplace romance altogether, you're out of luck. Secrecy or finding a new job are your only alternatives.

WHAT WILL COWORKERS THINK ABOUT YOUR CROSS-SEX FRIENDSHIPS?

Even when there is no romantic interest, cross-sex friends run into trouble when other colleagues misinterpret the friendliness. Let's say you pal around with an opposite-sex coworker in your office. You share inside jokes, hook up for a Starbucks run in the afternoon, and visit each other's offices frequently. In other words, you're friends. In many workplaces, rumors would start to fly, and it's important not to let gossip bring down your friendship.

The first step is to get out in front of the rumors. Directly tell your coworkers that you are just friends. Invite coworkers to join you on your Starbucks runs, so they understand it's not "alone time" for you and your friend. Leave the door open during office visits. If a coworker alludes to your workplace romance, set him or her straight. If you're married or in a relationship, introduce your spouse or partner to your workplace friend. Most important, don't try to keep your friendship a secret. Secrecy will only increase the likelihood of suspicion and gossip.

17

REVISING SEXUAL HARASSMENT TRAINING

You do not examine legislation in the light of the benefits it will convey if properly administered, but in the light of the wrongs it would do and the harms it would cause if improperly administered.

—Lyndon B. Johnson[1]

Started in 1921, Wonder Bread was an American phenomenon. The first brand to offer sliced bread, the bleached white, high-sugar (or high-fructose corn syrup) bread was touted as a healthy alternative to milk, eggs, and potatoes. The nutrients in Wonder Bread were advertised to enrich your body in eight ways (by the 1960s when more nutrients were added, Wonder Bread claimed to help your body in a remarkable twelve ways). As far as Americans were concerned, the more Wonder Bread they consumed, the better. During the 1930s and 40s Americans obtained more calories from commercially available white bread than from any other food. By the 1950s and early 60s, Americans ate so much that 25 to 30 percent of their daily calories came from white bread.[2] Then something changed. While not all bad for you, Americans gradually began to discover the unhealthy aspects of white bread. By 2010 sales of sliced wheat bread exceeded sales of sliced white bread in the United States.[3] In January 2012 Wonder Bread's parent company, Hostess Brands, filed for bankruptcy protection.[4] Most Americans apparently realized the benefits of this bread did not outweigh its drawbacks. In its day, Wonder Bread was perceived as a miracle food chosen by responsible parents, and it remains the icon to which we compare all new inventions (the greatest thing since sliced bread). It's not hard to understand why a "more is better" attitude prevailed with regard to Wonder Bread.

Today organizational practices designed primarily to protect women in the workplace are the Wonder Bread of the feminist movement. They're not all bad, but just like Wonder Bread, we need to assess what's in them before we start consuming them in large amounts. Add a little whole wheat, take out some of the sugar and overprocessing, and they could be a whole lot better for both women and the organization.

By all means, I'm not suggesting we stop eating bread. Nor should we abandon the programs that train employees about sexual harassment. However, as with Wonder Bread, the contents are key. We can no longer assume sexual harassment training is 100 percent beneficial for women, men, and organizations, and that more sexual harassment training is better. However, if we just modify the contents and adjust the ingredients of these training programs, then we can confidently roll them out to improve relations between men and women at work.

Recall there are four ways that sexual harassment impacts the sex partition. In order to break down the sex partition, all four of these must be addressed by training programs. The first, awareness of sexual harassment issues along with concern that one could be charged with sexual harassment, instills fear and causes men to avoid interactions with women. The second problem surrounds poor training methods and how they contribute to these fears. Third, the belief that women need protection in the workplace leads some to perceive women as weaker than men. And, most important, those who are sexually harassed naturally want nothing to do with their opposite-sex coworkers. Therefore, altering the content of sexual harassment training involves much more than merely ensuring that the information in these training programs is correct (though that would be a good first step).

SEXUAL HARASSMENT TRAINING AS IT SHOULD BE

First and foremost, training needs to be effective in reducing harassing behavior. Despite the demands for sexual harassment training in the workplace, little research has examined the efficacy of this training, and the few exceptions do not offer cause for optimism. Recall one study found sexual harassment training added to confusion about what constitutes sexual harassment.[5] In yet another study, sexual harassment training increased participants' ability to identify sexually harassing behaviors, but it had no impact on participants' tolerance for sexual harassment.[6] Still more research indicates that watching a sexual harassment training video had no impact on one's knowledge about sexual harassment or likelihood to engage in harassing behaviors.[7]

It seems odd, given the strong demand for training, that more efforts have not been devoted to ensuring its effectiveness. If we're dishing out training that polarizes men and women at work and possibly increases perceptions of women as weak, it doesn't seem too much to ask that the training should at least reduce harassing behavior. However, research does not seem to support this link.

LESSONS FROM SOCIAL PSYCHOLOGY

Why is sexual harassment training not as effective as we'd like? I believe the lack of efficacy in sexual harassment training may result from the lack of effort invested in studying how to frame the training in order to change behavior. The goal of sexual harassment training has unfortunately become the reduction of legal liability, not the reduction of harassing behavior.

Scholars can also be blamed. A great deal of academic research has been focused on sexual harassment, and a search of scholarly articles with the words "sexual harassment" in the title reveals there are over ten thousand such articles. While these papers focus on important topics related to sexual harassment (for example, characteristics of harassers and victims, organizations where sexual harassment is most likely to occur, case studies of sexual harassment, strategies for the harassed), I have found little that offers suggestions for improving sexual harassment training programs. Discovering strategies to reduce harassing behavior in the workplace, without repercussions for the sex partition, must become a higher priority.

Although an extensive literature on how to psychologically influence human behavior awaits, sexual harassment trainers (often legal experts) haven't tapped into this treasure trove of information. Psychology research can provide suggestions about how to influence behavior as well as provide insight on how to reduce unintended effects of training sessions.

For example, much can be learned from the work of Robert Cialdini, a preeminent researcher in the area of influence. His work not only illustrates how to best formulate a message in order to influence behavior but also how an incorrectly formulated message can have unintended effects on behavior change. As an example of unintended effects, Cialdini describes the Iron Eyes Cody television ad, which was intended to influence viewers to stop littering but may have resulted in the opposite effect.[8] This ad, which aired frequently in the 1970s and 1980s, was rated by *TV Guide* as one of the top television commercials of all time. In this ad, a traditionally dressed American Indian was shown canoeing along a river strewn with garbage. The Indian came ashore near a littered side of highway and watched as a bag of garbage was thrown from the window of a passing car. The garbage splattered at the Indian's feet. The ad then focused on the Indian's face and a tear was shown rolling down his cheek. The slogan, "People Start Pollution, People Can Stop It," appeared on the screen. (Several copies of this ad are available for free viewing on YouTube.com.)

Despite its popularity, Cialdini's research indicates this ad may inadvertently have increased littering behavior.[9] What's the problem with this ad? Well, according to Cialdini, there are two types of norms that motivate human behavior, and the creators of this ad pitted two kinds of norms against one another. The first type, injunctive norms, describe how someone should behave in a particular situation to gain approval or disapproval. The second type, descriptive norms, refer to how people typically behave in a situation. People like to meet with social approval (adhering to injunctive norms), but they also like to do what is popular (adhering to descriptive norms).

Although the Iron Eyes Cody ad provided injunctive norms against littering (the Indian crying clearly exhibited his disapproval), it also depicted the descriptive norm that many people litter. By depicting an abundance of litter on the ground as well as litter being thrown from a car, the ad inadvertently suggested that most people litter or that littering is popular. These opposing forces within the ad ultimately undermine the effectiveness of the message, and the ad may actually persuade people (who want to behave like everyone else) that everyone litters, so littering is acceptable.

Whether it's littering or sexual harassment, if we try to mobilize action against the problem by demonstrating the prevalence of the problem, we undermine the message. Much of the sexual harassment training I have viewed consists of videos of one employee sexually harassing another and then an explanation of why this behavior is wrong. Much like the Iron Eyes Cody advertisement, sexual harassment training provides both the injunctive norm that sexual harassment is unacceptable at work and the descriptive norm that depicts harassment as commonplace at work. Recall the employee who described that in his employer's sexual harassment training program, "The perverted scenarios were presented as if they were common."

As a result, the desire to do as others do may lead those who attend harassment training to consider harassment acceptable behavior. At the very least, the depictions of sexual harassment in training sessions detract from the effectiveness of the anti-harassment message. Therefore, endless video vignettes of sexual harassment in the workplace may not be the most effective strategy to discourage harassing behavior. Instead, messages that sexual harassment is wrong, accompanied by videos or photos of employees behaving appropriately at work, would be more effective at changing behavior.

Another descriptive norm portrayed in sexual harassment training is the objectification of women. Although the injunctive message sent by sexual harassment training is not to objectify women (or men) in the workplace, the training often depicts scenes of objectification in the workplace. Objectification of women occurs when women are thought of as merely physical objects of male sexual desire, and for decades, feminists have argued against the objectification of women in advertising and pornography. In sexual harassment training videos, several scenes (purportedly of what not to do in the workplace) objectify women. In training videos, I've watched scenes of men catcalling women, men inappropriately touching women at work, and men hanging photos of scantily clad women in their work areas. All of these situations depict the objectification of women.

Objectification is of particular concern in the workplace, because objectification has been linked to reduced perceptions of competence. One telling study of the consequences of objectification examined issues encountered by United States vice presidential candidate Sarah Palin.[10] In this study, half of the participants were asked to write about Palin, while the other half were asked to write specifically about Palin's appearance. Those who focused on Palin's appearance were considered to have objectified her. Participants were then asked to rate Palin's competence and state whether they intended to vote for the McCain-Palin ticket. Those who focused on Palin's appearance rated her less competent and were less likely to vote for her than those who were not focused on her appearance. (Similar results have been found when substituting Angelina Jolie for Sarah Palin. Those writing about Jolie's appearance also rated her less competent.) In addition to the obvious drawbacks of perceptions of incompetence in the workplace, these perceptions also contribute to the sex partition. Recall that mentors and sponsors prefer to assist only the most promising employees. Those who are objectified may have more difficulty finding mentors and sponsors.

Perhaps more directly related to friendship development, objectification also results in the dehumanization of the woman.[11] That is, objectified women are perceived as lacking the characteristics that make someone human (for example, lacking traits such as helpfulness or impulsiveness) and instead are perceived as more robotic. Thus the objectification may have both intrapersonal and interpersonal impact. Removing objectification from sexual harassment training should aid in increasing perceptions of women's competence and help in reducing the sex partition.

WHAT DO WHITE BEARS HAVE TO DO WITH SEXUAL HARASSMENT TRAINING?

Have you ever tried *not* to think about something? Try it right now. Try *not* to think about a white bear. You thought about a white bear, didn't you? Most people do. Subjects in one study illustrated this effect when they were asked to talk about whatever they were thinking about for five minutes. Furthermore, they were asked *not* to think about white bears. If they happened to think of a white bear, they were instructed to ring a bell. Results of the study indicated that subjects were not able to suppress the thought of the white bear. Clearly, most of the participants would not have thought of a white bear on their own during those five minutes. However, their effort to suppress the image of a white bear seemed to cause a preoccupation with it.[12]

Studies like this one suggest that the very act of asking employees to suppress their sexual thoughts about cross-sex coworkers could paradoxically make thinking these thoughts more likely. Although no studies to date have examined this effect with sexual harassment training, it is not hard to imagine a similar result. After all, we're instructing employees to *not* think about women in sexual terms. That is, after being instructed for two hours not to think of opposite-sex employees in sexual terms, employees, who may have never previously thought of employees in sexual terms, may begin to do just that. Indeed, it is possible that the results of the study presented in the earlier chapter, where women were perceived as weaker after viewing sexual harassment training, may be explained by this effect. That is, participants may have been more likely to think about women in sexual terms after the sexual harassment training, and this objectification resulted in ratings of the women as weaker. However, more research will be needed to determine if sexual harassment training suffers from the white-bear effect.

DON'T EXAGGERATE

Accuracy is another aspect of sexual harassment training that should be addressed. Sometimes, in an effort to eradicate all harassing behavior, organizations overstate what constitutes harassment. Unfortunately, this just leaves employees confused and nervous in cross-sex interactions. Recall Josh who was called in by his HR department for complimenting a female colleague's business suit. Others were warned about having lunch with an opposite-sex colleague.

This is overkill. Sexual harassment training needs to be clear about what constitutes harassing behavior, but it needs to be equally clear about what does NOT constitute harassing behavior. Compliments about attire do not constitute harassment. Having lunch does not constitute harassment. Meeting alone with an opposite-sex employee is not sexual harassment. Employees and managers need to feel free to interact with their coworkers.

THE GOAL SHOULD BE INCLUSIVENESS

Earlier I described how my male colleagues' joking around stopped in the presence of a female coworker. I blame this behavior on the current message many organizations are sending about inappropriate joking at work. In one widely used sexual harassment training video, the narrator describes how if your inappropriate comments or jokes are overheard by someone, that's sexual harassment. The implication here is that the joking is only inappropriate if it's overheard. By emphasizing the overhearing aspect instead of the joking itself, we may be limiting our legal liability, but we're not creating an environment where women and men can really bond at work. Instead we're inadvertently suggesting that coworkers segregate their joking sessions to ensure that they won't be overheard by the opposite sex.

In lieu of avoidance, the training sessions should emphasize inclusiveness. The reason we want to eliminate these jokes from the workplace is that we want men and women to be able to be privy to all interactions in the office. Indulge this analogy. Pretend you have a child, and you don't want your child to eat a lot of candy. You can basically take two routes. One is to threaten your child, telling him that if he is caught eating candy he will be severely punished. In this case, the child may not eat candy when adults are present, but he will be more likely to scarf down candy when no one is looking. A second strategy is to explain that candy is bad for your teeth and your body, and if you eat too much of it you'll get sick. I believe the second strategy is more effective.

Just like the child who eats candy when his parents aren't present, employees feel free to joke as long as there is no potential tattletale present. We need to explain to employees why inappropriate jokes are harmful—even if they are not overheard. Instead of threatening punishments if someone, presumably of the opposite sex, overhears the jokes, let's explain why the jokes themselves serve to polarize the sexes at work.

SEXUAL HARASSMENT TRAINING—IMPROVED

In sum, there is ample room for improvement in sexual harassment training programs. Unfortunately, improving these programs has not been a high priority. Regulations that address frequency and length of sexual harassment training programs must also begin to address the *contents* of these programs. For those who really want to institute change in their organization, the following suggestions provide solid first steps in amending sexual harassment training.

Standardize training. First and foremost, training should be standardized. The EEOC recommends that all employers offer sexual harassment training to their employees. Some states legislate who should have the training, the frequency of training, and the length of the training, but somehow there is less concern with the actual content of training. There is a plethora of misinformation being conveyed to employees that may inadvertently result in segregating male and female employees from one another. Training should have to meet certain standards. Criteria for what should and should not be covered in sexual harassment training should be provided to organizations. Off-the-shelf courses could be preapproved. This would go a long way toward reducing misinformation and making the training as effective as possible.

Those accused have rights too. Employees should be assured that all accusations will be investigated, and that those accused of sexual harassment will not be presumed guilty. Due process should be guaranteed. Guaranteeing an investigation that is fair to the accuser and the accused will help reduce the fear of sexual harassment charges.

Eliminate scare tactic terms such as "zero tolerance." Some organizations tout their adoption of a zero-tolerance policy toward sexual harassment. Sexual harassment isn't like taking drugs or carrying a weapon. It's not that clear cut. What does zero tolerance even mean when applied to sexual harassment? Zero tolerance is particularly murky for the hostile environment-type harassment. The EEOC says the behavior must be frequent or severe to constitute harassment. How can you have zero tolerance for a behavior that must be repeated? The term zero tolerance further implies that isolated incidents of teasing or offhand comments could result in severe punishments.

Do NOT overidentify or provide misinformation about what constitutes sexual harassment. While this may seem obvious, in an effort to minimize the likelihood of lawsuits, organizations tend to overstate exactly what constitutes harassment. In addition to covering what constitutes harassing behavior, it is important to also cover what is *not* sexually harassing behavior. Employees should be made aware that the EEOC's definition of sexual harassment includes that "the law doesn't prohibit simple teasing, offhand comments, or isolated incidents that are not very serious. Harassment is illegal when it is so frequent or severe that it creates a hostile or offensive work environment or when it results in an adverse employment decision (such as the victim being fired or demoted)."

The goal of training should not be limiting legal liability. The goal of training is to create a positive working environment that is more hospitable toward both sexes. This message makes it clear that the goal is inclusiveness, and that segregating your networks so you won't be charged with sexual harassment is not acceptable.

Do not generate perceptions of women as fragile. Make it clear that sexual harassment training is not provided just for the protection of women. Although most sexual harassment training is already gender neutral (portraying both men and women equally as victims of harassment), more work is needed in this area. For example, presenting research that indicates both men and women suffer the same repercussions after experiencing harassing behavior would help dispel myths that training is to protect women who "can't take a joke."

Take steps to avoid backlash or anger at having to attend sexual harassment training. Keep sexual harassment training interesting and not an insult to one's intelligence. Perhaps eliminating the time requirement and permitting a shorter training period would aid in reducing criticism. Furthermore, a genuine interest in workplace relations (as opposed to a legal motive) would help reduce backlash.

In addition, providing useful information that employees can use will make the training sessions more interesting and informative. Useful information on broaching workplace romance or communicating with the opposite sex would make these training sessions more interesting and applicable for many employees.

Access both descriptive and injunctive norms in the training. While it's important to access injunctive norms (that sexual harassment is not acceptable), it is also important to access descriptive norms (that most people do *not* sexually harass). Sexual harassment training too often focuses only on the injunctive norms. Photos or vignettes incorporated in sexual harassment training often depict instances of sexual harassment in the workplace. However, very little time is spent focused on images of positive relationships at work. A photo of a mentor dining with an opposite-sex mentee, accompanied by an explanation of the value of mentor relationships and that most often they are not accompanied by sexual harassment, would send a positive message.

For elementary through high school, use the label "sexual bullying" instead of "sexual harassment." Bullying is a major problem in schools, and clearly steps should be taken to eradicate it. There seems no added benefit to introducing the sexual harassment label and sexual harassment training in addition to training aimed at eliminating bullying and sexual bullying. Referring to school bullying as harassment may add to the confusion surrounding the definition of sexual harassment in the workplace.

Do not ignore workplace relationships. Workplace relationships will occur regardless of policies. Instead of merely discouraging office romance, offering employees suggestions on how to manage these relationships might help avoid misunderstandings.

Encourage cross-sex friendships and discourage gossip. Sexual harassment training should emphasize to employees that their concerns regarding sexual harassment should not inhibit the development of cross-sex friendship. Increasing awareness of the importance of bridging the gap between the sexes at work may go a long way to breaking down the sex partition. Furthermore, gossip or suspicion suggesting close cross-sex friends are involved in a romantic or sexual relationship should be discouraged. Instead, cross-sex friends should not receive any more scrutiny than same-sex friends.

STARTING A DIALOGUE
ABOUT THE
SEX PARTITION

Change happens by listening and then starting a dialogue with
the people who are doing something you don't believe is right.

—Jane Goodall, anthropologist[1]

Indian union minister Farooq Abdullah found himself embroiled in contro-
versy following comments he made regarding India's new sexual harassment
laws. India recently instituted new sexual harassment legislation aimed at making the workplace more hospitable toward women. So what got Abdullah in so
much hot water? He spoke out about the sex partition. He described how the
new regulations made him feel about women in the office: "I am scared to talk to
a woman these days. I don't even want to keep a woman secretary. Who knows,
I might end up in jail because of a complaint. No, I am not blaming the girls, I
am blaming society."[2]

According to the *Times of India*, criticism immediately poured in regarding
Abdullah's comments, and women's activist groups demanded his resignation. The chairperson of India's National Commission for Women labeled his
comments "disgusting"[3] and Abdullah's son tweeted that he hoped his father
would apologize for his "misplaced attempt at humor."[4] Others suggested his
comments were a warning that women who complain of harassment will lose
their jobs.

Under pressure, Abdullah did apologize for his comments. But did we need
an apology from someone who just opened up about his concerns? One social
activist, in her attempts to slam Abdullah, was quoted as saying, "When men
say they are afraid of hiring or talking to women as Farooq Abdullah did, they

are visibly a victim of their own insecurity."[5] She's absolutely right. Men like Abdullah are feeling insecure, and Abdullah was merely voicing this insecurity. What's wrong with that?

Instead of condemning Abdullah, I believe he should be commended for starting a dialogue regarding men's insecurity regarding sexual harassment. His comments should be seized as an opportunity to allay his fears and the fears of other men who shared his concerns. At this point, we don't even know why Abdullah feared talking to women. Did he fear false sexual harassment charges or was he afraid he would inadvertently harass someone? If he had been able to explain, it would have presented a great opportunity not only to dispel his fears, but to explain the importance of his interactions with female employees.

But that didn't happen. Abdullah was shut down. Because sexual harassment laws are new to India, Abdullah didn't realize the scorn he would face by discussing his fears. Since sexual harassment laws have a longer tenure in the United States, men here have already learned that it's taboo to speak of such things. Men in the United States just reduce their interactions with female employees and don't talk about it.

Unfortunately, an open dialogue on these issues is the first step in eradicating them. Let's face it, men still run the majority of organizations, and they need to understand that interactions with women, including social interactions, are essential to women's success. Segregating your socializing by gender is discriminatory, even if it's just lunch or water cooler talk.

We can begin to improve this situation by talking about it. We can start talking about interactions between men and women, and what makes them difficult. And by talking about it, we can make it better.

STARTING DIALOGUES AT WORK

We can start a dialogue on a societal level, like Farooq Abdullah attempted, or at an organizational level, as we discussed in previous chapters. However, the most important dialogues are those with our own coworkers and friends. Whether about issues of romantic interest, business trip issues, issues surrounding sexual harassment, or just misunderstandings resulting from gender differences, it's important to get these issues out of the closet. When you see an example of the sex partition in action, let your coworkers know. Not in a harsh "you need to be punished for this" kind of way, but in a "I bet you didn't even realize you were doing this" kind of way.

I started just such a dialogue with my friend Kevin. Kevin is a technology executive and has a pair of season tickets to Los Angeles Dodgers baseball games. His wife often attends games with him, but the Dodgers have a lot of home games. When she can't take any more baseball, he offers this extra ticket to an employee on his staff. I noticed that his baseball buddies were always male, and I suspected the sex partition was to blame. I decided to talk to Kevin about how he chose employees to join him at the games. Clearly, the employees who joined him for games had the advantage of getting to know the boss better, and potentially putting forth their ideas for the organization. When an important assignment surfaced, Kevin may be more likely to give it to the guy he got to know at the baseball game.

I explained this all to Kevin and asked him why he never took female employees to the games. His gut reaction was it would be awkward to invite a female employee, and if he did, he wasn't sure his wife would be okay with it. It was too complicated. The female employee might think it was a date. If she was married, her husband might think Kevin was making a move. In other words, the sex partition was keeping female employees from the baseball invitation.

I got Kevin thinking about it and suggested he start by talking to his wife. Not surprisingly, when he spoke to his wife, she agreed it wasn't fair that he didn't offer the tickets to women in the office. After all, he and his employees did discuss business at the games, and his male employees had more of a chance to get to know him. She was all for Kevin giving the female employees a chance.

One possible solution that initially seems fair would be for Kevin to e-mail his entire staff when he had an extra ticket. The first to respond would land the extra seat. While that's certainly better than excluding women completely, it's not ideal. Women might be reluctant to jump on the ticket offer for the same reasons Kevin was reluctant to ask them directly. That is, a female employee may have concern that Kevin or the other employees would get the wrong idea if she volunteered to go to the game with him. This time an open dialogue with the employees would be necessary to clear the air.

I told Kevin he should approach his employees, apologize for his men-only baseball outings, and openly express his concerns. He should explain how he was afraid that if he offered the ticket to a woman she might think it was a date. Or she would feel like she had to go even if she hated baseball. Or that her husband might come beat him up. Or that rumors would fly in his department. The female employees would appreciate his honesty. Through this type of open dialogue, the employees can establish a fair method of distributing Kevin's extra tickets.

Several dialogues were required here. First, someone had to point out to Kevin that the sex partition was impacting his behavior. Awareness is a catalyst. It gets people thinking about their behavior in a way they hadn't before. Sometimes that's all it takes. In Kevin's situation, further talks with his spouse and employees were required. However, it's identifying these situations, and pointing them out, that gets the ball rolling in the right direction.

If someone is excluding women in your office, it's important to speak up. Sometimes, particularly if it's a senior employee, direct confrontation can be awkward. In this case, you should speak to someone in your human resources department. Explain that women are being excluded from a particular event—and while the event might not be directly work related, those attending the event are receiving work perks. Human resources can intervene, and hopefully no one needs to know you were the whistle-blower.

Most people don't realize the repercussions associated with their choices. Pointing them out can go a long way to increasing women's inclusion. However, be prepared. If Kevin gives his extra baseball ticket to you, it may be a little uncomfortable. Once again, the best advice for overcoming this discomfort is to talk about it. Most important, get out in front of rumors. Talk to your coworkers about your impending outing with Kevin. Tell your fellow employees about your fears that people will think you're trying to sleep your way to the top. Start a dialogue.

STARTING DIALOGUES WITH KIDS

Starting a dialogue with our children can also help future generations break down the sex partition. Kids tend to like kids who are similar to themselves. However, if a child comes home and reports that he doesn't want to be friends with a new classmate because he has a different skin color or because he's wheelchair bound, most parents are propelled into action. They start a dialogue with their children about race and diversity. Parents are not alone in this task, as numerous websites and books offer guidance for parents desiring to talk to their children about precisely these issues.

Now imagine a boy comes home from school and says he doesn't want to be friends with a new classmate because she's a girl. The reaction will likely be quite different. Parents aren't typically propelled into action with this comment. No dialogue ensues. No talking about the importance of having friends of both genders follows. In fact, the parents may think it's cute that the young boy is avoiding girls. At best, the young boy may get a humorous warning regarding his likely future interest in the opposite sex, such as, "Someday soon you'll feel differently about girls."

Indeed, I don't know of any books or websites that guide parents on how to talk to their children about accepting diversity when it comes to male versus female. Let's not let that stop us. We need to start a dialogue with our children about how girls aren't so different from boys.

We must explain to our kids that befriending an opposite-sex classmate doesn't mean you "like" the girl or boy. If a boy pokes fun at a classmate for befriending a girl, it's not cute. It's sexist. If he made fun of someone for befriending a classmate with a different skin color it would obviously be racist. So why is it so hard to recognize that it's sexist to make fun of someone who befriends the opposite sex? We need to talk to all of our kids, boys and girls, about these topics.

Schools and teachers can also help bring male and female students together. Recently my son and his friends were complaining they had to sit on the floor during music class. It seems the classroom was short on chairs that day, so boys had to sit on the floor, leaving the chairs for the girls. Although, I'm sure the teacher thought that she was training the boys to be chivalrous, she was really doing a disservice to the girls and contributing to the sex partition. I explained to my son and his friends that girls are just as capable of sitting on the floor as boys. They're not more fragile, weaker, or less flexible. They don't need your seats. They are, indeed, just like boys in this situation. We talked about fairer methods to distribute the available seats—methods that didn't alienate the boys from the girls. Giving the seats to those with the largest instruments seems like a much fairer division, and one that doesn't segregate the sexes.

Helping our kids understand the value of having a diverse set of friends will help them throughout their lives. Ask your children what they gain from their friendships. What do their friends gain from them? What might you miss out on if all your friends were exactly like you? It's important children understand that everyone needs friends, and it's cool to have friends who aren't exactly like you. We need to explain that each sex makes up half of the population, and eliminating half of the population from our pool of potential friends severely limits their possible friendships. Starting young will help break down the sex partition for future generations.

BREAKING DOWN THE SEX PARTITION

For both adults and children, it's important to remember that the sex partition isn't a physical barrier, it's a social construction. People created it, and people can break it down. Women have ample experience breaking down barriers, and now they need to set their sights on this one. Female leaders were so scarce a half century ago that a 1965 *Harvard Business Review* article entitled "Are Women Executives People?" questioned, "Do women execs act like people, think of themselves as people, and does the business community treat them as people?"[6] It's hard to imagine now, but trailblazing female executives went to work with coworkers questioning whether they were "people." Due to the efforts of previous generations, women no longer head to work with concerns about being perceived as a person. Unfortunately, we have new barriers to break now.

We need to begin trailblazing a new path. Women who befriend or socialize with their male colleagues, particularly one-on-one, may have to bear the brunt of some rumors or negative remarks. They may have to endure uncomfortable situations. However, as this behavior becomes more common, it will be questioned less and less. Female executives a half century ago endured negative comments and attitudes about their nontraditional roles, but their experiences made it easier for us today. Now we need to trail-blaze a path through the sex partition. It will be worth our efforts.

We must tread carefully in breaking down the sex partition. One of my primary concerns about venturing into this new territory was summarized in a comment left by a reader of a piece I wrote on the sex partition for *The Guardian*. The comment read: "Hey Babe, let's go break down the sex partition . . ." This resonated with me, because it encapsulates one of the biggest dangers of implementing change. Encouragement to socialize with opposite-sex employees cannot be interpreted as a pass to sexually harass. I can't emphasize enough that breaking down the sex partition doesn't mean we need to set the clock back on sexual harassment. No one should have to endure harassing behavior in order to establish cross-sex networks. Developing a new approach to sexual harassment training and enforcement that does not segregate the sexes is yet another trail we must blaze.

There's no easy fix for the sex partition. The suggestions in this book will take concerted efforts on behalf of women, men, and organizations. What's the alternative? Pretending no sex partition exists in the workplace? It would certainly be easier to sweep these issues under the rug and continue with the status quo. That's the strategy we've been using to date, and it doesn't seem to be working so well. Breaking down the sex partition is essential if women are to achieve parity with men in the workplace. Yes, it will be difficult, but it will be worth the effort. There's really no alternative.

APPENDIX A

Details of Study of Sexual Harassment Training and Perceptions of Female Friends

This appendix outlines the details of the study described in chapter 4. Since a few readers are interested in the nitty-gritty details of the research methods and statistical analyses involved in this type of study, I've included them here. If numbers aren't your thing, then you may want to pass on this section.

HYPOTHESIS

The goal of this study was to assess what impact, if any, sexual harassment training would have on perceptions of female friends. I hypothesized that after viewing sexual harassment training, both men and women would perceive men as emotionally stronger than women. In particular, I predicted that for men and women who watched the sexual harassment training video, female friends would be rated lower in terms of emotional strength than male friends. This effect would be significantly less for those who watched the fire-safety video.

PARTICIPANTS AND PROCEDURES

Respondents were 111 students (forty-two men and sixty-nine women) at a state university in California. The sample consisted of students over eighteen years of age who had some full- or part-time employment experience. The mean age was 21.2 years (SD = 2.5), and participants were ethnically diverse, with 43.9 percent identifying as White, 26.3 percent Hispanic, 21.1 percent Asian, 4.4 percent African-American, and 3.5 percent identifying as "other."

Students volunteered to participate in this study to meet requirements for various courses. (Several psychology courses require students to participate as subjects in research studies.) Upon completion of the survey, students were granted course credit.

The web-based study randomly assigned participants to either the experimental or control conditions. Those in the experimental condition (fifty-two participants) watched a short sample video on sexual harassment training. The video seemed like a well-produced sexual harassment training video, and the company who produced the training video touts that they have tens of thousands of clients, including Fortune 500 companies. The remaining fifty-nine control participants watched a fire-safety video available on YouTube.com.

To disguise the intent of the study, participants were told that its purpose was to evaluate the effectiveness of the video. Participants were then asked to rate the effectiveness of the training, how much they enjoyed the training, and how much they learned from the training. After completing the video and the follow-up questions, participants were given another survey, which, to them, seemed unrelated to the previous one on sexual harassment training. It wouldn't be unusual for students completing surveys for course credit to be provided surveys for different studies in one sitting, so this most likely was not questioned. Participants were surveyed about their closest male friend and closest female friend. More specifically, they were asked to rate how well certain attributes described this friend.

MEASURE

Strength: Two items, emotionally strong and fragile (reverse-coded) were summed to assess the emotional strength of the closest male and female friend. Respondents indicated how well each of these attributes described their closest male and female friend on a 7–point scale (1= not at all, 7 = very much). Ratings for close female friends were then subtracted from ratings of close male friends to produce the differential.

RESULTS

In order to examine the effects of the experimental condition and participant gender on ratings of strength of the closest female friend relative to the closest male friend, factorial analysis of variance (ANOVA) was applied. More specifically, a 2 (sexual harassment video or fire-safety video) x 2 (gender of participant) factorial ANOVA was used to examine the strength differential. Results revealed significant main effects with regard to the experimental condition (F (1, 107) = 7.86, p = 0.006). Those who watched the sexual harassment training video were more likely to rate their close female friends lower on strength than their male friends (M = 1.69, SD = 0.44) than were those who watched the fire-safety video (M = 0.001, SD = 0.41). In other words, in the experimental condition, participants rated male friends, on average, 1.69 units higher on emotional strength than women. In the control condition, men were rated only 0.001 higher than women on strength. Results indicated no significant effects (at the p <.05 level) for participant gender nor were there any significant interaction effects. Therefore, there were no gender differences exhibited in the effect of sexual harassment training on perceptions of female strength.

LIMITATIONS AND FUTURE RESEARCH

The sample in this study was comprised of university students, and it is unknown how this study would generalize to older populations. Furthermore, I do not know what aspects of the sexual harassment training video account for the results in this study. Further research should determine whether the mere mention of sexual harassment results in similar results or whether some aspect of the video resulted in the perceptions of weak women. This study was exploratory in nature and should be replicated before any further conclusions can be drawn.

APPENDIX B

Details of Study of Cross-Sex Coworkers on a Business Trip

This appendix outlines the recruitment of participants for the study of business trips outlined in chapter 7. Participants were recruited from Amazon's Mechanical Turk and each was paid fifty cents for their participation. The advertisement for respondents asked that only those who had participated in a business trip with an opposite-sex colleague could participate. Participants were then asked to write about their experience on this business trip.

Mechanical Turk is a crowdsourcing web service where individuals can post tasks that require human intelligence or a particular skill. Individuals can then complete the tasks in exchange for payment. In the case of this study, Mechanical Turk users in the United States who had participated in a business trip with an opposite-sex colleague were required to answer questions about their trip in order to be paid.

One concern about online data collection is how representative the sample is. That is, if the participants recruited are not representative of the population in general, then the results are also not generalizable. However, research has found the demographics of Mechanical Turk participants are "at least as representative of the U.S. population as traditional subject pools, with gender, race, age, and education of Internet samples all matching the population more closely than college undergraduate samples and Internet samples in general."[1] Furthermore, the design of Mechanical Turk virtually eliminates the possibility of multiple entries by the same individual. In addition, the anonymity that is afforded through Mechanical Turk may lead participants to respond with greater honesty.

Responses in this survey were completely anonymous. Therefore, the names included in the book are not the actual names of participants.

Twenty-six men, twenty-four women, and one who refused to identify his or her gender were recruited. Forty-three participants reported their occupations. Occupations were varied and a list of occupations can be found in table B.1 below.

Participants were instructed to describe their experience on a business trip with a coworker of the opposite sex. In particular they were asked to mention if there was anything that made them uncomfortable on the trip. Participants typed in a paragraph or two to describe their experiences.

Qualitative analysis using multiple readings of the comments was used to identify the major concepts that emerged. A process of open coding was then applied.[2] Codes were generated from a microanalysis involving a line by line reading of the transcripts. The codes were reviewed, and more abstract categories, which applied to several responses, were determined. These categories are described in the text. The names used in the text are not the names of the actual participants.

Table B.1. Participant Professions

Sales (9)
Healthcare (4)
Marketing (3)
Accountant (2)
Business (2)
Store manager (2)
Technology (4)*
Assistant manager in telecommunications
Assistant to director of a nonprofit
Business owner
Columnist
Customer service
Event coordinator
Government
Industrial hygienist
Lawyer
Massage therapist
Merchandise distributor
Personal assistant
Psychologist
Public relations
Tax consultant
Telemarketer
Reinsurance broker

* Two IT directors, one programmer, and one IT advisor

NOTES

CHAPTER 1

1. Lewis, 1988, p. 71.
2. In an earlier publication in *Human Relations*, this barrier was referred to as the "glass partition" (Elsesser & Peplau, 2006).
3. Baruch-Feldman et al., 2002; Elsesser, 2003; Markiewicz, Devine & Kausilas, 2000; Podolny & Baron, 1997.
4. Catalyst, 2012.
5. Hewlett et al., 2010.
6. Williams, 1992.
7. Institute for Women's Policy Research, 2012.
8. Catalyst, 2013.
9. Catalyst, 2013.
10. Catalyst, 2014.
11. Richardson, 2014.
12. Parker, 2013.
13. Elsesser & Peplau, 2006, p. 1083.
14. Kanter, 1977.
15. Baruch-Feldman et al., 2002; Beehr et al., 2000; Madjar, 2008; Stewart & Barling, 1996.
16. Baruch-Feldman et al., 2002; Ducharme & Martin, 2000; Harris, Winskowski & Engdahl, 2007; Shirom et al., 2011; Unden, 1996.
17. Elsesser, 2003.
18. Fernandez & Weinberg, 1997.
19. Blair-Loy, 2001; Fernandez & Weinberg, 1997.
20. Crispin & Mehler, 2011.

21. Booth, Francesconi & Frank, 2003.
22. Granovetter, 1973, 1974; Lin, Ensel & Vaughn, 1981.
23. Marsden & Hurlbert, 1988.
24. Sias & Cahill, 1997.
25. Lalanne & Seabright, 2011; Markiewicz, Devine & Kausilas, 2000.
26. Lalanne & Seabright, 2011.

CHAPTER 2

1. Brock, 1994, p. 10.
2. Elsesser & Peplau, 2006.
3. Hewlett et al., 2010.
4. Hossack, 1993.
5. United States Equal Employment Opportunity Commission, 2014.
6. Alford v. Aaron's Rents, Inc, 2008.
7. Harris v. Forklift Systems, Inc., 1993.
8. For more details, see Harris v. Forklift Systems, Inc., 1993.
9. Harris v. Forklift Systems, Inc., 1993.
10. Rotundo, Nguyen & Sackett, 2001.
11. Rotundo, Nguyen & Sackett, 2001, p. 920.
12. www.eeoc.gov/laws/types/sexual_harassment.cfm.

CHAPTER 3

1. Attributed by Bowden, 2011.
2. Portions of this quote appeared in Elsesser & Peplau, 2006.
3. Schneider, 1996, p. 9.
4. Schneider, 1996, p. 37.
5. Schneider, 1996, p. 37.
6. Schneider, 1996, p. 37.
7. Faragher, 2005.
8. Faragher v. City of Boca Raton, 1998.
9. Kass, 2011.
10. Walsh, 2012.
11. United States Equal Employment Opportunity Commission, 2014.
12. Abcarian & Baum, 2011.
13. *The Sean Hannity Show*, 2011.

14. *The Sean Hannity Show*, 2011.
15. www.eeoc.gov/laws/types/sexual_harassment.cfm
16. Abcarian & Baum, 2011.
17. Abcarian & Baum, 2011.
18. Stewart, 2011.
19. Vance, 2010.
20. Vance, 2010.
21. Parker, 2011.
22. *Washington Post*–ABC News Poll, 2011.
23. Eisenman, 2011.
24. Eisenman, 2011.
25. Eisenman, 2011.
26. Schneider, 1996, p. 37.
27. Hajdin, 1997, p. 221.
28. Elsesser & Peplau, 2006, p. 1090.
29. English, 2003, p. 67.
30. Madera et al., 2007.
31. Golden, Johnson & Lopez, 2001; Madera et al., 2007; Pryor & Day, 1988.
32. Frieze, Olson & Russell, 1991; Kanazawa & Kovar, 2004; Marlow, Schneider & Nelson, 1996.
33. Frieze, Olson & Russell, 1991.
34. Ellis, Barak & Pinto, 1991.
35. Bryant & Lewis, 2005; Rodgers, 1999.
36. Rodgers, 1999.
37. Rodgers, 1999.
38. Bryant & Lewis, 2005, p. 6.
39. Williams, Giuffre & Dellinger, 1999, p. 86.
40. Elsesser & Peplau, 2006.

CHAPTER 4

1. Dunn, 1994.
2. Silverstein, 1998.
3. Paglia, 1992, p. 47.
4. Roiphe, 2011.
5. Ellison v. Brady, 1991.
6. Veniegas & Peplau, 1997.
7. Chan et al., 2008.
8. Chan et al., 2008.

CHAPTER 5

1. Attributed to Plato by Douglas, 1917.
2. Goldstein, 2008.
3. Barone, 2005.
4. Baer, 2003.
5. Whittle, 2008.
6. Eisenman, 2001, p. 79.
7. Bingham & Scherer, 2001.
8. Bingham & Scherer, 2001, p. 144.
9. Hurley & Fagenson-Eland, 1996.
10. Bryan, Matson & Weiss, 2007.
11. Eisenman, 2001.
12. English, 2003, p. 68.
13. Bisom-Rapp, 2001.
14. Pilgram & Keyton, 2009.
15. Pilgram & Keyton, 2009, p. 232.
16. Perry et al., 2010.
17. Dziech & Weiner, 1990.
18. Dziech & Weiner, 1990, p. 164.
19. Dziech & Weiner, 1990, p. 119.
20. Jan, 2006.
21. Cramer, 2011.
22. Foxnews.com, 2011.
23. Murphy, 2013.

CHAPTER 6

1. Posner, R., from Carr v. Allison Gas Turbine Div., Gen. Motors Corp., 1994.
2. Marchuk v. Faruqi & Faruqi, LLP, 2013.
3. The allegations and quotes regarding Marchuk are from a complaint Marchuk filed in United States District Court for the Southern District of New York in March, 2013 (Marchuk v. Faruqi & Faruqi, LLP, 2013).
4. Chan et al., 2008.
5. Bergman et al., 2002.
6. Conley, 1999, p. 105–106.
7. Conley, 1999, p. 185–186.
8. Wolf, 2004.

CHAPTER 7

1. *60 Minutes Overtime*, 2013.
2. Trunk, 2007.
3. Trunk, 2007.
4. Lyvers et al., 2011.
5. Crowe & George, 1989.
6. *60 Minutes Overtime*, 2013.
7. English, 2003, p. 64.

CHAPTER 8

1. Kipnis, 2004.
2. Hewlett et al., 2010.
3. Elsesser & Peplau, 2006; English, 2003.
4. Clifford, 2012.
5. Clifford, 2012.
6. Sorkin, 2012.
7. Cropper, 1997.
8. Elsesser & Peplau, 2006, p. 1087.
9. Elsesser & Peplau, 2006, p. 1088.
10. Koblin, 2010.
11. Koblin, 2010.
12. Hewlett et al., 2010.
13. Hewlett et al., 2010.
14. Hewlett et al., 2010, p. 38.
15. Hewlett et al., 2010.
16. Careerbuilder.com, 2011; Vault.com, 2011.
17. Obama, 2008, p. 514.
18. Bureau of Labor Statistics, 2006; U.S. Department of Labor, 2010.
19. Zajonc, 1968.
20. Saegert, Swap & Zajonc, 1973.
21. See Brehm, 1992, for review.
22. For more information on Miller v. Department of Corrections, see Diaz, 2006, and Dolan, 2005.
23. Careerbuilder.com, 2011.
24. Anderson & Hunsaker, 1985; Quinn, 1977.
25. Quinn, 1977.
26. Mead, 1980, p. 55.

27. Mead, 1980, p. 56.
28. Massengill & Petersen, 1995.
29. Schaefer & Tudor, 2001.
30. Trounson, 2003.
31. Brehm & Brehm, 1981.
32. Driscoll, Davis & Lipetz, 1972.
33. Mainiero, 1986.

CHAPTER 9

1. Rudner & Cho, 2003.
2. Nelson v. Knight DDS, P.C.
3. Associated Press, 2013a.
4. Rubin, 1985, p. 156.
5. Kalmijn, 2002.
6. See Monsour, 2002, for a review.
7. Werking, 1997.
8. For information regarding Kelly Flinn and Marc Zigo, see Sciolino, 1997a, 1997b.
9. Merle, 2005.
10. Yaniv, 2009.
11. For more information on the affairs of congressional representatives, see Clement, 2014; Pergram & Brown, 2010; and Schouten, 2011.
12. Dworkin, 1997.
13. Alderman, 1995.
14. Levine, 2010.
15. Captivate, 2010.
16. Vault.com, 2010.
17. Captivate, 2010.
18. Captivate, 2010.
19. For the *Wall Street Journal* article, see Shellenbarger, 2011.
20. Work spouse survey results can be found at Captivate, 2010.
21. Keedle, 2011.
22. Rosenthal & Jacobson, 1992.
23. Captivate, 2010.
24. Drphil.com, 2012.

CHAPTER 10

1. Wilde, 1892.
2. For quotes from *When Harry Met Sally*, see Ephron, Reiner & Scheinman, 1989.

3. Bleske-Rechek et al., 2012.
4. Guerrero & Chavez, 2005; Reeder, 2000; Sapadin, 1988.
5. Elsesser & Peplau, 2006.
6. Fisher, Moore & Pittenger, 2012.
7. Curtis, 1998.
8. Abbey, 1987.
9. Kowalski, 1993.
10. Abbey, 1987.
11. Cogan, 2013.
12. Kolhatkar, 2004.
13. Kolhatkar, 2004.
14. Abbey, 1982; Perilloux, Easton & Buss, 2012.
15. Perilloux, Easton & Buss, 2012.
16. Perilloux, Easton & Buss, 2012.
17. Maccoby, 1988.
18. Adler, Kless & Adler, 1992.
19. Maccoby, 1988.
20. Adams, 1985.
21. Adams, 1985, p. 609.
22. Adams, 1985, p. 609.
23. Hughes, Morrison & Asada, 2005, p.49.
24. Bradac, 1983.
25. Brown and Auerback, 1981, p. 108.
26. Brown and Auerback, 1981, p.108.
27. Bisson & Levine, 2009; Hughes, Morrison & Asada, 2005.
28. Lehmiller, VanderDrift & Kelly, 2011; McGinty, Knox & Zusman, 2007.
29. Bisson & Levine, 2009.
30. Preston & Marelich, 2008.
31. O'Meara, 1989, p. 535.
32. Bisson & Levine, 2009.

CHAPTER 11

1. Barry, 1999.
2. Churchill, 1950, p. 609.
3. DiPietro, 1981.
4. Maccoby, 2002.
5. Maccoby, 1998.
6. Helgeson, 2012, p. 262.
7. Jacklin & Maccoby, 1978.
8. Maccoby & Jacklin, 1987.

9. Maccoby, 1998.
10. Maccoby, 1998.
11. Marcus & Overton, 1978.
12. Maccoby, 1998.
13. Tannen, 1990.
14. Wright, 1982.
15. Markiewicz, Devine & Kausilas, 2000.
16. Greif, 2008, p. 18.
17. Wright, 1982.
18. Markiewicz, Devine & Kausilas, 2000.
19. Ibarra, 1993.
20. For more information on Katz's trial, see Zagier, 2014.
21. Reeder, 2003.
22. Tannen 1990, 1994.
23. Tannen, 1990, 1994.
24. Misner, Walker & De Raffele, 2012.
25. Helweg-Larsen et al., 2004.
26. Hewlett et al., 2010.
27. Hewlett et al., 2010.
28. Quoted in Clark, 2009.
29. Hewlett et al., 2010.
30. Clark & Mills, 1993.
31. Elsesser & Lever, 2011.

CHAPTER 12

1. Attributed by Cardiff, 1964.
2. Cooper, 1997; Ellemers et al., 2004; Elsesser & Lever, 2011.
3. Staines, Tavris & Jayaratne, 1974.
4. Parks-Stamm, Heilman & Hearns, 2008.
5. Ellemers et al., 2004.
6. Barash, 2007, p. 158.
7. Barash, 2007, p. 157.
8. Elsesser & Lever, 2011.
9. Schieman & McMullen, 2008.
10. Ellemers et al., in press.
11. Duguid, 2011.
12. Cech & Blair-Loy, 2010.
13. Elsesser & Lever, 2011.
14. McPherson, Smith-Lovin & Cook, 2001.
15. Morry, 2005, 2007.

16. Ibarra, 1993.
17. Kanter, 1977; Lincoln & Miller, 1979.
18. Ibarra, 1995.
19. Thomas, 1990.
20. Teahan, 1975.
21. Elsesser & Peplau, 2006.
22. Rumens, 2008.
23. Rumens, 2008, p. 86.
24. O'Boyle & Thomas, 1996, p. 247.
25. Pirlott & Neuberg, 2014.
26. Rumens, 2008, p. 87.
27. Woods & Lucas, 1994.

CHAPTER 13

1. Kintz, 2012.
2. Manjoo, 2013.
3. Edwards, 2012.
4. Brass, 1985, p. 340.
5. Kanter, 1977, p. 282.
6. Ibarra, 1992, p. 441.
7. Lewis & Fagenson, 1995.
8. Lewis & Fagenson, 1995, p. 41.
9. Chao, Walz & Gardner, 1992.
10. Greve, Benassi & Dag Sti, 2010.
11. Greve, Benassi & Dag Sti, 2010.

CHAPTER 14

1. Attributed by Hershberg, 1993, p. 89.
2. Cathey, 2013.
3. Cooper, 2008.
4. Cooper, 2008.

CHAPTER 15

1. Kaye & Giulioni, 2012, p. 87.
2. Allen et al., 2004.
3. Dreher & Cox, 1996; Ragins & Cotton, 1999.

4. Chao, Walz & Gardner, 1992; Ragins & Cotton, 1999; Scandura & Williams, 2001.
5. Scandura & Williams, 2001.
6. Catalyst, 2003.
7. Linehan & Scullion, 2008; Lyness & Thompson, 2000.
8. Wells, Lindsay & Ferguson, 1979.
9. Zenger, 2012.
10. Klein & Kim, 1998; Wayne, Shore & Liden, 1997.
11. Boyd & Taylor, 1998.
12. Sparrowe & Liden, 1997.
13. Dougherty & Dreher, 2007.
14. Hewlett et al., 2010.
15. Hewlett et al., 2010, p. 4.
16. Hewlett et al., 2010, p. 6.
17. Hewlett et al., 2010.
18. Hewlett, 2013, p. 41–42.
19. Hewlett, 2013.
20. Hewlett, 2013.
21. Tripathy, Bagchi & Mehta, 2010.

CHAPTER 16

1. Davies et al., 2009.
2. Associated Press, 2013b.
3. Perry, 2013a.
4. Perry, 2013b.
5. Graves & Shepard, 1992, p. A1.
6. Abcarian & Baum, 2011.
7. Wolf, 2004.
8. United States Equal Employment Opportunity Commission, 1990.
9. Duke & Brown, 2007.
10. California Senate Bill No. 967.

CHAPTER 17

1. Although this quote is widely attributed to Johnson, the original source is unknown.
2. Bobrow-Strain, 2012a, 2012b.
3. Velasco, 2012.

4. Associated Press, 2012.
5. Pilgram & Keyton, 2009.
6. Kearney, Rochlen & King, 2004.
7. Perry, Kulik & Schmidtke, 1998.
8. Cialdini, 2003.
9. Cialdini, 2003.
10. Heflick & Goldenberg, 2009.
11. Heflick & Goldenberg, 2009.
12. For more on the white bear study, see Wegner et al., 1987.

CHAPTER 18

1. Jane Goodall, attributed by Brooks, 2008, p. 23.
2. Chakrabarty, 2013.
3. Chakrabarty, 2013.
4. Abdullah, 2013.
5. Times News Network, 2013.
6. Bowman, Worthy & Greyson, 1965.

APPENDIX B

1. Paolacci, Chandler & Ipeirotis, 2010, p. 414.
2. Strauss & Corbin, 1990.

REFERENCES

Abbey, A. (1982). Sex differences in attributions for friendly behavior: Do males misperceive females' friendliness? *Journal of Personality & Social Psychology* 42, 830–838.

Abbey, A. (1987). Misperceptions of friendly behavior as sexual interest: A survey of naturally occurring incidents. *Psychology of Women Quarterly* 11, 173–194.

Abcarian, R., & Baum, G. (2011, November 7). Herman Cain accuser goes public with sexual harassment claim. *Los Angeles Times*.

Abdullah, O. (2013). Twitter post from @abdullah_omar dated December 5, 2013.

Adams, R. G. (1985). People would talk: Normative barriers to cross-sex friendships for elderly women. *Gerontologist* 25, 605–611.

Adler, P., Kless, P., & Adler, P. (1992). Socialization to gender roles: Popularity among elementary school boys and girls. *Sociology of Education* 65, 169–187.

Alderman, L. (1995). Surviving an office romance without jeopardizing your job. *Money* 24, 37–40.

Alford v. Aaron's Rents, Inc. (2008). D. Illinois 3:08–MJR-DGW-683.

Allen, T. D., Eby, L. T., Poteet, M. L., Lentz, E., & Lima, L. (2004). Career benefits associated with mentoring for proteges: A meta-analytic review. *Journal of Applied Psychology* 89, 127–136.

Anderson, C. I., & Hunsaker, P. L. (1985). Why there's romancing at the office and why it's everyone's problem. *Personnel* 62, 57–63.

Associated Press. (2012, January 11). Maker of Twinkies, Wonder Bread files for bankruptcy. *USA Today*.

Associated Press. (2013a, July 12). Iowa dentist who fired pretty and "irresistible" employee acted legally. *New York Daily News*.

Associated Press. (2013b, December 9). Ex-San Diego mayor Bob Filner faces sentencing for sexual harassment. *Guardian* (London).

Baer, R. (2003). *See No Evil: The True Story of a Ground Soldier in the CIA's War on Terrorism*. New York: Three Rivers Press.

Barash, S. (2007). *Tripping the Prom Queen: The Truth about Women and Rivalry*. New York: St. Martin's Griffin.

Barone, M. (2005, September 19). Blame aplenty. *U.S. News & World Report*, p. 56.

Barry, D. (1999). *Dave Barry Turns 50*. New York: Ballantine Books.

Baruch-Feldman, C., Brandolo, E., Ben-Dayan, D., & Schwartz, J. (2002). Sources of social support and burnout, job satisfaction, and productivity. *Journal of Occupational Health Psychology* 7, 84–93.

Beehr, T. A., Jex, S. M., Stacy, B. A., & Murray, M. A. (2000). Work stressors and coworker support as predictors of individual strain and job performance. *Journal of Organizational Behavior* 21, 391–405.

Bergman, M. E., Langhout, R. D., Palmieri, P. A., Cortina, L. M., & Fitzgerald, L. F. (2002). The (Un)reasonableness of reporting: Antecedents and consequences of reporting sexual harassment. *Journal of Applied Psychology* 87, 230–242.

Bingham, S. G., & Scherer, L. L. (2001). The unexpected effects of a sexual harassment educational program. *Journal of Applied Behavioral Science* 37, 125–153.

Bisom-Rapp, S. (2001). Fixing watches with sledgehammers: The questionable embrace of employee sexual harassment training by the legal profession. *UALR Law Review* 24, 147–168.

Bisson, M. A., & Levine, T. R. (2009). Negotiating a friends with benefits relationship. *Archives of Sexual Behavior* 38, 66–73.

Blair-Loy, M. (2001). It's not just what you know, it's who you know: Technical knowledge, rainmaking and gender among finance executives. *Research in the Sociology of Work* 10, 51–83.

Bleske-Rechek, A., Somers, E., Micke, C., Erickson, L., Matteson, L., Schumacher, B., Stocco, C., & Ritchie, L. (2012). Benefit or burden? Attraction in cross-sex friendship. *Journal of Social & Personal Relationships* 29, 569–596.

Bobrow-Strain, A. (2012a). Atomic bread baking at home: A Yucatan-based American tries to recreate the '50's-era market-tested UDA white pan loaf No. 1 and in doing so reveals how today's miracle food can become tomorrow's catastrophe. *Believer Magazine*.

Bobrow-Strain, A. (2012b). *White Bread: A Social History of the Store-Bought Loaf*. Boston, MA: Beacon Press.

Booth, A. L., Francesconi, M., & Frank, J. (2003). A sticky floors model of promotion, pay, and gender. *European Economic Review* 47, 295–322.

Bowden, P. (2011). *Telling It Like It Is*. Seattle: Amazon Digital Services.

Bowman, G. W., Worthy, N. B., & Greyson, S. A. (1965). Problems in review: Are women executives people? *Harvard Business Review* 43, 52–67.

Boyd, N. G., & Taylor, R. R. (1998). A developmental approach to the examination of friendship in leader-follower relationship. *Leadership Quarterly* 9, 1–25.

Bradac, J. J. (1983). The language of lovers, flovers, and friends: Communicating in so-cial and personal relationships. *Journal of Language & Social Psychology* 2, 141–162.

Brass, D. J. (1985). Men's and women's networks: A study of interaction patterns and influence in an organization. *Academy of Management Journal* 28, 327–343.

Brehm, S. S. (1992). *Intimate Relationships*. New York: McGraw-Hill.

Brehm, S. S., & Brehm, J. W. (1981). *Psychological reactance: A theory of freedom and control*. New York: Academic Press.

Brock, D. (1994). *The Real Anita Hill: The Untold Story*. New York: Free Press.

Brooks, Y. (2008). *Do Animals Have Rights?* London: Arcturus.

Brown, M., & Auerback, A. (1981). Communication patterns in initiation of marital sex. *Medical Aspects of Human Sexuality* 15, 108–109.

Bryan, L. L., Matson, E., & Weiss, L. M. (2007). Harnessing the power of informal employee networks. *McKinsey Quarterly* 4.

Bryant, A., & Lewis, M. L. (2005). *Flirting 101: How to Charm Your Way to Love, Friendship and Success*. New York: Thomas Dunne Books.

Bureau of Labor Statistics. (2006). *100 Years of U.S. Consumer Spending: Data for the Nation, New York City, and Boston*.

California Senate Bill No. 967, Chapter 748. Retrieved from: https://leginfo.legislature .ca.gov/faces/billNavClient.xhtml?bill_id=201320140SB967

Captivate. (2010). Work Spouse Survey.

Cardiff, I. (1964). *The Wisdom of George Santayana*. New York: Open Road Media.

Careerbuilder.com. (2009). Forty percent of workers have dated a co-worker, finds an-nual careerbuilder.com Valentine's Day survey [press release].

Careerbuilder.com. (2011). Nearly one in five workers have dated co-workers at least twice during their career, finds annual careerbuilder Valentine's Day survey [press release].

Carr v. Allison Gas Turbine Div., Gen. Motors Corp., 32 F.3d 1007, 1008–1009 (7th Cir. 1994).

Catalyst. (2003). *Women in U.S. Corporate Leadership: 2003*. New York: Catalyst.

Catalyst. (2012). *2012 Catalyst Census: Fortune 500 Women Executive Officers and Top Earners*. New York: Catalyst.

Catalyst. (2013). *2013 Catalyst Census: Fortune 500 Women Executive Officers and Top Earners*. New York: Catalyst.

Catalyst. (2014). *Women CEO's of the Fortune 1000*. New York: Catalyst.

Cathey, G. (2013). The top 100 most connected people on LinkedIn. Retrieved from http://booleanblackbelt.com/2013/05/the-top-100-most-connected-people-on -linkedin/.

Cech, E. A., & Blair-Loy, M. (2010). Perceiving glass ceilings? Meritocratic versus structural explanations of gender inequality among women in science and technology. *Social Problems* 57, 371–397.

Chakrabarty, R. (2013, December 7). Farooq Abdullah faces flak for "sexist" remark, his apology does not cut ice. *Times of India*.

Chan, D. K-S., Lam, C. B. Chow, S. Y., & Cheung, S. F. (2008). Examining the job-related, psychological, and physical outcomes of workplace sexual harassment: A meta-analytic review. *Psychology of Women Quarterly* 32, 362–376.

Chao, G. T., Walz, P. M., & Gardner, P. D. (1992). Formal and informal mentorships: A comparison on mentoring functions and contrast with nonmentored counterparts. *Personnel Psychology* 45, 619–636.

Churchill, W. (1950). *The Second World War*, vol. 3. New York: Houghton Mifflin.

Cialdini, R. B. (2003). Crafting normative messages to protect the environment. *Current Directions in Psychological Science* 12, 105–109.

Clark, L. (2009, May 18). Childless women "vilified by bosses": Why NOT having a family could ruin your career. *Daily Mail* (London).

Clark, M. S., & Mills, J. (1993). The difference between communal and exchange relationships: What it is and is not. *Personality and Social Psychology Bulletin* 19, 684–691.

Clement, S. (2014, April 10). Odds are Vance McCallister won't survive Smoochgate. *Washington Post.*

Clifford, S. (2012, May 14) Chairman of Best Buy resigns after an internal audit. *New York Times.*

Cogan, M. (2013, February 27). House of cads: Psycho-sexual ordeal of reporting in Washington. *New Republic.*

Conley, F. K. (1999). *Walking out on the Boys.* New York: Farrar, Straus & Giroux.

Cooper, C. (2008). Elucidating the bonds of workplace humor: A relational process model. *Human Relations* 61, 1087–1115.

Cooper, V. (1997). Homophily or the queen bee syndrome: Female evaluation of female leadership. *Small Group Research* 28, 483–499.

Cramer, M. (2011, December 2). First grader accused of sexual harassment. *Boston Globe.*

Crispin G., & Mehler, M. (2011). 10th annual CareerXroads source of hire report: By the numbers. Retrieved from http://www.careerxroads.com/news/SourcesOfHire11 .pdf.

Cropper, C. M. (1997, Oct 26). Earning it: That unwritten code against fraternization. *New York Times.*

Crowe, L. C., & George, W. H. (1989). Alcohol and human sexuality: Review and integration. *Psychological Bulletin* 105, 374–386.

Curtis, K. (1998, September 3). Safeway clerks object to smile rule. *Associated Press.*

Davies, R. T., Ford, P., Nation, T., & Harper, G. (2009). The Waters of Mars [television series episode]. *Doctor Who.* BBC Wales.

Diaz, V. (2006) Playing favorites in the workplace: Widespread sexual favoritism as actionable discrimination under Miller v. Department of Corrections. *Southern California Review of Law and Social Justice* 16, 165–196.

DiPietro, J. A. (1981). Rough and tumble play: A function of gender. *Developmental Psychology* 17, 50–58.

Dolan, M. (2005, July 19). Affairs at work subject to suits. *Los Angeles Times*.

Dougherty, T. W., & Dreher, G. F. (2007). Mentoring and career outcomes. In B. R. Ragins & K. E. Kram (eds.), *The Handbook of Mentoring at Work* (pp. 51-94). Thousand Oaks, CA: Sage.

Douglas, C. N. (1917). *Forty Thousand Quotations: Prose and Poetical*. New York: Halcyon House.

Dreher, G. F., & Cox, T. H., Jr. (1996). Race, gender, and opportunity: A study of compensation attainment and the establishment of mentoring relationships. *Journal of Applied Psychology* 81, 297.

Driscoll, R., Davis, K. E., & Lipetz, M. E. (1972). Parental interference and romantic love: The Romeo and Juliet effect. *Journal of Personality & Social Psychology* 24, 1-10.

Drphil.com. (2012). How to keep boundaries with a "work spouse."

Ducharme, L. J., & Martin, J. K. (2000). Unrewarding work, co-worker support, and job satisfaction: A test of the buffering hypothesis. *Work and Occupations* 27, 223-243.

Duguid, M. (2011). Female tokens in high-prestige work groups: Catalysts or inhibitors of group diversification? *Organizational Behavior and Human Decision Processes* 116, 104-115.

Duke, L., & Brown, D. L. (2007). Tapping into the secrets of the stall. *Washington Post*.

Dunn, K. (1994, November). Just as fierce. *Mother Jones*.

Dworkin, T. M. (1997). It's my life—leave me alone: Off-the-job employee associational privacy rights. *American Business Law Journal* 35, 47-103.

Dziech, B., & Weiner, L. (1990). *The Lecherous Professor: Sexual Harassment on Campus*. Chicago: University of Illinois Press.

Edwards, D. (2012). *I'm Feeling Lucky: The Confessions of Google Employee Number 59*. New York: Mariner Books.

Eisenman, R. (2001). The sexual harassment seminar: A cultural phenomenon of indoctrination into feminist ideology. *Sexuality and Culture* 5, 77-85.

Eisenman, R. (2011). My perceptions of biased sexual harassment proceedings, or how I almost got punched by a university administrator. *Sexuality & Culture* 15, 391-394.

Ellemers, N., Rink, F., Derks, B., & Ryan, M. (2012). Women in high places: When and why promoting women into top positions can harm them individually or as a group (and how to prevent this). *Research in Organizational Behavior*.

Ellemers, N., van den Heuvel, H., de Gilder, D., Maass, A., & Bonvini, A. (2004). The underrepresentation of women in science: Differential commitment or the queen bee syndrome? *British Journal of Social Psychology* 43, 315-338.

Ellis, S., Barak, A., & Pinto, A. (1991). Moderating effects of personal cognitions on experienced and perceived sexual harassment of women at the workplace. *Journal of Applied Social Psychology* 21, 1320-1337.

Ellison v. Brady (1991). CA 9, 54 FEP Cases 1346.

Elsesser, K. M. (2003). Receipt and provision of social support in the workplace: Outcomes and gender comparisons. (Unpublished doctoral dissertation). University of California, Los Angeles.

Elsesser, K. M., & Lever, J. (2011). Does gender bias against female leaders persist? Quantitative and qualitative data from a large-scale survey. *Human Relations* 64, 1555–1578.

Elsesser, K. M., & Peplau, L. A. (2006). The glass partition: Obstacles to cross-sex friendships at work. *Human Relations* 59, 1077–1100.

English, H. (2003). *Gender on Trial: Sexual Stereotypes and Work/Life Balance in the Legal Workplace.* New York: ALM.

Ephron, N. (writer), Reiner, R. (producer and director) & Scheinman, A. (producer) (1989). *When Harry Met Sally* [motion picture]. United States: Columbia Pictures.

Faragher v. City of Boca Raton. (1998). 524 U.S. 775.

Faragher, B. A. (2005). Faragher v. City of Boca Raton: A personal account of a sexual discrimination plaintiff. *Hofstra Labor and Employment Law Journal* 22, 417–427.

Fernandez, R. M., & Weinberg, N. (1997). Sifting and sorting: Personal contacts and hiring in a retail bank. *American Sociological Review* 62, 883–902.

Fisher, T. D., Moore, Z. T., & Pittenger, M. J. (2012). Sex on the brain?: An examination of frequency of sexual cognitions as a function of gender, erotophilia, and social desirability. *Journal of Sex Research* 49, 69–77.

Foxnews.com. (2011, December 4). Boy, 9, suspended from school for sexual harassment after calling teacher "cute."

Frieze, I. H., Olson, J. E., & Russell, J. (1991). Attractiveness and income for men and women in management. *Journal of Applied Social Psychology* 21, 1039–1057.

Golden, J. H., Johnson, C. A., & Lopez, R. A. (2001). Sexual harassment in the workplace: Exploring the effects of attractiveness on perceptions of harassment. *Sex Roles* 45, 767–784.

Goldstein M. (2008, December 10). Memorandum available at http://www.senate.ucla.edu/issues/documents/12–10–08GoldsteintoCroughanSexualHarassment.pdf.

Granovetter, M. (1973). The strength of weak ties. *American Journal of Sociology* 78, 1360–1380.

Granovetter, M. (1974). *Getting a Job: A Study of Contact and Careers.* Cambridge, MA: Harvard University Press.

Graves, G., & Shepard, C. E. (1992, November 22). Packwood accused of sexual advances; Alleged behavior pattern counters image. *Washington Post,* p. A1.

Greif, G. (2008). *Buddy System: Understanding Male Friendships.* New York: Oxford University Press.

Greve, A., Benassi, M., & Dag Sti, A. (2010). Exploring the contributions of human and social capital to productivity. *International Review of Sociology* 20, 35–38.

Guerrero, L. K., & Chavez, A. M. (2005). Relational maintenance in cross-sex friendships characterized by different types of romantic intent: An exploratory study. *Western Journal of Communication* 69, 339–358.

Hajdin, M. (1997). Why the fight against sexual harassment is misguided. In L. LeMoncheck & M. Hajdin (eds.), *Sexual Harassment: A Debate* (pp. 199–226). Lanham, MD: Rowman & Littlefield.

Harris, J. I., Winskowski, A. M., & Engdahl, B. E. (2007). Types of workplace social support in the prediction of job satisfaction. *Career Development Quarterly* 56, 150–156.

Harris v. Forklift Systems, Inc. (1993). 114 S.Ct. 367.

Heflick, N. A., & Goldenberg, J. L. (2009). Objectifying Sarah Palin: Evidence that objectification causes women to be perceived as less competent and less fully human. *Journal of Experimental Social Psychology* 45, 598–601.

Helgeson, V. (2012). *The Psychology of Gender*. Upper Saddle River, NJ: Pearson Education.

Helweg-Larsen, M., Cunningham, S. J., Carrico, A., & Pergram, A. M. (2004). To nod or not to nod: An observational study of nonverbal communication and status in female and male college students. *Psychology of Women Quarterly* 28, 358–361.

Hershberg, J. G. (1993). *James B. Conant: Harvard to Hiroshima and the Making of the Nuclear Age*. New York: Knopf.

Hewlett, S. A. (2013). *Forget a Mentor, Find a Sponsor: The New Way to Fast-Track Your Career*. Boston: Harvard Business School.

Hewlett, S. A., Peraino, K., Sherbin, L., & Sumberg, K. (2010). The sponsor effect: Breaking through the last glass ceiling. *Harvard Business Review Research Report*.

Hossack, R. (1993). Male executive: Challenged by a gender bind. *CMA Magazine* 67, p. 5.

Hughes, M., Morrison, K., & Asada, K. J. K. (2005). What's love got to do with it? Exploring the impact of maintenance rules, love attitudes, and network support on friends with benefits relationships. *Western Journal of Communication* 69, 49–66.

Hurley, A. E., & Fagenson-Eland, E. A. (1996) Challenges in cross-gender mentoring relationships: Psychological intimacy, myths, rumours, innuendoes and sexual harassment. *Leadership & Organization Development Journal* 17, 42–49.

Ibarra, H. (1992). Homophily and differential returns: Sex differences in network structures and access in an advertising firm. *Administrative Science Quarterly*, 422–447.

Ibarra, H. (1993). Network centrality, power, and innovation involvement: Determinants of technical and administrative roles. *Academy of Management Journal* 36, 471–501.

Ibarra, H. (1995). Race, opportunity, and diversity of social circles in managerial networks. *Academy of Management Journal* 38, 673–703.

Institute for Women's Policy Research. (2012). *The gender wage gap by occupation*. Retrieved from http://www.iwpr.org.

Jacklin, C. N., & Maccoby, E. E. (1978). Social behavior at 33 months in same-sex and mixed-sex dyads. *Child Development* 49, 557–569.

Jan, T. (2006, February 11). In Brockton, boy's parents hire lawyer. *Boston Globe*.

Kalmijn, M. (2002). Sex segregation of friendship networks: Individual and structural determinants of having cross-sex friends. *European Sociological Review* 18, 101–117.

Kanazawa, S., & Kovar, J. L. (2004). Why beautiful people are more intelligent. *Intelligence* 32, 227–243.

Kanter, R. M. (1977). *Men and Women of the Corporation*. New York: Basic Books.

Kass, A. (2011, June 9). Aaron's to appeal $95 million sexual harassment verdict. *Atlanta Journal-Constitution*.

Kaye, B., & Giulioni, J. W. (2012). *Help Them Grow or Watch Them Go: Career Conversations Employees Want*. San Francisco: Berrett-Koehler.

Kearney, L. K., Rochlen, A. B., & King, E. B. (2004). Male gender role conflict, sexual harassment tolerance, and the efficacy of a psychoeducative training program. *Psychology of Men and Masculinity* 5, 72–82.

Keedle, J. (2011). Work life: Polygamy in the workplace. Timesunion.com.

Kintz, J. (2012). *This Book Title Is Invisible*. Seattle, WA: Amazon Digital Services.

Kipnis, L. (2004, January 2). Should students be allowed to hook up with professors? Slate.com. Retrieved from: http://www.slate.com/articles/arts/culturebox/2004/01/off_limits.html.

Klein, H. J., & Kim, J. S. (1998). A field study of the influence of situational constraints, leader-member exchange, and goal commitment on performance. *Academy of Management Journal* 41, 88–95.

Koblin, J. (2010, July 21). Intrigue at the Times Magazine: Marzorati's departure followed soured morale and a controversial deputy. *New York Observer*.

Kolhatkar, S. (2004, November 25). Revolt of Fox's hens. *New York Observer*.

Kowalski, R. M. (1993). Inferring sexual interest from behavioral cues: Effects of gender and sexually relevant attitudes. *Sex Roles* 29, 13–36.

Lalanne, M., & Seabright, P. (2011). The old boy network: Gender differences in the impact of social networks on remuneration in top executive jobs. *TSE Working Paper* 11.

Lehmiller, J. J., VanderDrift, L. E., & Kelly, J. R. (2011). Sex differences in approaching friends with benefits relationships. *Journal of Sex Research* 48, 275–284.

Levine, I. S. (2010, December 16). The work spouse: Indispensable friend or playing with fire? *Psychology Today* [blog].

Lewis, A. E., & Fagenson, E. A. (1995). Strategies for developing women managers: How well do they fulfill their objectives? *Journal of Management Development* 14, 39–53.

Lewis, C.S. (1988). *Four Loves*. Orlando, FL: Harcourt Books.

Lin, N., Ensel, W. M., & Vaughn, J. C. (1981). Social resources and strength of ties: Structural factors in occupational status attainment. *American Sociological Review* 46, 393–405.

Lincoln, J., & Miller, J. (1979). Work and friendship ties in organizations: A comparative analysis of relational networks. *Administrative Science Quarterly* 24, 181–198.

Linehan, M., & Scullion, H. (2008). The development of female global managers: The role of mentoring and networking. *Journal of Business Ethics* 83, 29–40.

Lyness, K. S., & Thompson, D. E. (2000). Climbing the corporate ladder: Do female and male executives follow the same route? *Journal of Applied Psychology* 85, 86–101.

Lyvers, M., Cholakians, E., Puorro, M., & Sundram, S. (2011). Beer goggles: Blood alcohol concentration in relation to attractiveness ratings for unfamiliar opposite sex faces in naturalistic settings. *Journal of Social Psychology* 151, 105–112.

Maccoby, E. E. (1988). Gender as a social category. *Developmental Psychology* 24, 755–765.

Maccoby, E. E. (1998*). The two sexes: Growing up apart, coming together.* Cambridge, MA: Harvard University Press.

Maccoby, E. E. (2002). Gender and group process: A developmental perspective. *Current Directions in Psychological Science* 11, 54–58.

Maccoby, E. E., & Jacklin, C. N. (1987). Gender segregation in childhood. In H. W. Reese (ed.), *Advances in Child Development and Behavior*, vol. 20 (pp. 239–288). New York: Academic Press.

Madera, J. M., Podratz, K. E., King, E. B., & Hebl, M. R. (2007). Schematic responses to sexual harassment complainants: The influence of gender and physical attractiveness. *Sex Roles* 56, 223–230.

Madjar, N. (2008). Emotional and informational support from different sources and employee creativity. *Journal of Occupational & Organizational Psychology* 81, 83–100.

Mainiero, L. A. (1986). A review and analysis of power dynamics in organizational romances. *Academy of Management Review* 11, 750–762.

Manjoo, F. (2013). The happiness machine: How Google became such a great place to work. Slate.com.

Marchuk v. Faruqi & Faruqi LLP. (2013). 13 CIV 1669. Complaint [U.S. District Court for the Southern District of New York].

Marcus, D. E., & Overton, W. F. (1978). The development of cognitive gender constancy and sex role preferences. *Child Development* 49, 434–444.

Markiewicz, D., Devine, I., & Kausilas, D. (2000) Friendships of women and men at work: Job satisfaction and resource implications. *Journal of Managerial Psychology* 15, 161–184.

Marlow, C. M., Schneider, S. L., & Nelson, C. E. (1996). Gender and attractiveness biases in hiring decisions: Are more experienced managers less biased? *Journal of Applied Psychology* 81, 11–21.

Marsden, P. V., & Hurlbert, J. (1988). Social resources and mobility outcomes: A replication and extension. *Social Forces* 66, 1038–1059.

Massengill, D., & Petersen, D. J. (1995). Legal challenges to no fraternization rules. *Labor Law Journal* 46, 429.

McGinty, K., Knox, D., & Zusman, M. E. (2007). Friends with benefits: Women want "friends," men want "benefits." *College Student Journal* 41, 1128–1131.

McPherson, M., Smith-Lovin, L., & Cook, J. M. (2001). Birds of a feather: Homophily in social networks. *Annual Review of Sociology* 27, 415–444.

Mead, M. (1980). A proposal: We need taboos on sex at work. In D. A. Neugarten & J. M. Shafritz (eds.), *Sexuality in Organizations: Romantic and Coercive Behaviors at Work* (pp. 53–58). Oak Park, IL: Moore.

Merle, R. (2005, March 8). Boeing CEO resigns over affair with subordinate. *Washington Post.*

Misner, I., Walker, H. M., & De Raffele, F. J., Jr. (2012). *Business Networking and Sex: Not What You Think.* Irvine, CA: Entrepreneur Media.

Monsour, M. (2002). *Women and Men as Friends.* Mahwah, NJ: Erlbaum.

Morry, M. M. (2005). Relationship satisfaction as a predictor of similarity ratings: A test of the attraction-similarity hypothesis. *Journal of Social & Personal Relationships* 22, 561–584.

Morry, M. M. (2007). The attraction-similarity hypothesis among cross-sex friends: Relationship satisfaction, perceived similarities, and self-serving perceptions. *Journal of Social & Personal Relationships* 24, 117–138.

Murphy, D. (2013, December 15). Georgia student suspended for sexual harassment after hugging teacher. *New York Daily News.*

Nelson v. Knight DDS, P.C. and Knight. (2013). Supreme Court of Iowa, No. 11–1857.

Obama, B. (2008). *The Audacity of Hope: Thoughts on Reclaiming the American Dream.* New York: Vintage.

O'Boyle, C. G., & Thomas, M. D. (1996). Friendships between lesbian and heterosexual women. In J. S. Weinstock & E. D. Rothblum (eds.), *Lesbian Friendships* (pp. 240–248). New York: New York University Press.

O'Meara, J. D. (1989). Cross-sex friendship: Four basic challenges of an ignored relationship. *Sex Roles* 21, 525–543.

Paglia, C. (1992). *Sex, Art, and American Culture: Essays.* New York: Vintage Books.

Paolacci, G., Chandler, J., & Ipeirotis, P. G. (2010). Running experiments on Amazon Mechanical Turk. *Judgment and Decision Making* 5, 411–419.

Parker, A. (2013, January 3). Day of records and firsts as 113th Congress opens. *New York Times.*

Parker, K. (2011, November 21). He said, she said, we shrug; Why Americans can't make up their minds on sexual harassment. *Newsweek*, p. 18.

Parks, M. (2006). 2006 workplace romance: Poll findings. *Society for Human Resource Management.*

Parks-Stamm, E. J., Heilman, M. E., & Hearns, K. A. (2008). Motivated to penalize: Strategic rejection of successful women. *Personality and Social Psychology Bulletin* 34, 237–247.

Patai, D. (1998). *Heterophobia.* Lanham, MD: Rowman & Littlefield.

Pergram, C., & Brown, S. (2010, May 18). Indiana rep. Mark Souder resigns after affair with staffer. Foxnews.com.

Perilloux, C., Easton, J. A., & Buss, D. M. (2012). The misperception of sexual interest. *Psychological Science* 23, 146–151.

Perry, E. L., Kulik, C. T., Bustamante, J., & Golom, F. D. (2010). The impact of reason for training on the relationship between "best practices" and sexual harassment training effectiveness. *Human Resource Development Quarterly* 21, 187–208.

Perry, E. L., Kulik, C. T., & Schmidtke, J. M. (1998). Individual differences in the effectiveness of sexual harassment awareness training. *Journal of Applied Social Psychology* 28, 698–723.

Perry, T. (2013a, July 31). Eighth woman accuses Mayor Bob Filner of sexual misconduct. *Los Angeles Times.*

Perry, T. (2013b, August 23). San Diego mayor Bob Filner out Aug. 30, apologizes to victims. *Los Angeles Times.*

Pilgram, M., & Keyton, J. (2009). Evaluation of sexual harassment training instructional strategies. *NASPA Journal about Women in Higher Education* 2, 222–239.

Pirlott, A. G., & Neuberg, S. L. (2014). Sexual prejudice: Avoiding unwanted sexual interest? *Social Psychological & Personality Science* 5, 92–101.

Podolny, J. M., & Baron, J. N. (1997). Social networks and mobility in the workplace. *American Sociological Review* 62, 673–693.

Preston, K. S. J., & Marelich, W. D. (2008). "Friends with benefits": A new scale to assess attitudes toward casual sex relationships. Poster presentation at the biennial conference of the International Association for Relationship Research, Providence, Rhode Island.

Pryor, J. B., & Day, J. D. (1988). Interpretations of sexual harassment: An attributional analysis. *Sex Roles* 18, 405–417.

Quinn, R. E. (1977). Coping with cupid: The formation, impact, and management of romantic relationships in organizations. *Administrative Science Quarterly* 22, 30–45.

Ragins, B. R., & Cotton, J. L. (1999). Mentor functions and outcomes: A comparison of men and women in formal and informal mentoring relationships. *Journal of Applied Psychology* 84, 529–550.

Reeder, H. (2000). "I like you . . . as a friend": The role of attraction in cross-sex friendship. *Journal of Social & Personal Relationships* 17, 329–348.

Reeder, H. (2003). The effect of gender role orientation on same- and cross-sex friendship formation. *Sex Roles* 49, 143–152.

Richardson, K. M. (2014). Report of the Eighth Annual NAWL National Survey on Retention and Promotion of Women in Law Firms. National Association of Women Lawyers. Retrieved from http://www.nawl.org/p/bl/et/blogid=10&blogaid=56.

Rodgers, J. E (1999, January 1). Flirting fascination. *Psychology Today.*

Roiphe, K. (2011, November, 12) In favor of dirty jokes and risqué remarks. *New York Times.*

Rosenthal, R., & Jacobson, L. (1992). *Pygmalion in the classroom.* New York: Irvington.

Rotundo, M., Nguyen, D., & Sackett, P. R. (2001). A meta-analytic review of gender differences in perceptions of sexual harassment. *Journal of Applied Psychology* 86, 914–922.

Rubin, L. B. (1985). *Just friends: The role of friendship in our lives.* New York: Harper & Row.

Rudner, R., & Cho, M. (2003). *Best of the Improv,* vol. 3. Koch Vision.

Rumens, N. (2008). The complexities of friendship: Exploring how gay men make sense of their workplace friendships with straight women. *Culture & Organization* 14, 79–95.

Saegert, S. C., Swap, W., & Zajonc, R. (1973). Exposure, context and interpersonal attraction. *Journal of Personality & Social Psychology* 25, 234–242.

Sapadin, L. (1988). Friendship and gender: Perspectives of professional men and women. *Journal of Social & Personal Relationships* 5, 387–403.

Scandura, T. A., & Williams, E. A. (2001) An investigation of the moderating effects of gender on the relationships between mentorship initiation and protégé perceptions of mentoring functions. *Journal of Vocational Behavior* 59, 342–363.

Schaefer, C. M., & Tudor, T. M. (2001). Managing workplace romance. *SAM Advanced Management Journal*, 4–10.

Schieman, S., & McMullen, T. (2008). Relational demography in the workplace and health: An analysis of gender and the subordinate-superordinate role-set. *Journal of Health & Social Behavior* 49, 286–300.

Schneider, K. T. (1996). Bystander stress: The effect of organizational tolerance of sexual harassment on victims' coworkers. (Doctoral dissertation). Retrieved from ProQuest Dissertations and Theses.

Schouten, F. (2011, February 10). GOP rep. Chris Lee resigns over shirtless photo on web. *USA Today*.

Sciolino, E. (1997a, May 11). From a love affair to a court-martial. *New York Times*.

Sciolino, E. (1997b, May 18). For honorable discharge, B-52 pilot will resign and avoid court-martial. *New York Times*.

Sean Hannity Show. (2011, November 3). Retrieved from http://www.hannity.com/show/2011/11/03.

Shellenbarger, S. (2011, February 9). Does your work wife get a valentine? Some co-workers want to acknowledge a deep—yet platonic—bond on the romantic holiday. *Wall Street Journal*.

Shirom, A., Toker, S., Alkalay, Y., Jacobson, O., & Balicer, R. (2011). Work-based predictors of mortality: A 20-year follow-up of healthy employees. *Health Psychology* 30, 268–275.

Sias, P. M., & Cahill, D. J. (1997). From coworkers to friends: The development of peer friendships in the workplace. *Western Journal of Communication* 62, 273–299.

Silverstein, S. (1998, June 27). Fear of lawsuits spurs the birth of new industry. *Los Angeles Times. 60 Minutes Overtime.* (2013, March 10). Two uber-successful women on their mentors.

Sorkin, A. R. (2012, August 16). Restoration Hardware co-chief steps down after an inquiry. *New York Times*.

Sparrowe, R. T., & Liden, R. C. (1997). Process and structure in leader-member exchange. *Academy of Management Review* 22, 522–552.

Spherion. (2011). Love conquers all—Except the need for job security. Retrieved from http://www.prnewswire.com/news-releases/love-conquers-allexcept-the-need-for-job-security-115894574.html.

Staines, G., Tavris, C., & Jayaratne, T. E. (1974). The queen bee syndrome. *Psychology Today* 7, 55–60.

Stewart, J. B. (2011, September 21). Voting to hire a chief without meeting him. *New York Times.*

Stewart, W., & Barling, J. (1996). Daily work stress, mood and interpersonal job performance: A mediational model. *Work & Stress, 10,* 336–351.

Strauss, A., & Corbin, J. (1990). *Basics of Qualitative Research: Grounded Theory Procedures and Techniques.* Newbury Park, CA: Sage.

Tannen, D. (1990). *You Just Don't Understand: Women and Men in Conversation.* New York: William Morrow.

Tannen, D. (1994). *Talking from 9 to 5: Women and Men at Work.* New York: Avon.

Teahan, J. E. (1975). Role playing and group experience to facilitate attitude and value changes among black and white police officers. *Journal of Social Issues* 31, 35–45.

Thomas, D. A. (1990). The impact of race on managers' experiences of developmental relationships (mentoring and sponsorship): An intra-organizational study. *Journal of Organizational Behavior* 11, 479–492.

Times News Network. (2013, December 6). Farooq Abdullah apologizes for "sexist" remark. *Times of India.*

Tripathy, R. M., Bagchi, A., & Mehta, S. (2010). *A study of rumor control strategies on social networks.* Proceedings of the 19th ACM International Conference on Information and Knowledge Management, 1817–1820.

Trounson, R. (2003, July 18). UC bans dating of faculty, students. *Los Angeles Times.*

Trunk, P. (2007). The ill-advised but often-sought business trip tryst. Retrieved from http://blog.penelopetrunk.com/2007/02/12/the-ill-advised-but-often-sought -business-trip-tryst/.

Unden, A. (1996). Social support at work and its relationship to absenteeism. *Work & Stress* 10, 46–61.

United States Department of Labor. (2010). *Women in the Labor Force in 2010.*

United States Equal Employment Opportunity Commission. (1990). Policy guidance on current issues of sexual harassment. Retrieved from http://www.eeoc.gov/policy/ docs/currentissues.html.

United States Equal Employment Opportunity Commission. (2014). *Sexual harassment charges FY 2010–FY 2013.* Retrieved from http://www.eeoc.gov/eeoc/statistics/ enforcement/sexual_harassment_new.cfm.

Vance, A. (2010, August 6). H.P. ousts chief for hiding payments to friend. *New York Times.*

Vault.com. (2010). Almost 70% of employees say shaky economy hasn't affected their willingness to take romantic risks at work.

Vault.com. (2011). 2011 Office Romance Survey Results.

Velasco, S. (2012, January 11). Are Twinkies in decline? Hostess files for Chapter 11. *Christian Science Monitor.*

Veniegas, R. C., & Peplau, L A. (1997). Power and the quality of same-sex friendships. *Psychology of Women Quarterly* 21, 279–297.

Walsh, D. (2012, May 2). Sacramento jury awards $167 million to former Mercy Hospital employee. *Sacramento Bee.*

Washington Post–ABC News Poll. (2011). Retrieved from http://www.washingtonpost.com/wp-srv/politics/polls/postabcpoll_111311.html.

Wayne, S. J., Shore, L. M., & Liden, R. C. (1997). Perceived organizational support and leader-member exchange: A social exchange perspective. *Academy of Management Journal* 40, 82–111.

Wegner, D. M., Schneider, D. J., Carter, S. R., & White, T. L. (1987). Paradoxical effects of thought suppression. *Journal of Personality & Social Psychology* 53, 5–13.

Wells, G. L., Lindsay, R. C., & Ferguson, T. J. (1979). Accuracy, confidence, and juror perceptions in eyewitness identification. *Journal of Applied Psychology* 64, 440.

Werking, K. J. (1997). *We're Just Good Friends: Men and Women in Nonromantic Relationships.* New York: Guilford Press.

Whittle, B. (2008, November 21). Training day. *National Review Online.*

Wilde, O. (1892). *Lady Windermere's Fan.* In Peter Raby (ed.), *The Importance of Being Earnest and Other Plays.* London: Penguin, 1940.

Williams, C. L. (1992). The glass escalator: Hidden advantages for men in the "female" professions. *Social Problems* 39, 253–267.

Williams, C. L., Giuffre, P. A., & Dellinger, K. (1999). Sexuality in the workplace: Organizational control, sexual harassment and the pursuit of pleasure. *Annual Review of Sociology* 25, 73–93.

Wolf, N. (2004). The silent treatment. *New York Magazine.*

Woods, J. D., & Lucas, J. H. (1994). *The Corporate Closet: The Professional Lives of Gay Men in America.* New York: Free Press.

Wright, P. H. (1982). Men's friendships, women's friendships and the alleged inferiority of the latter. *Sex Roles* 8, 1–20.

Yaniv, O. (2009, October 25). ESPN fires Steve Phillips after ex-Mets GM admits affair with production assistant Brooke Hundley. *New York Daily News.*

Zagier, A. S. (2014, May 2). St. Louis trial highlights gender bias in pay. *USA Today.*

Zajonc, R. B. (1968). Attitudinal effects of mere exposure. *Journal of Personality & Social Psychology* (Monograph Suppl., Pt. 2), 1–29.

Zenger, J. (2012, October 16). Solving the bad boss problem: Could the answer begin with you? Forbes.com.

ACKNOWLEDGMENTS

Those who have read this book understand that having a network is necessary for success in pretty much any endeavor. Everyone needs help (from both men and women), and thankfully I had lots of help with this book. My family deserves a very special thank-you for their encouragement, love, and support throughout the writing process. My husband, Bill, has spent an inordinate amount of time discussing different aspects of the sex partition with me. He came up with the partition metaphor, read several drafts of the book without complaint, and offered innumerable valuable comments. Thank you, Bill. Your enthusiasm and support are much appreciated. To my son, Bradley, thanks for being the greatest kid in the universe, for your excitement about Mom's book, and for your treasured thoughts on everything from the cover to the anecdotes about you. And to the late Lucy Marie Dog, border collie extraordinaire: Thanks to you, I was never alone while writing.

Having never published a book before, some extra hand-holding was needed with the publishing process. Thanks to Janet Lever for introducing me to my fabulous agent, Helen Zimmermann. And thanks to Helen for all her support, for patiently answering all my frantic newbie author questions, and for pointing out that a book that describes a problem must also offer solutions.

Thanks to my editor at Globe Pequot, Lara Asher—it was great to work with someone who could relate to the sex partition. Lara's positive feedback was a motivating force. After the acquisition of Globe Pequot, thanks to everyone at Taylor Trade for staying on top of all aspects of the book's progression. I appreciate your attention to detail and all of your expertise in transforming my words into an actual book.

I started my research on the sex partition while in the doctoral program at UCLA and want to thank Anne Peplau, my advisor, for her help and enthusiasm for this line of research. Long after I graduated, Anne continues to offer her inspiring support. Furthermore, without the support and research privileges provided to me by the UCLA Center for the Study of Women, I would not have been able to complete the research for this book.

Thanks, also, to those who provided endorsements while I was trying to find a publisher, including Barbara Gutek, Pepper Schwartz, Matthew Lieberman, Heidi Reeder, Anne Peplau, and Richard Lippa. I'm also indebted to friends and relatives who offered their thoughts, read drafts, or shared their contacts with me, especially Chuck Elsesser, Tom Elsesser, Kathleen Tkac, Elaine Gibson, Geoff Gibson, Susan Wall, and Peter Muller.

I am particularly grateful to everyone who opened up and shared their stories with me. I wish I could recognize you by name, because your stories truly made the sex partition come to life. Last but not least, thanks to everyone who reads this book. I appreciate you taking the time to understand the sex partition, and why it's an important issue for women at work.

INDEX

ABOUT THE AUTHOR

Kim Elsesser, PhD, is a research scholar at the Center for the Study of Women at the University of California-Los Angeles (UCLA), where she teaches courses on gender issues. Prior to her work in gender research, Elsesser cofounded a profitable proprietary trading group while employed at Morgan Stanley. Her experiences as a quantitative equity trader inspired much of her research on working women.

Elsesser has published in the *New York Times* and the *Guardian*, has discussed gender issues on Fox News *America Live*, NPR's *Talk of the Nation*, and BBC World Service's *Business Daily*, and was named one of CNN's "Most Intriguing People." She holds a PhD in psychology from UCLA, two graduate degrees from the Massachusetts Institute of Technology (MIT), and an undergraduate degree from Vassar College. She lives in Pasadena, California.